Dictionaries of Civilization

D1494601

Contents

Introduction

Despite its immense geographical extension, China, known to its inhabitants as Zhongguo, "The Middle Kingdom," is among the oldest civilizations that have a continuous history, in China's case from the end of the 3rd century BC to the 21st century. The idea of a universal kingdom that would unite "everything beneath the celestial vault" (tianxia), which took shape between the 5th and the 3rd century BC, was realized for the first time in 221 BC when the ruler of the Qin kingdom—source of our word China—ended the struggle among numerous kingdoms and declared himself "First august emperor." The Qin dynasty created the administrative and legislative structure of ancient China and standardized the writing system, a fundamental factor promoting union in a country that spoke different languages and innumerable dialects. The next dynasty, the Han (206 BC–AD 220), laid the theoretical basis for the empire, elevating Confucianism, a moral and religious system born in the 5th century BC, to state ideology. At the head of the social organization was the sovereign, mediator between the two universal entities, the earth and the heavens. Inventions, innovations, and discoveries that dated to preimperial times were attributed to mythical rulers, often presented as ancestors of the ruling house. The present thus drew its legitimacy from the past, an idea that involved the reworking of the historical past so as to present an ideal image. It also led to the custom of making a record of all facts, events, and figures deemed worthy of being remembered. This systematic recording of both empirical data and the results of experimentation, along with the efficient organization of the processes of manufacturing, gave China a superiority over the West in the technical-scientific field that continued until the 15th–16th centuries.

Daoism, the other major indigenous system of thought in ancient China, favored investigations into proto-scientific fields, spurring exploration of the rhythms of nature and the universe. The disintegration of the empire following the collapse of the Han dynasty stimulated cultural exchanges with bordering peoples, making possible the arrival of Buddhism, the universalistic religion from India, which eventually made its way into the heart of China.

The temporary weakness of Confucian ideology did nothing to weaken the ideal of a single, united Chinese empire, although more than 350 years were to pass before this was accomplished. The brief Sui dynasty (AD 581–618) introduced large-scale reforms that favored the three centuries of government of the next dynasty, the Tang (618–907). This was the golden age of ancient China, characterized by territorial expansion, religious tolerance, and cosmopolitan and liberal policies. For the first and only time in Chinese history, the situation was created that made possible the ascent to the imperial throne of a woman.

The end of the Tang dynasty was followed by nearly fifty years of disintegration, after which China was finally reunited, but at the same time threatened by the foreign populations to the north. The Song dynasty (960–1279) was forced to pay heavy tributes and to move the capital to southern China (1127). During this period of great patronage of the arts, the culture of the literati was codified, being expressed in established formulas incomprehensible to the uninitiated. The dynasty was overcome by the Mongol invasion, and Kublai Khan, grandson of Genghis, took the throne of the empire, beginning almost a century of foreign domination with the Yuan dynasty (1279–1368); the administration used foreigners to rule over the Chinese. It was during this very period, when foreign discrimination impeded every creative impulse in the country, that the astonishing inventions of ancient China made their arrival in the West. The Ming dynasty (1368–1644) brought a return to Chinese traditions, but its Sinocentric policies closed China off from the outside world and quashed all attempts at reform.

It is at that point that this book ends, just before the traumatic impact of the last dynasty, the Qing (1644–1911), instituted by another foreign people, the Manchu, using the technological superiority of the Western powers. This last period merits treatment of its own in a separate volume, as does the predynastic period, which was a time of great cultural diversity, as is slowly being discovered today through the intense activity of excavations. In China, the transmission of knowledge through an intellectual elite composed of public officials led to the standardization of literary and historical works. These historical sources are today flanked by material documents that make it necessary to integrate and sometimes alter our knowledge of many aspects of ancient Chinese civilization. The iconography encountered in the Mawangdui tombs—taken as an example since it is cited several times in this book—has revealed the existence of a fantastic world parallel to the Confucian universe that rationalized magical-religious factors. The principal archaeological sources are tombs, temples, and cave temples, along with unexpected treasures. What remains of ancient imperial and private collections presents a broad panorama of the arts of painting and calligraphy, while in terms of architectural works there are few remains because of the perishable nature of the primary construction material, wood.

To the Western world, China long remained a fantastic land, distant from reality. The difficulties in translating the literary sources and the complexity of the two principal schools of thought, Confucianism and Daoism, slowed the formation of a more in-depth vision of ancient China. Today, archaeological material from excavations and more accurate philological studies offer the opportunity to compose a lively and dramatic image of a great and ancient empire.

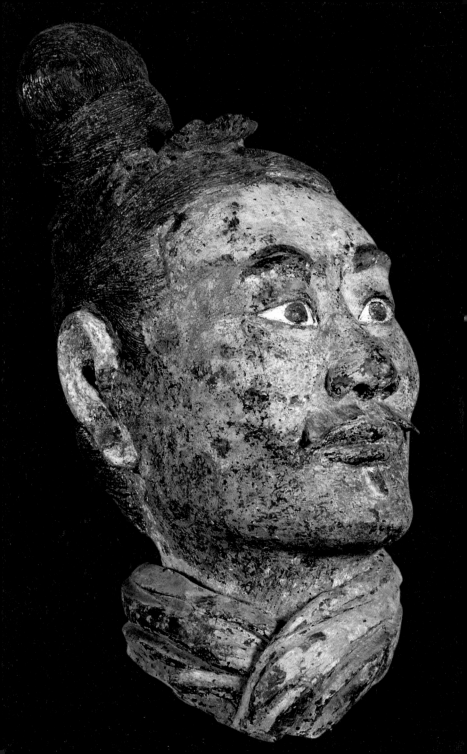

People

Qin Shi Huangdi
Li Si
Wudi
Sima Qian
Cao family
Taizong
Xuanzang
Wu Zetian
Li Bai
Huizong
Su Shi
Zhu Xi
Kublai Khan
Hongwu
Yongle

◄ Head with green flesh
tones, Qin dynasty, terracotta,
lacquer, pigment, Museum of
Qin Terracotta Warriors and
Horses, Lintong.

"He changed the calendar and chose black as the color . . . and chose six as the basic number: seals and official hats measured all six inches, carts six feet" (Sima Qian)

Qin Shi Huangdi

First emperor of China

Period
Qin (221–206 BC)

Reign
247–221 BC (ruler of Qin); 221–210 BC (emperor of China)

Family name
Zhao or Qin

Given name
Zheng

Terms
Small seal script (*xiaozhuan*)

Related entries
Li Si, Mandate of heaven, Controlling water, War, Great Wall, The quest for immortality, Xianyang

In 221 BC, having defeated the six principal contenders for supreme power, the leader of the Qin dynasty assumed the new title of *Shi Huangdi*, "first august emperor," and laid the basis for an empire whose structure remained intact for more than two thousand years. To increase the central power, the first emperor divided the country into thirty-six administrative units, the governors of which had to report to central authorities and were supported in their tasks by generals in charge of military control. The laws of the individual kingdoms in force until then were replaced by a penal code destined to remain at the base of the Chinese judicial system until the threshold of the 20th century. Coins, weights, and measures, even the width of cart axles were standardized; the writing forms in use were standardized, creating so-called small seal script, making possible the codification of a unitary literary language for the empire. The first emperor undertook massive construction projects, building new roads and canals that eased the movement of people and goods; existing fortresses were strengthened and connected to form a barrier along the northern border, the Great Wall. Sumptuous palaces and an immense mausoleum were built to preserve the imperial power for eternity. The enormous strain placed on the people of China to provide the money and labor demanded by these undertakings led to a general insurrection and thus the end of the dynasty only a few years after the first emperor's death.

▶ *Ding* tripod, Qin dynasty, from the pit with acrobats near the tomb of Qin Shi Huangdi at Lintong, bronze, 64 cm diam., Chinese History Museum, Beijing.

Ding tripods are among the most ancient ritual food vases; they were used for meat offerings in the royal tombs of the Shang epoch.

The earliest sources that tell of the Nine Legendary Tripods, cast during the mythical Xia dynasty, date to the 6th–4th centuries BC. The tripods were said to have been handed on from dynasty to dynasty, symbols of the passage of political power and the right to rule.

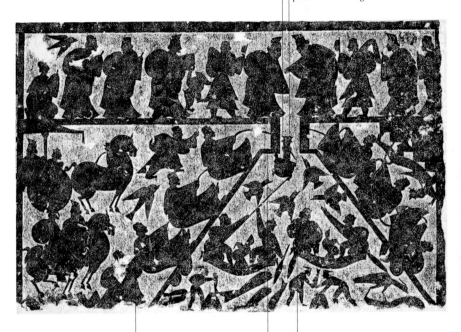

The historian Sima Qian (mid-2nd century BC) lamented the loss of the Nine Tripods and repeated the legend according to which they had sunk in the Si River near Pencheng 150 years before the unification of the country by the Qin.

During the Han period it was said that Qin Shi Huangdi had sent thousands of men to remove the tripods from the river, but at the critical moment a dragon had bitten through the cables, making the tripods fall back into the waves.

This scene depicts the moment in which the cables broke and the men tumbled back. The image is thus symbolic of heaven's disapproval of the Qin government and legitimizes the Han seizure of power.

▲ *The Emperor Seeks the Tripods,* Eastern Han dynasty, 2nd century AD, rubbing of a stone bas-relief, from the eastern wall of Room 2, Wu Liang Shrine, Shandong.

As soon as he ascended the throne of Qin, in 247 BC, the first emperor had work begin on his tomb at Mount Li, near the capital of Xianyang. The work continued until 208 BC.

The emperor arranged to have himself surrounded by all the comforts that he would require in the afterlife; the two quadrigas would prove useful for the inspection trips he would take in the other world.

The horse trappings and accessories for the carts are decorated with inlaid gold and silver. Both carts were covered by very thin bronze canopies.

Carts, charioteers, and horses were all painted, increasing the realistic effect of the quadrigas.

▲ The two quadrigas as they were found, in 1980, in the western area of the mausoleum of the first emperor at Lintong, Shaanxi, Qin dynasty.

▲ One of the quadrigas after its restoration, Museum of Qin Terracotta Warriors and Horses, Lintong.

The two bronze single-shaft carts, made to a scale of 1:2, are perfectly working models that reproduce the royal carriages down to the smallest detail.

The three enormous pits of the mausoleum, containing more than seven thousand terracotta soldiers, are famous throughout the world, but few know that the statues were all covered by a natural lacquer that had been applied as an undercoat for the layer of paint made using precious mineral pigments.

When the statues were removed from the moist soil, the layer of lacquer dried out and flaked off the surfaces, remaining stuck to the ground that had held them for more than two millennia.

Only in recent years, and with the use of various chemical methods, has it been possible to reattach the paint to the terracotta. The archers were restored in situ in 1999 using a procedure developed especially for the terracotta army.

▲ Archer, restored and photographed *in situ*, Qin dynasty, Pit 2 of the mausoleum of the first emperor, lacquered and painted terracotta, Museum of Qin Terracotta Warriors and Horses, Lintong.

"In the state of the intelligent ruler there is no literature . . . the law is the only teaching. There are no quoted sayings of the early kings, the magistrates are the only instructors" (Han Fei)

Li Si

Prime minister of Qin Shi Huangdi

Period
Qin (221–206 BC)

Life
circa 280–208 BC

Terms
Legalism
(*fajia*, lit., "school of law")
Book of Lord Shang (Shangjunshu)
Book of Master Han Fei (Han Feizi)
Law (*fa*)
Methods (*shu*)

Related entries
Qin Shi Huangdi, Officials and literati, Writing, Confucianism

The intransigent politics of Qin Shi Huangdi received theoretical support from the Legalist school, represented at court by Prime Minister Li Si. The oldest text related to this movement is the *Book of Lord of Shang*, the creator of which had served the Qin king in the 4th century BC. The author of the principal Legalist work, Han Feizi, was put to death in 233 BC by Li Si, following a court intrigue. In the ideal Legalist state, power is concentrated in the hands of the ruler, who makes use of the "law," inflexible and equal for everyone with the exception of the ruler himself, and of "methods," deceptive tactics by which he maintains control of the state, manipulating human instincts. The Legalist state does not recognize cultural differences and does not have room for individual expression. This was also the ideological thinking behind the standardization of weights and measurements and writing. Later Chinese historians credited Li Si for having created the new uniform writing system, but also found fault with him for persecuting literati and for destroying works of literature and history from earlier periods. Following the death of Qin Shi Huangdi, Li Si took part in the plot that brought the second emperor to the throne. Later, he himself fell victim to a plot, shortly before the collapse of the Qin dynasty, which also marked the end of the supremacy of the Legalist school.

▶ Measurement unit with edict of the first emperor, Qin dynasty, from Zhuguo, Zoucheng province, engraved clay, 20.5 cm diam., Shandong Provincial Museum, Shandong.

Chinese historiography relates that Li Si, promoter of a centralized state, urged the first emperor to silence dissent by means of a drastic measure: the burning of books, an event that took place in 213 BC.

The victims of this pyre of books included not only the chronicles of feudal states but also Confucian classics; only the chronicles of the Qin and scientific texts were spared.

During the years of persecution, Fu Sheng had hidden a copy of the Classic of Documents inside the walls of his home, and he spent the rest of his life, well into his nineties, teaching its contents.

Fu Sheng is seated cross-legged on a simple mat. On the low table in front of him are the tools of a man of letters: a pen and an ink stone. On the floor near the mat is the famous book he managed to keep hidden.

According to legend, in 212 BC, the year after the book burning, 460 Confucian scholars were buried alive for having defended their ideas.

▲ Portrait of Fu Sheng, Tang dynasty, 9th century AD, ink and color on silk, 25.4 x 44.7 cm, Municipal Museum of Art, Osaka.

> *"We therefore direct the leaders of provinces and districts to examine officials and private citizens . . . for those able to become our generals, our ministers, our ambassadors"* (Han emperor Wudi)

Wudi

Emperor

Period
Western Han
(206 BC–AD 8)

Reign
141–87 BC

Family name
Liu

Given name
Shizong

Posthumous name
Emperor Wu

Terms
Region (*bu*, then *zhou*)
Imperial university
(*taixue*)
*The Five Classics
(Wujing)*:
*Book of Changes
(I Ching); Book of
Documents (Shujing);
Book of Songs
(Shijing); Record of
Rites (Liji);* and *Spring
and Autumn Annals
(Chunqiu)*

Related entries
Qin Shi Huangdi,
Officials and literati,
Confucianism,
Commerce, Chang'an
(Western Han), Mogao

The first emperors of the Han dynasty had a conciliatory attitude toward bordering peoples and lands, most of all the Xiongnu tribes of northern China; Wudi replaced this with an expansionist policy that, over the 54-year course of his reign, fully doubled the size of China. In terms of domestic affairs, Wudi's centralizing policies brought about a gradual decline in the local centers of power and weakened the power of merchants by way of the institution of state monopolies on the minting of coins and the sale of salt, iron, and alcohol. China's administrative units were divided into thirteen "regions," regularly visited by inspectors directly subordinate to the central government. Like his predecessors, Wudi was in constant search of educated and competent officials; governors were instructed to call attention to noteworthy people, who then had to take a national civil-service examination in the capital. In 124 BC the emperor created the imperial university, where chosen candidates were given lessons in the Confucian *Five Classics*. These works, which collected the essence of the traditions of the past, confirmed the validity of the current social order, most especially the imperial institutions. Beginning with Wudi, the empire's cultural identity was founded on the principles of Confucianism, safeguarded by the class of officials and literati.

In 138 BC the Han emperor Wudi sent Zhang Qian with a hundred men on an embassy to the Yuezhi, located in ancient Bactria in Central Asia, to make an alliance with them against the powerful Xiongnu nomads.

General Zhang Qian was captured by the Xiongnu, and ten years passed before he succeeded in escaping and reaching the Yuezhi, only to find they had no intention of becoming involved in a war with the Xiongnu.

The mission failed in its objective but was of fundamental importance to the Chinese government, which as a result obtained its first eye-witness account of the populations of the "western lands."

Zhang Qian, having dismounted his horse, kneels before the horseback emperor; between them, near the center of the scene, is an inscription that explains the subject.

The painting implies that the true goal of the mission was religious, but not until the middle of the 1st century AD, meaning almost two hundred years after the mission, do Chinese historical sources begin speaking of any Buddhist involvement.

◀ Boar (?), Western Han dynasty, 2nd century BC, stone, 163 cm long, tomb of General Huo Qubing, Xi'an.

▲ Han Emperor Wudi Sends Zhang Qian to the Western Regions, Tang dynasty, circa AD 705–713, painting on the northern wall of Cave 323 at Mogao, Dunhuang, Gansu.

Dian was one of the kingdoms located in the southwestern regions of the empire that maintained their independence until the ascent of Wudi to the throne of Han.

Despite influence from the surrounding populations as well as from the distant Han empire, the Dian had developed an autonomous and highly developed use of bronze.

The container was made to hold the Dian unit of exchange, money-cowries. At the center of the lid is a gilt rider mounted on a small platform.

Along with various types of weapons used most of all in hunting and in wars against neighboring peoples, agricultural tools have been found with containers, musical instruments, and buckles.

The ritual, musical, and warlike traditions of the Dian are known today through the decorations modeled on containers; the separate elements were cast using the "lost-wax" technique and were then soldered to the surface.

This kind of wide-horned bovine with its muscular neck area often appears in the iconography of Dian art and is related to religious practices not yet understood.

▲ Container for money-cowries, Han dynasty, circa 150–50 BC, from Tomb 10 at Shizhaishan, Jinning, partially gilt bronze, 50 cm high, Yunnan Provincial Museum, Kunming.

"I have brought together the scattered fragments of ancient lore . . . I studied the events of history and set them down in significant order" (Sima Qian)

Sima Qian

The *Records of the Grand Historian* by Sima Qian relate the outlines of the historical and cultural events of the ancients and do so in a realistic and straightforward language often enlivened by dialog. The period covered begins with the semimythical days of the Yellow Emperor and ends at the period when the book was compiled, the reign of the Han emperor Wudi. Sima Qian's father handed on to him his post as court astronomer-astrologer and also began collecting the material relating to the past that Sima Qian concluded by way of careful research in the imperial archives as well as a long journey to track down witnesses. The work contributed to the further consolidation of Confucian thought as the basis of political and social order, since it presented the historical evolution from the ethical and moral point of view of contemporary ideology, which saw, for example, the succession of dynasties as the inevitable result of the absence of "virtue" with the consequent loss of the right to govern. The structure and style of the *Records of the Grand Historian*, a result of the private initiative of one official, became exemplary for the official historiography of all later dynasties: after every dynastic change, the new government took upon itself the compilation of a history of the preceding dynasty with the aim of learning from the past but also legitimizing the present.

Historian

Period
Western Han
(206 BC–AD 8)

Life
circa 140–90 BC

Terms
Records of the Grand Historian
(Shiji)
Virtue (*ren*)

Related entries
Wudi, Signs from the heavens, Mandate of heaven, Officials and literati, Confucianism

Portrait of Sima Qian, Ming dynasty, 7th century, ink and

Sima Qian was aware of the importance of his work to historiography. Although he had to suffer the penalty of castration for having interceded on behalf of a general who had fallen into disgrace, he kept working to bring his work to completion.

The stories, myths, and legends evoked by Sima Qian became the source of inspiration for innumerable artists and artisans.

Sima Qian's work is divided into five sections (annals, chronological tables, treatises, genealogies of noble families, biographies), which are in turn divided into 130 chapters. This arrangement was followed by later historians.

▲ Reverse of a mirror decorated with historiated scenes, Western Han dynasty, bronze, 18.6 cm diam., Freer Gallery of Art, Smithsonian Institution, Washington, DC.

Sima Qian created some of the ideological premises that still dominate Chinese historiography today, first among them the idea of the cultural and political unity of China from its very beginning.

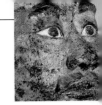

"Here is the wine! So let us sing, because life is as short as the morning dew, and the past is so very sad" (Cao Cao)

Cao family

Around the end of the Western Han period, the central government passed into the hands of the court eunuchs, while various military leaders vied for domination of the empire's peripheral zones. In AD 196, General Cao Cao, who controlled vast areas of central-northern China, forced the Han emperor Xiandi to relocate the capital to Xuchang (Henan) and then assumed all power himself. In AD 200, Cao Cao defeated the soldiers of his principal rival, but his attempts to advance south of the Yangtze River to again unite the country under a single ruler were foiled, and he met final failure in AD 208, when his army was defeated by the combined forces of his two major opponents, the future founders of the kingdoms of Shu (AD 221) and Wu (AD 222). When he died, in AD 220, his son Cao Pi assumed the title of emperor of the Wei dynasty, thus formally ending the four hundred years of Han rule. Cao Cao and his sons Cao Pi and Cao Zhi were among the most highly regarded poets of the period, grouped together stylistically under the name of the last dynastic era of the Han, Jian'an (AD 196–220). The poetic art of the Jian'an style is expressed in verses of five characters that reflect the passage from earlier poetry based on popular songs to the learned poetry of the literati. It is poetry that often laments the precarious nature of life and exalts wine for its ability to provide moments of illusory joy.

Family of politicians and poets

Period
End of the Eastern Han (AD 25–220), beginning of the Three Kingdoms period (AD 220–265)

Dates
Cao Cao: AD 155–220
Cao Pi: AD 187–226
Cao Zhi: AD 192–232

Terms
Jian'an style (*Jian'an fenggu*)

Related entries
Poetry, Novels, Theater, Luoyang

◄ Square table with scene of Cao Cao (see page 22), Ming dynasty, 15th–16th century, lacquered wood with mother-of-pearl inserts, 52 cm high, Lee Family Collection, Tokyo.

During the period of disorder following the fall of the Han dynasty, powerful men quickly rose to power in various regions of China and struggled to reunite the country, battling their rivals in large fratricidal battles.

Warrior and strategist but also poet and reformer, the figure of Cao Cao has fascinated Chinese historians and literati, most of all beginning in the Song epoch.

The scene depicts Cao Cao, standing, offering defeated general Guan Yu a splendid palace, a famous sorrel horse, and brocaded clothing.

The balustrade with stone pillars marks off the edge of the stone terrace that served as the base for timber constructions.

▲ Top of the square table (see page 21), Ming dynasty, 15th–16th century, lacquered wood with mother-of-pearl inserts, 52 cm high, Lee Family Collection, Tokyo.

Cao Cao is one of the leading characters in the Romance of the Three Kingdoms, *attributed to the man of letters Luo Guanzhong, and is also among the traditional characters in the musical theater and opera of Beijing.*

Historiography describes Cao Cao as a brilliant strategist, but the novel—and even more the theatrical productions—presents him as a cruel and suspicious tyrant, a personification of evil.

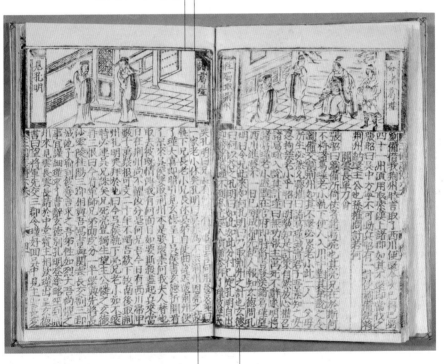

This incomplete example, today preserved in Spain, is the only known version of this edition. The version on which Western translations are based dates to the early Qing period.

The novel, which tells of the period of wars that followed the fall of the Han dynasty in AD 220, reaches epic proportions; many historical figures are endowed with supernatural powers.

▲ Double page from the *Romance of the Three Kingdoms,* Ming dynasty, Ye Fengchun edition, 1548, Real Biblioteca del Escorial, Madrid.

"Dynasties have always waxed and waned, but what deed of the kings of old could compare with the emperor of Tang returning to life?" (Journey to the West)

Taizong

Emperor

Period
Tang (AD 618–907)

Reign
AD 626–649

Family name
Li

Given name
Shimin

Temple name
Taizong

Posthumous name
Emperor Wen

Terms
Historiography office (*shiguan*)
Equal-field system (*juntian*)

Related entries
Xuanzang, Wu Zetian, Officials and literati, Education and exams, Confucianism, Commerce, Chang'an (Tang)

▶ Vase with dragon-shaped handles, Tang dynasty, 7th century AD, glazed terracotta, 55 cm high, Shaanxi History Museum, Xi'an.

Although he ascended the throne with a coup d'état, forcing his father, former military commander under the short Sui dynasty and then founder of the Tang dynasty, to abdicate in his favor, the second Tang emperor, Taizong, is described by Confucian historiography as one of China's most excellent rulers. A learned man with a pragmatic approach to matters of general interest, Taizong was open to criticism and new ideas. He strengthened the organization of the national exam system, and having understood the value of history as a tool of moral education and political legitimization, he set up a historiography office charged with writing down histories of preceding dynasties and making records of current events. China's growing economy was boosted by fiscal and agrarian reforms (like the equal-field system) that favored the well-being of the common people and permitted the large-scale expansion of the empire. With the help of the military, Taizong extended Chinese domination to the areas of today's Inner Mongolia and Xinjiang; diplomatic contact with bordering foreign powers as well as with distant lands contributed to China's fame as the most highly evolved and cosmopolitan power in the ancient world.

Taizong's cosmopolitan policies are also revealed by such measures as his official recognition, in AD 642, of music from Central Asia. At Chang'an, ten orchestras were granted permission to perform.

The bearded man is playing the pipa, *a stringed instrument originally from the Near East, while the woman holds a small drum to strike with a stick or by hand.*

The two musicians, perhaps found in the same tomb, are dressed in the style of the Kucha oasis, with narrow-sleeved, tight-fitting clothes and ample skirts that spread out around the kneeling figures.

▲ Pair of musicians, Tang dynasty, first half 7th century AD, glazed terracotta, 17 cm high, Musée Guimet, Paris.

The six horses were originally located in the northern area of the tomb of Emperor Taizong at Zhaoling, in the area of Chang'an.

The subjects are carved with a dynamic realism that displays both the details of the saddles and the muscles of the horses in movement.

The horses have fascinating names, such as Purple of the Misty Dew; their manes are woven to form the so-called three flowers (sanhua), indicating they belong to the imperial stables.

In 1914, a group of smugglers broke the reliefs while attempting to take them to the United States. Two of the six sculptures are today in Philadelphia; the others were taken to a museum in Xi'an.

General Qiu Xinggong is depicted withdrawing an arrow from the chest of an imperial horse, wounded in battle.

In AD 636 the emperor asked the famous painter Yan Liben to paint the six horses he had ridden during the military campaigns that had preceded his ascent to the throne. These portraits served as the models for the stone sculptures.

▲ The six war horses of the emperor Taizong, copies from the Song epoch (AD 973) of originals dating to the Tang dynasty (circa AD 636–645), stone bas-reliefs, each circa 170 x 220 cm, Forest of Stone Tablets Museum, Xi'an, and University of Pennsylvania Museum, Philadelphia.

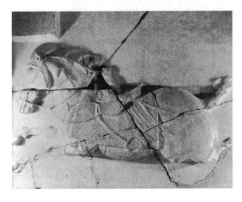

In AD 641 Emperor Taizong received an emissary from the first king of Tibet, sent to escort Princess Wencheng to Tibet.

The princess married the king of Tibet, following the "matrimonial diplomacy" tradition of the Chinese emperors. The union proved very happy, but other Chinese brides were consumed by nostalgia for home in the cold tents of their nomadic husbands.

▲ Yan Liben (attrib.), *The Emperor Receives the Tibetan Ambassador* (painted section), Tang dynasty, 7th century AD, horizontal scroll, ink and color on silk, 38.5 x 129 cm, Palace Museum, Beijing.

Ambassador Ludongzan, depicted with two members of his retinue, wears a long brocade cloak and bears a letter from the king.

Emperor Taizong, depicted larger than his retainers, sits on a sedan chair carried by six women; other women hold large fans and a parasol.

The attribution of an ancient work of art to any one artist is almost always uncertain, given the habit of artists of reproducing famous paintings to closely study their details and understand their essence.

Most of the figures are depicted with subtle but homogeneous features; the leading figures in the work are given strikingly individual features, while the faces and clothes of the others are not differentiated.

Error29

"He is about to leave the emperor to set off for the West, with constant faith and awareness of the Great Emptiness" (Journey to the West)

Xuanzang

Buddhist monk

Period
Tang (AD 618–907)

Life
AD 602–664

Lay name
Chen Yi

Terms
Record of the Western Regions (Xiyuji)
Journey to the West (Xiyouji)

Related entries
Qin Shi Huangdi, Officials and literati, Confucianism, Commerce, Chang'an (Western Han), Images of the Buddha

While basing his government on the norms of Confucianism, Emperor Taizong personally preferred the Daoist school and permitted the expression of other religions. In consideration of the great social importance of the Buddhist faith in China, a large temple was built in the capital of Chang'an dedicated to the memory of the emperor's mother. When the Chinese Buddhist monk Xuanzang returned to the capital in AD 645, after a 16-year trip to India, he was offered a position at court. When the monk declined the position, the ruler suggested he write his *Record of the Western Regions* (completed in AD 646), which relates primarily the history, customs, products, geography, and climate of the countries he had visited. Xuanzang had chosen the land route across the Gobi Desert and the Tian Shan and Pamir mountains and had found support from such powerful rulers as the king of Turfan and the great khan of the Western Turks, at the time on friendly terms with the Chinese emperor. He had spent years in India studying the most important centers of Buddhist knowledge and devotion. Xuanzang brought to China 657 works from the Buddhist canon, and with the support of Taizong, who put the temple dedicated to his mother at his disposal, he undertook the translation of 75 of these sacred texts, an activity that occupied him until the end of his life.

▶ *The Healing of Horse Diseases by the Stableboy of the Heavenly Stables, the Monkey Sun Wukong,* 20th century, New Year's woodblock print (*Nianhua*) produced at Fengxiang, Shaanxi.

The monkey Sun Wukong is the second main character in the novel: the playful and irreverent monkey had been chosen by the Buddha to protect the monk during his trip.

Xuanzang's trip inspired the man of letters Wu Cheng'en (1500?–1582) to write the novel Journey to the West, *a bestseller that still fascinates the world's readers.*

Named "Stableboy of the Heavenly Stables" by the Buddha, the monkey is still honored as the patron divinity of horses. Sun Wukong, the "monkey king," has also become part of traditional Chinese theater and delights audiences with his ingenuity and his agile acrobatics.

▲ Illustration for the novel *Journey to the West (Xiyouji)*, Li Zhuowu xiansgheng piping Xiyouji edition, Ming dynasty, early 17th century, Bibliothèque Nationale, Paris.

In the novel Xuanzang is the reincarnation of a disciple of the Buddha who is escorted on his long trip by three notorious monsters with supernatural powers and features that are part animal and part human.

The monk travels on a cloud accompanied by a tiger and a small meditating Buddha seated on another cloud. The striding figure expresses vigor and dynamism.

A small perfume holder hanging from a chain fixed to a stick swings over a stack of written scrolls, apparently sacred texts of the Buddhist canon that the monk carries like a backpack.

The pilgrim's features are almost caricatural to indicate his foreign provenance; thick lips over square teeth, a large nose, and thick eyebrows.

Xuanzang was not the first Chinese pilgrim on the Silk Route: the monk Faxian reached India during his long trip, from 399 to 413, followed in 518 by the monk Huisheng.

In his left hand he holds a flyswatter, while his right rests on a walking stick.

▲ *Itinerant Monk* (detail), end Tang dynasty, 9th century, from Dunhuang, Gansu, ink and color on paper, 49.6 x 29.4 cm, Musée Guimet, Paris.

The texts brought by Xuanzang were preserved in this pagoda, built by the successor of Taizong.

The pagoda is part of a complex dedicated to the ruler's mother called the Temple of Great Goodwill (Da Ci'en Si).

The pagoda rises from its square base, narrowing upward floor by floor. The building has been destroyed and rebuilt several times, with two floors being added to the original five.

Inside, a winding wooden staircase leads to the seventh floor. Beginning at a small central space of each floor, four narrow passages lead the visitor to door windows, which open on the four sides of the construction.

▲ The Big Wild Goose Pagoda (*Dayanta*), Tang dynasty, circa AD 652, brick, 64 m high, Xi'an, Shaanxi.

The stone architraves over the ground-floor doors are decorated with motifs of Buddhist inspiration, which legend attributes to the famous painter Yan Liben.

"If a wife does not serve her husband, the proper relationship between man and woman and the natural order of things are neglected and destroyed" (Ban Zhao)

Wu Zetian

Wife of Emperor Gaozong, empress

Period
Tang (AD 618–907)

Reign
AD 690–705

Family name
Wu

Proper name
Mei, later Zhao

Posthumous name
Empress Zetian

Terms
Great Cloud Sutra (Dayunjing)

Related entries
Taizong, Officials and literati, Education and exams, Confucianism, Buddhism, Women, Commerce

Formerly a concubine of the emperor Taizong, Wu Zetian managed to rise to the rank of principal wife of his successor, Gaozong, who fell ill in 660 and handed the reins of government over to her. At Gaozong's death, in 683, Wu Zetian accepted the formal nomination of her son Zhongzong, but at his first sign of autonomy she replaced him with another son. In 690 she began a new dynasty, the Zhou, and took the throne. The only woman in Chinese history to assume sovereignty, Wu Zetian was later treated harshly by Confucian historians for having deserted the traditional role of a woman. A better reason for such condemnation was the cruelty with which she imposed her will, a cruelty that did not stop even when dealing with her own family members. Her reign did have positive aspects: Wu Zetian favored the ascent of a new elite by promoting the system of national exams and transferring the capital to Luoyang, thus distancing the court from the direct influence of the ancient northwestern clans. Chinese Buddhism experienced its period of greatest prosperity during her reign. Temples were built throughout the country dedicated to the *Great Cloud Sutra*, which contains a prophecy concerning the reincarnation of a goddess in the form of a universal sovereign. In 705 the empress fell ill and was forced to abdicate, and the Tang dynasty was revived.

▶ The Sacred Way (*shendao*) that leads to the tomb of Emperor Gaozong and Empress Wu Zetian, Tang dynasty, AD 684–706, Qianling, Shaanxi.

Two twin stele were erected opposite the southern entrance of the combined tomb of Gaozong and Wu Zetian: one bears 8,000 characters celebrating the emperor's deeds; the other, dedicated to the empress, bears no writing.

The top of the stele is decorated symmetrically with dragons carved in high relief.

The two stele mark the end of the Sacred Way, which leads to the sepulchral tumulus and is flanked by many large human and zoomorphic figures carved fully round.

Why did the empress leave vacant the space usually dedicated to the glorification of the ruler? Various possible explanations have been advanced.

Perhaps she believed her merits could be judged only by future generations, and in fact during the 10th and 11th centuries thirteen epitaphs were inscribed on the stele, although with the passage of time they have almost disappeared.

▲ Stele without writing, Tang dynasty, AD 684–706, stone, 630 x 210 x 149 cm, Qianling, Shaanxi.

Princess Li Yongtai was a granddaughter of the empress Wu Zetian and favorite daughter of the unfortunate emperor Zhongzong, deposed by his own mother.

A pair of mandarin ducks symbolizes the conjugal harmony between Princess Yongtai and her husband, Wu Yanji, buried in the adjacent tomb.

The princess died in AD 701 at Luoyang, at only 17, and was buried definitively in 706, a year after the death of her grandmother—who, according to certain sources, was responsible for the princess's premature death.

On the eastern side of the exterior face of the sarcophagus, which is engraved inside and out with scenes depicting the private life of the princess, two servants are presented watching over an interior door as though it were Yongtai's bed chamber.

▲ Two servants in front of a door with two knockers, Tang dynasty, AD 706, detail of the engravings on the sarcophagus of Li Yongtai, Qianling, Shaanxi.

"I sat drinking and did not notice the dusk until falling petals filled the folds of my dress. Drunken, I rose; I walked toward the moonlit stream" (Li Bai)

Li Bai

The poems of one of the greatest poets of Chinese literature are fresh and spontaneous, full of wonder and playfulness, of love for life and for wine. Li Bai, who was fascinated by Daoism, speaks with the moon and meets with mountains, using all the traditional poetic genres, but giving preference to the ancient style, which involves fewer restrictions in terms of the length of verses, rhythm, and the parallelism of words. His poems are often retrospective and express nostalgia for the glorious past and melancholy over the flow of time, but there are also the pleasures of idleness and inebriety. Parting with friends, traveling, and being far from home are themes that Li Bai shared with many poet-officials of the period who were forced to perform their duties in far-off locales. Li Bai, however, traveled as a matter of choice and never took the national exam in order to obtain a position. Such was his fame that he was summoned by the emperor Xuanzong (reigned AD 712–756) to the Hanlin Painting Academy at Chang'an, but the position proved brief. Exiled because of his presumed involvement in the great An Lushan rebellion, which shook the Tang empire at the middle of the 8th century, Li Bai was pardoned several years before his death. Legend has it that while out boating, and drunk, he met his death by drowning, falling overboard in the attempt to embrace the moon's reflection on the water.

Poet

Period
Tang (AD 618–907)

Life
AD 701– 762

Family name
Li

Proper name
Bai, also
pronounced Po

Nickname (*Zi*)
Taibai or Taipo

Terms
Ancient-style poetry
(*guti shi*)

Related entries
Officials and literati,
Poetry, Landscape
painting, Chang'an
(Tang)

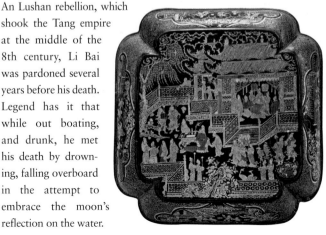

◄Lid of a box, Yuan dynasty, black lacquer with mother-of-pearl inserts, 27.3 x 22.2 cm, Lee Family Collection, Tokyo.

Two maid servants are busy heating the wine, made of grains and always served warm.

▲ Attributed in the past to Du Dashou, *The Poet Li Bai Drinking with the Emperor Minghuang*, Ming dynasty, early 15th century, horizontal scroll, ink and color on silk, 29.6 x 83 cm, Museum of Fine Arts, Julia Bradford Huntington James Fund, Boston.

The emperor, although relaxed, sits composedly on a stool in the inner court of the palace; the poet, without his outer clothes, is sprawled across a nearby bench.

Li Bai's fondness for wine was the subject of many legends. The state of drunkenness was not deplored in China, being considered instead one of the ways to stimulate the free flow of creativity.

Du Fu, another great poet of the period, claimed that one cup of wine was enough for Li Bai to write one hundred poems.

Only once did Li Bai and Du Fu actually meet, but Du Fu, a poet of dramatically realistic works with an innovative form, was profoundly struck by the encounter.

Li Bai

The painter Liang Kai, a highly esteemed academy master during the period of the Southern Song, specialized in the depiction of figures, landscapes, and Buddhist and Daoist subjects. At the height of his fame he retired to private life.

The seal has never been deciphered, but there is no question that it was composed using the square Mongolian script created by the Tibetan monk Phags-pa, circa 1269.

The head is defined with a few simple lines that give a concise but at the same time magical image of the great poet.

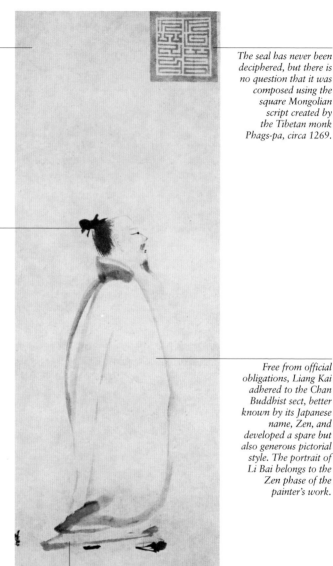

Free from official obligations, Liang Kai adhered to the Chan Buddhist sect, better known by its Japanese name, Zen, and developed a spare but also generous pictorial style. The portrait of Li Bai belongs to the Zen phase of the painter's work.

▲ Liang Kai, *Li Bai Reciting His Poems*, Southern Song dynasty, early 13th century, ink on paper, 81.1 x 30.5 cm, National Museum, Tokyo.

The robe the poet wears, which covers him head to foot, is created with a quick gesture using diluted ink; shading at the collar and along the bottom give it profondity and volume.

"Last night the spring wind entered my room again. I cannot bear to remember the bright moon of my lost kingdom, the marble steps and carved balustrades" (Li Yu)

Huizong

Huizong, passionate connoisseur of the arts and himself a talented artist, gave new impulse to China's traditional artistic disciplines as well as to artisan creations. He took personal care of the wares made in porcelain kilns and founded a famous painting academy in the capital of Bianliang, today's Kaifeng. Under his rule the scholastic system was improved, as was the structure of the national exams, but he also found time for new subjects, such as archaeological research and the encyclopedic collection of scientific and historical information. In truth, the business of state was neglected, and the court was not aware of the danger looming in the new state of Jin, founded by the Jurchen nomads to the north of China. The Jin pressed on the Liao, a dynasty formed by the Khitans, another nomadic people that occupied large areas in northern China. In the hope of finally driving the Khitans out of Chinese territory, the Southern Song dynasty allied itself with the Jin. The undertaking succeeded despite the poor military contribution of the Song, but the Jurchen then invaded China, conquering the capital in 1127. Huizong, who had abdicated in 1126, was deported along with his successor and lived out the last eight years of his life in prison, reduced to the status of an ordinary man.

Emperor and artist

Period
Northern Song
(AD 960–1127)

Reign
AD 1100–1126

Family name
Zhao

Given name
Ji

Temple name
Huizong

Related entries
Zhu Xi, Calligraphy, Landscape painting, Collectors of antiquities, Foreign dynasties, Kaifeng

◀ Emperor Huizong, *Five-colored Parakeet on a Blossoming Apricot Tree*, painted section, Northern Song dynasty, late 11th–early 12th century, ink and color on silk, 52 x 125 cm, Museum of Fine Arts, Boston.

41

The emperor's elegant and refined taste is best expressed in his personal calligraphic style, known as "slender gold" (shoujin).

The characters are composed of sharply defined and vigorous strokes, making them appear engraved rather than brushed on the absorbent support.

The structure and proportions are perfectly balanced, and despite their markedly personal style the characters are easily legible.

The emperor's paintings are equally lucid and precise, but also so detailed they seem static, lacking the dynamic touch that characterizes his calligraphy.

▲ Emperor Huizong, *Five-colored Parakeet*, calligraphic section, Northern Song dynasty, late 11th–early 12th century, ink and color on silk, 52 x 125 cm, Museum of Fine Arts, Boston.

The emperor took a personal interest in the painting academy he founded, sometimes instructing and correcting the painters and often suggesting themes to work on, including auspicious events, such as this work.

The white wings of the cranes stand out luminously against the blue background without need of further definition. The emperor adopted the "boneless" (mogu) style of painting, which did without the classic black outlines given figures.

The unusual angle of the painting reflects the emperor's respect for the private life of all citizens. He once severely criticized a painter who had depicted scenes of daily life inside homes for having invaded privacy.

Huizong wanted to commemorate two propitious events that had happened in the capital of Kaifeng: the appearance of an auspicious cloud (white edged in red) that enclosed the palaces of the capital, and the flight of a flock of cranes across a clear sky.

▲ Emporer Huizong, *Auspicious Cranes*, painted section, Northern Song dynasty, late 11th–early 12th century, ink and color on silk, 51 x 138 cm, Provincial Museum, Liaoning.

Wares from the kilns of Ru were reserved for the imperial court and were created only for about twenty years under the vigilance of Emperor Huizong. With the fall of the capital, production ended.

A stupendous gray-blue glaze covers the entire body of the vase, including the edges and the bottom. To avoid damaging the surfaces during firing in the kilns, these ceramics were placed atop tiny spurs called "sesame seeds."

Huizong, an avid collector of ancient bronze vases, introduced the production of ceramics in archaic shapes, such as this tripod, made to imitate a prototype dating to the Han dynasty.

The thick network of craquelures was meant to favor comparison with the veining of jade while also giving the vase a more antique appearance.

▲ Tripod vase, Northern Song dynasty, product of the Ru kilns, Henan, glazed ceramic, 12.9 cm high, Palace Museum, Beijing.

'But do you understand the nature of water and of the moon?—he asked—The first of them flows without ever ending, the other now waxes, now wanes, without ever increasing or diminishing" (Su Shi)

Su Shi

Su Shi lived during the reigns of five of the Northern Song emperors, and his public career, characterized by a series of highs and lows, reflected the transitory fortunes of the two principal opposing political trends that alternated in the rule of the country. A Confucian man of letters drawn to Buddhism and Daoism, Su Shi, best known in the West by his pseudonym, Su Dongpo, was a poet, calligrapher, painter, art critic, and essayist. He and his fellow artists, struck by the simplicity of the ancient works of art just then being discovered during the first archaeological excavations and inspired by neo-Confucian ideas, promoted a new theory of artistic creation, seen as a means for the spontaneous expression of human nature. The "imprint of the heart" left on the page expresses the essence of the person through the means of personal expression even though conditioned by taste and modesty. In that way art approaches the universal principle that exists beyond the concrete depiction of objects. Calligraphy, particularly in the loose but legible running-hand cursive style, and painting in ink were the expressive genres most agreeable to this concept and beginning in the Song period were considered superior to other genres. The literary production of Su Shi, a brilliant and candid man, is formally perfect but without prejudice and never dogmatic. He was one of the promoters of the free style in prose, and certain of his works have inspired later generations of artists.

Man of letters

Period
Northern Song
(AD 960–1127)

Life
AD 1037–1101

Family name
Su

Given name
Shi

Pseudonym
Su Dongpo

Terms
Imprint of the heart
(*xinyin*)
Universal principle (*li*)
Running hand
(*xingshu*)

Related entries
Huizong, Zhu Xi,
Education and exams,
Poetry, Calligraphy,
Landscape painting

◀ Su Shi, *Poetry in the Ancient Style of Li Bai*, written in running-hand cursive, Northern Song dynasty, dated to 1093, ink on paper, 34.0 x 111.1 cm, Municipal Museum of Art, Osaka.

Carved from a single piece, Su Shi's inkstone has a slight hollow in the front part where the ink stick was rubbed.

Two characters, dong jing ("eastern source"), engraved on the raised edge, refer to the famous man of letters, who chose "Eastern Slope" (Dongpo) as his nom de plume.

A few drops of water are poured onto the stone with grindings from an inkstick, and ink collects in the hollow rear of the stone, enclosed by a raised border.

An inscription on the front side highlighted in gold leaf repeats words from Emperor Qianlong of the Qing dynasty that support the presumed provenance of the stone.

The inkstone was a very personal object and a fundamental tool to the Chinese literati, and its usefulness counted as much as the simple elegance of its shape.

▲ Inkstone of Su Shi, shown top and bottom, Northern Song dynasty, 11th century, black stone, 11.4 x 7.9 x 3.3 cm, National Palace Museum, Taipei.

Several calligraphic works by Su Shi have survived, but of his paintings in black ink there is only this one black-and-white photograph; all trace of the work was lost several decades ago.

The rock and tree seem to have been made in a single circular gesture from left to right, ending in the short lines that suggest dried branches. The effect is dynamic and at the same time balanced.

The moment of inspiration distinguished painter-literati from painter-artisans, a distinction created by Su Shi that became fundamental to the history of Chinese painting in later dynasties.

Su Shi wrote, "In the moment in which you take brush in hand, staring fixedly, what you wish to paint will appear before your eyes, and you must get up in a hurry to pursue it."

The composition does not seem copied from life and corresponds instead to a mental image created by the artist, who had studied and memorized forms to create an ideal image.

▲ Su Shi, *Old Pine and Rock*, Northern Song dynasty, second half 11th century, ink on paper, *sine loco*.

> *"Knowledge and action always require each other, like eyes and legs. Without legs, the eyes cannot walk; without eyes, the legs cannot see"* (Zhu Xi)

Zhu Xi

Philosopher

Period
Northern Song (AD 960–1127)

Life
AD 1030–1100

Terms
School of universal principles (*lixue*)
Neo-Confucianism (*daoxue*)
Universal principle (*li*)
Vital force (*qi*)
Five relationships (*wulun*)
Four Books of Confucianism (*Sishu*): *Analects* (*Lunyu*), *Mencius* (*Mengzi*), and two chapters of the *Liji (Record of Rites)* entitled *The Doctrine of the Mean* (*Zhong Yong*) and *The Great Learning* (*Daxue*)

Related entries
Huizong, Su Shi, Confucianism, The five relationships

▶ Liu Minshu, *Portrait of Three Literati: Cheng Hao, Cheng Yi, Zhu Xi*, Yuan dynasty, 13th–14th century, ink and color on silk, 122.2 x 68.6 cm, Freer Gallery of Art, Smithsonian Institution, Washington, DC.

During the Song period, Confucian teaching was thoroughly reexamined because, unlike both Buddhism and Daoism, its moral and ethical teaching could not respond to metaphysical questions and it did not include a cosmology. Zhu Xi offered a synthetic arrangement of the "school of universal principles" of the so-called neo-Confucians: beginning with the scrupulous analysis of Confucian texts, he identified the origin of all things in the "universal principle," which was manifested in "vital force" and which in turn permeates everything, making possible the birth, evolution, and destruction of things through an alternation of yin and yang. The universal principle is reflected in humans as an innate moral principle, while the quality of vital force determines social role. Since all humans are endowed with the moral principle, wisdom is not restricted to an elect few but is instead the concrete goal of every-

one. Education and the cultivation of the self take place through the process of socialization based on the obligations made clear in the "five relationships" and through the "investigation of things," which is the study of objects and concrete events. At first opposed, Zhu Xi's concepts were soon reevaluated, and the *Four Books* of Confucianism he had chosen from among the classic texts and had written commentaries on were included in the program of national examinations beginning in the Yuan dynasty.

As a result of the affirmation of neo-Confucianism, a trend began in the Song period of representing the "universal principle" by way of intimate and simple subjects.

An excellent sense of observation, united with the careful execution of details, distinguished the painters who specialized in the depiction of flowers and insects.

The bamboo, outlined in black and painted in rich tonalities of green, creates a diagonal, accentuated by the wasp at upper right.

A second diagonal is created between the grasshopper and the dragonfly. The center of the painting, the virtual meeting point, does not attract the eye, which is instead drawn first to the pleasing colors of the bamboo and then led to the study of the insects.

▲ Wu Bing, *Bamboo and Insects*, Southern Song dynasty, circa 1190–1194, album leaf, ink and color on silk, 24.2 x 27 cm, Cleveland Museum of Art.

In his maturity, Shen Zhou, one of the "four masters of the Ming dynasty," developed an expressive style in which he composed paintings with abstract calligraphic effects.

During the Ming period, a new neo-Confucian theory broke with the concept of the "investigation of things" of the Song period to turn to meditative introspection intended to cultivate the self and thus achieve wisdom: Daoism.

The clouds—the area left white above the foreground landscape—lighten the entire composition and give height and depth to the mountains.

An isolated pavilion invites meditation in a setting of wild beauty.

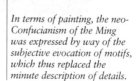

In terms of painting, the neo-Confucianism of the Ming was expressed by way of the subjective evocation of motifs, which thus replaced the minute description of details.

▲ Shen Zhou, *Clouds among Mountains and a Stream*, Ming dynasty, early 16th century, ink and color on paper, 148 x 68.2 cm, Museum of Art, Hong Kong.

"He is a man of good stature. . . . His limbs are well fleshed and modeled in due proportion. His complexion is fair and ruddy like a rose, the eyes black and handsome" (Marco Polo)

Kublai Khan

Although he declared himself a promoter of Mongolian politics, Kublai Khan became inserted in the tradition of Chinese civilization, assuming the Chinese dynastic name Yuan ("origin") in 1271 for his empire, at the time not yet entirely conquered. To avoid being absorbed by the numerically superior Chinese, the Mongols divided the population in four categories kept apart by impassable social barriers. The Mongols paid no taxes and occupied key hereditary positions in the government; their Central Asian allies also enjoyed fiscal privileges and were used in the administration as subordinates or as tax collectors, when they were not involved in commerce. The third category was composed of the inhabitants of northern China—Chinese, Jurchen, Khitans—and coming last were the "southerners," the Chinese inhabitants of the territory of the Song dynasty in the south, discriminated against and excluded from all important positions. The extension of the Mongol domination, from China to the Caucasus, and Kublai Khan's multiethnic state organization facilitated intercontinental exchanges: firearms, paper, and hydraulic and metallurgic techniques traveled all the way to Europe. Mongol inexperience in the field of rural politics, however, led to impoverishment, and after Kublai's death there were revolts of the peasant population, forced to abandon their fields to build canals and palaces and subjected to the payment of increasing tributes.

Emperor

Period
Yuan (1279–1368)

Reign
1271–1294

Family name
Borjigin

Given name
Kublai

Temple name
Shizu

Related entries
Foreign dynasties,
Theater, Beijing

◀ Mongol passport
(*paizi*), Yuan
dynasty, 13th
century, iron with
silver inlay, 18.1 cm
high, Metropolitan
Museum of Art,
New York.

The genre of portraiture of the imperial family began taking shape during the Song period and was continued during the Mongol domination, reflecting the identity of the foreigners, made clear in their facial features and clothing.

The imperial family was careful to maintain Mongol habits and customs, in part because they were deeply tied to them and in part to avoid being seen as having betrayed their culture in the eyes of the Mongol aristocracy.

The portraits of the Mongol emperors were held in state temples dedicated to Lamaism, which had become the official religion of the Mongols in 1253.

It seems the emperor truly loved his consort—which did not prevent him from frequenting concubines— and that her death threw him into a state of grave depression.

▲ Portrait of the Empress Zhabi, Consort of Shizu (Kublai Khan), Yuan dynasty, 13th century, album leaf, ink and color on silk, 61.5 x 48 cm, National Palace Museum, Taipei.

Beginning in the 10th century the representation of the life and customs of nomadic peoples became a common pictorial genre. Among that genre's favorite subjects were hunting and horseback sports, pastimes the Chinese had abandoned after the 8th century.

Perhaps the painter intended to emphasize the emperor's Mongolian origin. The subject of the painting itself must have seemed strange to the Chinese, but in addition there is the presence of a woman along with men of clearly foreign extraction.

The painter emphasizes the emperor's regality in every detail but presents him as busy in an informal activity in a wild setting, thus breaking with the schemes of royal portraiture known until then.

A hunting dog, a feline crouching behind a rider, and a falcon resting on the hand of a rider accompany the men during their hunt.

▲ Liu Guandao, *Kublai Khan Hunting*, Southern Song dynasty, dated 1200, vertical scroll, ink and color on silk, 182.9 x 104.1 cm, National Palace Museum, Taipei.

In 1298, held prisoner of war in Genoa, the Venetian Marco Polo dictated a report of his trip to the Orient and the seventeen years spent at the court of Kublai Khan to fellow prisoner, a Pisan named Rustichello.

Polo's description of the splendors of the court and the wealth of the cities seemed so incredible to 14th-century European readers that they took it for pure invention.

The Mongol khan was described with great respect: the Venetian emphasized not only the magnificence of the ruler, surrounded by splendid comforts, but gave admiring descriptions of his cosmopolitanism and his efficient administration.

▲ Workshop of the Boucicaut Master, *Kublai Khan in a Sedan Chair Carried by Elephants and His Followers on Horseback*, 1412, page with miniature from the *Livre des Merveilles du Monde* by Marco Polo, 15th century, Folio 42, Bibliothèque Nationale, Paris.

In his role of foreign merchant, Marco Polo found himself in a privileged position compared to the native Chinese, who were the victims of the hierarchy of Mongolian society.

The figures and settings of the Mongol court were of a style completely unknown to the 15th-century European artist, who had certainly never seen an elephant and who gave the Mongols classical European features.

"We have been chosen by our people to occupy the imperial throne of China in the dynastic name of the 'Great Luminosity'"
(Hongwu)

Hongwu

Son of poverty-stricken peasants, a Buddhist monk, then leader of one of the many secret societies that rose in rebellion at the end of the Yuan dynasty, this future ruler triumphed over the various factions struggling for power, then forced the Mongols to withdraw to the interior of Mongolia. Known by the dynasty-era name of Hongwu, the emperor improved the lot of the poor masses with the hereditary division of the population into farmers, soldiers, and artisans. The farmers were grouped in small autonomous administrative units, responsible for their own census and the collection of taxes. The soldiers were given allotments of previously untilled land so they could provide for their own sustenance. The artisans worked in the imperial factories or were at least obliged to perform temporary services. Most of the tax revenue came from the pockets of the merchants, looked upon as parasites. Hongwu, forced to depend on councilors from the literati class, but highly distrustful of them, eliminated all hereditary roles and strengthened the Confucian system of national exams. The heads of ministries and other high offices had to report directly to the emperor, to the detriment of the imperial chancellery. This dangerous concentration of power led, under his successors, to the growing power of the eunuchs.

Emperor

Period
Ming (1368–1644)

Reign
1368–1398

Family name
Zhu

Given name
Xingzong, later
Yuanzhang

Temple name
Taizu

Posthumous name
Gao

Era name
Hongwu

Terms
Luminosity (*ming*)
Vast military (*Hongwu*)

Related entries
Eunuchs, Officials and
literati, Ceramics,
Technology and
industries, Nanjing,
Beijing

◀ *Portrait of the Emperor Hongwu*, Ming dynasty, end 14th century, vertical scroll, ink and color on silk, 268.8 x 163.8 cm, National Palace Museum, Taipei.

Hongwu's tomb complex, built between 1381 and 1383, is near Nanjing, the city that he chose, as first emperor of the Ming dynasty, as his capital.

Geomancers identified a spot in the Purple Mountains (Zhongshan) as the ideal location to erect the tomb. The site was then occupied by the Ling Gu monastery, founded in the 6th century, but the emperor had it relocated to the north.

This enormous stele is enclosed within the walls of a pavilion that long ago lost its original timber roof; it marks the beginning of the Sacred Way that leads to the tomb complex.

The stele was erected by Hongwu's son, the emperor Yongle, three years after his illicit appropriation of the throne, and it commemorates the deeds and virtues of his father.

The turtle is the animal of the north, symbol of long life and constancy. The turtles that support imperial commemorative steles often have dragon-shaped heads.

▲ Commemorative stele to the emperor Hongwu, Ming dynasty, 1405, stone, 8.8 m high, Xiaoling tomb complex, Sifangcheng, Nanjing.

Wang Meng was one of the many literati who suffered harsh punishments following the installation of the Ming: imprisoned for having looked at paintings together with another man later condemned for treason, he died in prison.

Last of the "Four great masters of the Yuan dynasty," Wang Meng made liberal use of stylistic elements and techniques from the entire history of Chinese landscape painting to develop his own expressive style, admired and imitated by later painters.

The human presence is limited to small huts located on the edges of the composition.

The paintings made after the foundation of the dynasty in 1368 are dense, almost obsessive in their tendency to completely cram the surface, whereas this landscape is given luminosity and breadth by its few empty spaces.

The famous critic Dong Qichang (1555–1636) said of this painting, "Master Wang's brushstrokes are strong enough to lift a tripod; for five hundred years there has been no one like him."

▶ Wang Meng, *The Qingbian Mountains*, Yuan dynasty, dated 1366, ink on paper, 141 x 42 cm, Shanghai Museum.

Over the course of the Yuan dynasty, the Jingdezhen kilns, located in southern China, developed a porcelain with a transparent underglaze painted decoration that profoundly influenced ceramic production.

The underglaze technique involved a first firing at high temperature, after which the "bisque" was decorated and covered by a transparent glaze and fired a second time at lower temperature.

The copper-red decoration is typical of the Hongwu period. Its production required great skill since the tonalities and the quality of the color depended on constant atmospheric conditions during the firing in the kiln.

The inside of the bowl is decorated with peony flowers, while the outside is painted with chrysanthemums. Both motifs appear often in the repertory of the Ming and Qing dynasties.

▲ Bowl, Ming dynasty, Hongwu reign, 1368–1398, porcelain with copper-red underglaze decoration, 15.6 cm high, 40 cm diam., Metropolitan Museum of Art, New York.

"Let commerce flourish on our frontiers and foreigners from distant lands be welcome among us" (Yongle)

Yongle

Like some of the greatest Chinese rulers, Yongle usurped the throne from the legitimate successor, Hongwu's grandson, and succeeded in legitimizing his seizure of power with a farsighted government and large-scale territorial expansion. To more adequately protect the northern borders, he moved the capital northward from Nanjing to the former capital of the Mongols, which now took the name Beijing ("northern capital"). After the multiethnic governments of the Yuan, the Ming dynasty, with its homegrown roots, was strongly Sino-centric, in some cases resulting in political xenophobia. Emperor Yongle, curious and tolerant in terms of religion, was able to transform nationalism into a productive attitude. Under his rule six great maritime expeditions took Chinese emissaries as far as the eastern coast of Africa, demonstrating China's high level of technology as well as the intense diplomatic and mercantile activity of China at that time. The *Yongle Encyclopedia*, compiled by more than three thousand literati in four years of research and collected in 22,877 books, was to contain all the scientific knowledge of the time as well as the text of every book written in China. The manuscript, completed in 1408, was lost; fragments of a 16th-century copy are all that remain today.

Emperor

Period
Ming (1368–1644)

Reign
1403–1424

Family name
Zhu

Proper name
Di

Temple name
Chengzu

Posthumous name
Taizong

Name at the time
Yongle

Terms
Perpetual happiness
(*yongle*)
Yongle Encyclopedia
(*Yongle Dadian*)
Northern capital
(Beijing)

Related entries
Eunuchs, Officials and
literati, Ceramics,
Technology and
industries, Nanjing,
Beijing

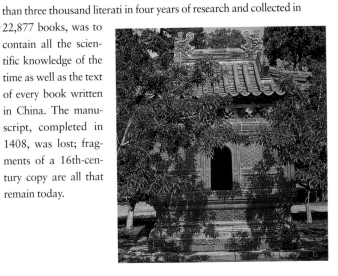

◀ Sacrificial oven (for burnt offerings) at the tomb of Emperor Yongle, Ming dynasty, 1409–1472, glazed terracotta, wood, bricks, Changling, Beijing.

It is not known when the Central Asian technique of cloisonné was introduced to China, but the oldest examples known today date to the early 15th century.

The technique of cloisonné consists in the creation of decorative designs on a metal vessel by soldering copper or bronze wires to it and filling the areas with a colored-glass paste that is then melted when the vessel is fired at a temperature of about 800°C.

Lotus flowers in red, blue, yellow, and white stand out against a background of deep turquoise, surrounded by volutes of green leaves.

Initially condemned as vulgar and showy, cloisonné wares were highly appreciated in the second half of the Ming dynasty as well as during the Qing.

The metallic wire of this plate has been gilded along the scalloped edges, on the two inner circles, and along the entire base.

▲ Dish with scalloped rim, Ming dynasty, early 15th century, cloisonné, 15.2 cm diam., Metropolitan Museum of Art, New York.

Between 1414 and 1433, the Muslim eunuch Zheng He (1371–1435), nominated admiral of the Chinese fleet by the emperor Yongle, led seven large-scale naval expeditions, reaching India and Persia and going as far as Africa.

At least sixty-two transoceanic ships, each more than 400 feet long with holds large enough for 1,500 tons, accompanied by more than one hundred smaller ships, carried crews numbering more than 30,000.

Despite the diplomatic and commercial successes obtained by the fleet, the most modern of its time, the costly trips were criticized after the death of Yongle and were ultimately suspended after the final 1433 expedition, in which the elderly admiral died.

Emperor Yongle clearly intended to use this enormous fleet to make clear the glory and power of the new China, which had freed itself from foreign rule only a few years earlier.

▲ Tribute Giraffe with Attendant, Ming dynasty, dated 1414, vertical scroll, ink and color on silk, 171.5 x 53.3 cm, Philadelphia Museum of Art.

Zheng He returned from his first expedition with two giraffes, highly prized by the Chinese because they were associated with the unicorn, a mythical animal that signaled the presence of a wise and benevolent ruler.

For the first time, direct official contacts were made between the Chinese court and several African countries, which sent ambassadors and precious gifts to Beijing.

Power and public life

◄Shang Xi, *Emperor Xuande during a Horseride* (detail), Ming dynasty, vertical scroll, ink and color on silk, 211 x 353 cm, Palace Museum, Beijing.

"The moon waxes and wanes, the sun is high or low. The celestial bodies and the abodes of the stars are orderly spread in place" (Thousand-Character Classic)

Signs from the heavens

Terms
Fixed star (*hengxing*)
Planet (*xingwing*)
Mansion (*xiu*)
Resonance (*ganying*)

Related entries
Telling time, Mandate of heaven, Sacred mountains

To the ancient Chinese, the universe was composed of three unities, the heavens, the earth, and humans. The position of the fixed stars and the dynamism of the planets determined the appearance of the sky and earth: according to a theory known as early as 350 BC, the square earth was surrounded by a spherical sky, hence the terrestrial equator crossed the route of the sun in the four points of the solstices and the equinoxes, the locations of the four mountains, or corners, of the earth. The earthly equator corresponded to the celestial equator, segmented in 28 groups of equatorial stars called mansions, each associated with a certain star. Every night of the lunar month, the moon stopped in one of these mansions. The manifestations of the heavens, meaning the superior force, were reflected in the history and destiny of humankind, and vice versa, following the principle known as "resonance"; observing and recording the positions of the stars, their movement, and any extraordinary celestial phenomena was thus of enormous importance. Comets and meteors appear in the ancient star charts, along with sun spots and even novas and super-novas, together with information on natural and atmospheric phenomena, such as rain, thunder, light-ning, and rainbows. All of the phenomena observed in the sky expressed the will of the heavens, without the modern distinctions made among astronomy, astrology, and meteorology.

▶ *Astral Map of Dunhuang* (detail), period of the Five Dynasties and the Ten Kingdoms, circa AD 940, ink and color on paper, British Library, London.

The manuscript illustrates fourteen cloud formations and twenty-nine configurations of comets. The figures are accompanied by their interpretation for divinatory purposes.

The appearance of a dog-shaped cloud is interpreted with regard to a military campaign: "If this [cloud] appears over the walls of the city, it will not be conquered."

Each of the fourteen cloud formations is related to one of the Warring States. Since the first cloud belongs to the kingdom of Chu, one can suppose that the treatise was compiled by an astronomer-astrologer before the end of its reign, in 223 BC.

▲ *Various Divinations of Astrology and Meteorology* (detail), Western Han dynasty, circa 168 BC, from Tomb 3 at Mawangdui, ink and color on silk, 150 x 48 cm, Hunan Provincial Museum, Changsha.

The drawings of the comets, the oldest in the world, are classified according to the appearance of the tail, present in all except the last, which has the shape of a swastika.

The Suzhou Planisphere was elaborated during the rule of the emperor Yuanfeng (1078–1085) of the Northern Song and was engraved in stone for purposes of preservation in 1247, after the transfer of the capital to Hangzhou.

The three characters that compose the title are pronounced tian we tu and mean "astronomical map."

The circular field, of about 85 cm in diameter, encloses all the heavenly bodies recorded by court astronomers in the sky over the capital of Kaifeng. The stars are grouped in configurations very much like the constellations defined by the ancient Greeks.

The median circle represents the celestial equator, which is intersected by the ecliptic.

At the center is the pole star, surrounded by a narrow ring that contains the stars that are always visible.

Forty-one columns with 209 characters explain the image, providing a review of the astronomical knowledge of the period.

▲ Suzhou Planisphere, Southern Song dynasty, 1247, rubbing of a stone bas-relief, 276 x 117 cm, Stone Carving Museum, Suzhou.

"The wind ceases, fallen flowers pile high. Outside my screen are heaps of them, red and snow white. Memory endures of the time the apple trees were in bloom. It is the lament of the dying spring" (Li Qingzhao)

Telling time

One of the major duties of each new dynasty was the compilation of a calendar to guarantee the favor of the heavens. The year of the Chinese lunisolar calendar was divided into six months of 30 days and six months of 29 days; every three years a short supplementary month was inserted to compensate for the difference between the solar year and the lunar month. In their calculations, Chinese astronomers made reference to Jupiter and to its movement in relationship to solar movements. Since Jupiter takes twelve times as long as the sun to complete its circuit, years were grouped in cycles of twelve. The sexagesimal cycle of years and days was arrived at through the combination of two indicators: the Ten Celestial Stems, created through a combination of the five phases and yin and yang, and the Twelve Terrestrial Branches, symbolized from the Eastern Han onward by twelve animals of the zodiac. The sexagesimal cycle of the days was divided into six weeks of ten days each, while the animals of the calendar were also used to indicate the hours, beginning at midnight. The denomination of time was not tied to the calendar but to the name or motto given to the dynasty era by the ruler. Wudi, who began all this, changed the name of the dynasty era fully eleven times, while beginning with the Ming only one name was used for the entire duration of the reign of each ruler.

Terms
Celestial Stems (*tian gan*)
Terrestrial Branches (*dizhi*)

Related entries
Wudi, Sima Qian, Signs from the heavens, Mandate of heaven, Yin and yang and the five phases

▼ Reverse of a mirror with the twelve animals of the zodiac, Sui dynasty, early 7th century, 21.5 cm diam., Musée Guimet, Paris.

From left to right, the twelve
models, with human bodies and
animal heads, represent the rat, ox,
tiger, rabbit (or hare), dragon,
snake, horse, sheep (or goat),
monkey, rooster (or phoenix), dog,
and pig (or boar).

The animals of the Chinese
calendar compose a cycle of
twelve years and not, as is
the case with the Western
zodiac cycle, twelve months.

The cyclical animals are sometimes
depicted along with animals
symbolic of the cardinal points,
such as, for example, on the cosmic
mirrors of the Tang period.

▲ Models of the twelve animals of
the calendar (shi'ershi), Tang
dynasty, 8th century AD, from the
outskirts of Xi'an, terracotta
painted after being fired,
38.5–41.5 cm high, 150 x 48 cm,
Shaanxi History Museum, Xi'an.

All twelve models are depicted wearing the robes of Tang-era officials, with sleeves so long they reach beneath the knees.

The presence in tombs of models making reference to the calendar and to the cardinal points may indicate the desire to regulate the world of the afterlife with the universal representation of space and time.

The panels covering the tower are left open along one side to reveal the mechanism that told time by way of manikins that exited tiny doors to hold up signs or ring bells and gongs, beat drums, or play stringed instruments.

The scientist Zhang Heng made the first armillary sphere in AD 125. It was used to demonstrate the movement of the stars in relation to the movement of the earth.

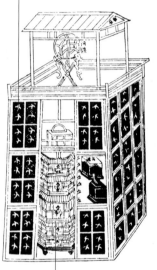

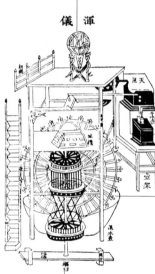

渾儀

By way of a series of gears, a water wheel transmits its power to the armillary sphere, the celestial globe, and the clock.

Small mechanical figures brusquely move—following the rhythm of an escapement mechanism—on the five levels that compose the clock.

Various sources document the existence of an astronomical tower built at Luoyang between AD 686 and 694, of which no trace has remained. The first European mechanical clocks date to the 14th century.

▲ Tower with astronomical instruments and a clock, Northern Song dynasty, 1088, from Su Song, *Essentials of a New Method for Mechanizing the Rotation of an Armillary Sphere and a Celestial Globe (Xin yi xiang fayao)*, 1094.

*'Light mists and heavy clouds, melancholy the long dreary day.
In the golden censer the burning incense is dying away. It is time
again for the lovely Double-Ninth Festival"* (Li Qingzhao)

Festivals

Most of the traditional Chinese festivals are based on the lunisolar
calendar, and the numbers of the dates of the festivals, considered
good luck, often replaced the actual names of the festivals. The celebration of the dead, however, followed the calendar of the 24
"seasons," which divided the 360-degree span of the solar year in
days of 15 degrees each. The names of the seasons of this calendar,
traditionally used in agriculture, refer to annual climatic changes.
The celebrations for the Spring Festival, which lasted 15 days, were
certainly the most important. The festival celebrated the beginning
of the new year, located between the winter solstice and the spring
equinox, which according to the Gregorian calendar occurs
between January 21 and February 21. In the past, the seventh day
of the festival marked the birthday for every Chinese regardless of
his or her actual date of birth. A child born in October, for example, would celebrate his second birthday in January (since the Chinese counted age beginning at the date of conception). The roots of
the Spring Festival probably lead back to the sacrificial ceremonies
in the Yin and Shang
periods (circa 17th–11th
centuries BC) when the
new year was welcomed
with offerings to divini-
ties as well as to ances-
tors. Many of the princi-
pal festivals were known
in the Han epoch and
reached their full devel-
opment in the Tang and
Song periods.

Terms
Season (*jieqi*)
Spring Festival
(*chunjie*)

Related entries
Telling time

▼ Wang Zhenpeng,
Spring Festival (detail),
Yuan dynasty, early
14th century, ink and
color on silk, 214 x 75
cm, Museum für
Völkerkunde, Leipzig.

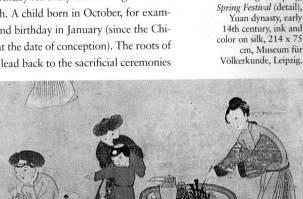

A precious antique bronze vase, a landscape in miniature, and other select objects placed on a table carved from a root clarify the meaning of the scroll and locate the scene in the home of an educated, well-to-do family.

The scene ends at a large bed with a painted screen flanked by two lamps. In the rear, a raised curtain offers a glimpse of the adjacent space.

Dressed in warm clothing and fur hats, these women celebrate the new year with tasty morsels and tea, poured into tiny colored cups by a maid.

The horns, gongs, drums, and cymbals played by the women also serve the purpose of entertaining the ladies seated around the table.

▲ Wang Zhenpeng, *Spring Festival* (detail), Yuan dynasty, early 14th century, ink and color on silk, 214 x 75 cm, Museum für Völkerkunde, Leipzig.

Evil spirits are afraid of loud noises and thus are driven off at the new year with fireworks, like those being thrown by children in the foreground, and also by loud music.

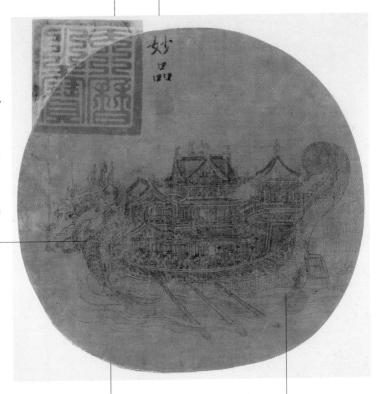

The Dragon Boat Festival falls on the fifth day of the fifth lunar month and marks the beginning of summer.

In his famous poem "Encountering Trouble" (Lisao), presented in the first person, Qu Yuan expresses his sorrow at having been unjustly exiled and at not having helped his ruler in the time of danger.

Most of all in southern China, the festival was celebrated with a race between boats decked out to look like dragons in memory of the illustrious poet of the reign of Chu named Qu Yuan (circa 340–278 BC).

In ancient China rivers were believed to be dragons that from time to time revealed their true aspect. When the great poet threw himself into the river, the local people raced to save him from the dragon, the event that is commemorated in the boat race.

Legend recounts that the writer committed suicide by throwing himself into a river.

▲ Wang Zhenpeng (attrib.), *A Grand Dragon Boat*, Yuan dynasty, late 13th–early 14th century, album leaf, ink, colors, and gold leaf on silk, 25.5 x 26.5 cm, Museum of Fine Arts, Chinese and Japanese Special Fund, Boston.

Despite its generic title, the painting probably depicts the Mid-Autumn, or Moon, Festival, being celebrated in a palace.

The Moon Festival usually falls in September, at the moment when the earth is at its greatest distance from the sun and thus the moon is at the height of its luminosity.

The Mid-Autumn Festival, still a very popular celebration, includes the eating of a traditional sweet called mooncake (yuebing).

The painter has splendidly rendered the nocturnal light of the scene, making the illuminated areas stand out through the use of white and bright colors, while the areas in shadow are rendered with a wide range of gray tonalities.

Court ladies and their female servants are shown parading toward a pavilion, where they will make offerings and compose verses in honor of the moon.

The festival is of special importance to women since, according to ancient myth, the moon is inhabited by Chang'e, a hero's wife who was forced to live there with a rabbit as her only companion after having illicitly swallowed the pill of immortality.

▲ Attributed in the past to Zhao Boju, *The Han Palace*, Southern Song dynasty, 12th century, album leaf mounted on a vertical scroll, image 24.5 cm diam., National Palace Museum, Taipei.

*"August is the Sky that observes the world below in its immensity.
It scans the four directions of the empire in search of He who will
diminish the suffering of the people"* (Book of Odes)

Mandate of heaven

The ideology of the "mandate of heaven" explains the rise and fall of
dynasties as the acquisition or loss of the moral right to rule, conferred
by heaven, which communicates its will through celestial signs: a conjunction of the planets Jupiter, Saturn, Venus, Mars, and Mercury
took place in 1059 BC, at the time of the ascent of the house of Zhou,
which eventually deposed the family of the Shang. In 205 BC a new
conjunction occurred and was thought to be related to the recent fall
of the Qin and the taking of power of the Han. This ancient ideology,
recorded in the *Classic of History*, was widely discussed by Confucius
and was integrated with cosmological and historical elements by a
scholar at the court of Emperor Wudi of the Han, giving life to a complex system of relationships between the heavens, earth, and humans.
Thanks to his virtues a new ruler received the mandate of heaven,
which gave him the right to take power. The emperor expressed the
will of the heavens and was the mediator between heaven and earth.

His primary mission was the
education of the people, and his
principal duties were the deter-
mination of the calendar, the
performance of sacrifices to the
heavens and the earth, which
coincided with the start of the
sowing and harvest seasons,
and the direction of public
works. Signals sent by the heavens were received and interpreted by court astronomer-
astrologers, who thus performed an activity of vital
importance to the survival of
the ruling house.

Terms
Mandate of heaven
(*tianming*)
Classic of History
(*Shujing*)

Related entries
Wudi, Signs from the
heavens

◄ Golden dragon,
symbol of the Chinese
emperor, Tang dynasty,
gilt bronze, 118 cm,
Collection of Board in
Charge of Cultural
Relics, Xi'an.

The privileged relationship
between the heavens and the
ruler was expressed not only
through worship of the state
but also by the celebratory
works made in the painting
academy, the products made
by the imperial state factories,
and the splendor of the
imperial collections.

This painting has a propitiatory
function and symbolizes divine
favor by way of the plant heavy
with rice.

The static composition is
based on vertical lines: the
central branch of the plant is
vigorous and healthy, and the
branches with the rice panicles
are clearly delineated.

The chromatic rendering plays
on the delicate contrasts
between tonalities of only two
colors, black and ocher, diluted
to various degrees in long, soft
brushstrokes.

▶ *Propitiatory Grain*, Yuan
dynasty, vertical scroll, ink and
color on silk, 190.2 x 67.9 cm,
National Palace Museum, Taipei.

*"From the jade tower rise skyward sounds of music and song.
Wind carries far the happy voices and laughter of court ladies"
(Gu Kuang)*

Court

The outward manifestations of imperial power were rites, ceremonies, and receptions that took place in accordance with a procedure that did not permit the smallest variation. Not only the actions performed in relation to the rule of the Son of Heaven, but every separate gesture had to be in keeping with the rigid rules in force at court, with protocols even regarding the food the emperor ate and the clothes he wore. Only the closest advisers were permitted near the emperor, who lived enclosed in the inner palace, protected by the imperial guard and surrounded by court ladies, the youngest children, and eunuchs. The government offices and audience rooms were located in the outer adjacent palace, where public functions took place and where the emperor received his officials. The structure of the palace, oriented on a north-south axis and enclosed within high walls, manifested the supremacy of the ruler, founded on his privileged relationship with cosmic forces. The wealth of the palace's decorations, its interior ponds and gardens, were the concrete demonstration of the state's magnificence. The empress, flanked by several secondary wives and by a variable number of concubines, was the highest authority of the "inner palace" and in some cases managed to exercise a notable influence on the emperor's decisions, a fact viewed negatively by Confucian historians, worried about the "illicit" competition between women and eunuchs.

Terms
Son of Heaven (*tianzi*)

Related entries
Mandate of heaven,
Chang'an (Tang),
Beijing

▼ *Concert at Court*,
Tang dynasty, ink and
color on silk, 48.7 x
69.5 cm, National
Palace Museum, Taipei.

Gu Kaizhi is considered one of the greatest painters in the history of Chinese art. None of his work survives, but there are copies inspired by them, including two versions of the Admonitions of the Instructress to the Court Ladies.

The handscroll in the British Museum contains nine of the original eleven scenes, which illustrate a political parody written in AD 292 by the poet and official Zhang Hua.

With a gesture the emperor dismisses a concubine.

The thin, undulating lines that define the figures, set against a bare background, seem to flow without ever coming detached from the background, a style destined to be characteristic of Chinese painting until the Tang period.

▶ Copy from the 6th–8th century AD of a work attributed to Gu Kaizhi, AD 344–406, The Admonitions of the Instructress to the Court Ladies (detail), handscroll, ink and color on silk, 25 cm high, British Museum, London.

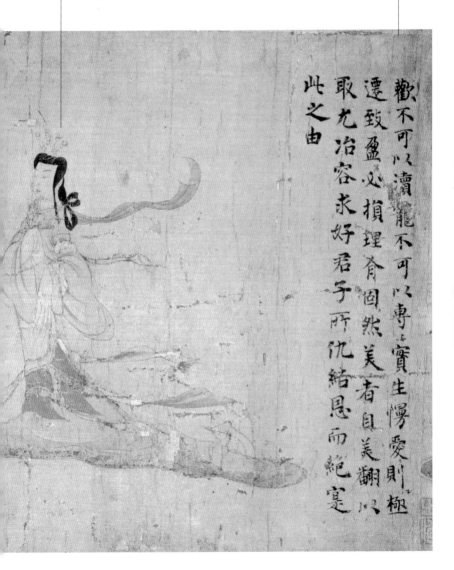

The work, painted in the period of disintegration of the empire and of weakness in the Confucian ideology, indicates that the stereotypical figurations of the Han period had been overcome, making possible the portrayal of individual personalities and emotions.

Each scene is preceded by an explanatory text.

此之由

遷致盈必損理有固然美者自美翻以

取尤冶容求好君子所沈結恩而絕寔

歡不可以瀆寵不可以專實生慢愛則極

The scenes, arranged in four rows, are inspired by a didactic text, Biographies of Exemplary Women (Lienü zhuan), *compiled by Liu Xiang, a 1st-century BC official.*

Although the stories cited relate to other times, even to mythical ages, the clothing styles and few elements of furnishing belong to the Han period.

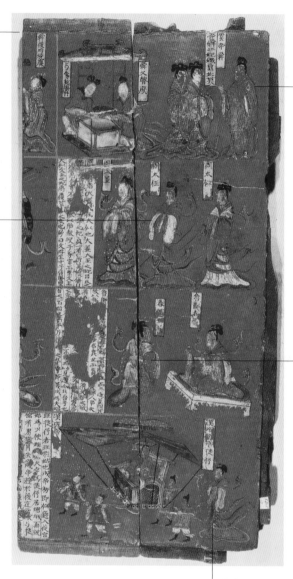

Illustrated are women who, according to the Confucian canon, were distinguished by their moral rectitude and virtue, beginning with the two concubines of the mythical Shun emperor, above, and by the three family founders of the Zhou dynasty in the second row.

This row relates the story of a virtuous woman in the feudal state of Lu, birthplace of Confucius.

▲ Four court scenes, Northern Wei dynasty, end 5th century, from the tomb of Sima Jinlong and his wife at Datong, Shanxi, panel from a lacquered screen, 81.5 x 40.5 cm, Provincial Museum, Shanxi.

The bottom row depicts Ban Jieyu, a learned woman who was among the ladies in waiting of the emperor Chengdi (37–7 BC). As revered as many were, concubines were not permitted to travel on the same litter as the emperor.

A hole in the headdress, characteristic of a court official, suggests that a feather was inserted here that identified his exact role.

The long tunic gathered in soft folds around the official's prostrate body gives only an approximate idea of his body, whereas his head and facial features are clearly defined.

At the level of the hands, joined in a sign of respect, is a small opening that may have been used as the base for a hu tablet, raised in the presence of the emperor (see page 203).

The hu table permitted access to the reception hall of the palace and was thus kept by special guards who gave it to the official when the ruler wished to speak with him.

A white slip decoration covers the entire figure, which after firing was painted in precious pigments, including green and blue made from cupriferous minerals. There are also traces of gold leaf.

▲ Model of an official, Tang dynasty, 8th century, terracotta, slip decoration, pigments, 56.5 cm long, Jan van Beers, London.

> "All the cities suffer a common ill: the ruler is surrounded by unworthy people. . . . Those who would dominate rulers first discover their fears and secret yearnings" (Han Fei)

Eunuchs

Terms
Filial piety (*xiao*)
Inner palace (*neigong*)
Treasure (*bao*)

Related entries
Court, Confucianism

Castration is a serious violation of Confucian ethics: a person who has been castrated is not authorized to perform rites for ancestors, since continuation of the family is one of the primary duties of "filial piety." Even so, while scorning the creation of eunuchs, who had been present even in the preimperial period, almost no Confucian man of letters ever gave thought to suggesting abolishing the practice. The Confucian councilors sought instead to limit the range of action of the eunuchs to the walls of the "inner palace," since the emperor had the exclusive right to surround himself with eunuchs. In some cases, however, they could not control the eunuchs, who, by exploiting rivalries among the women, the inexperience of an infant-emperor, or the incompetence of a ruler, managed to come into control of enormous wealth and limitless power: more than once the fall of a dynasty was attributed to intrigues among the eunuchs in the imperial palace. The first emperor of the Ming dynasty, Hongwu, drastically reduced the number of eunuchs and prevented them from interfering in state affairs. These provisions were revoked by his successors, and by the end of the dynasty more than 10,000 eunuchs lived in the inner palace, administering public affairs, the treasury, and the law.

▼ Eunuch tombs (*Tianyi Mu*), Beijing, Ming dynasty, early 17th century.

Originally figures like this were dressed and had arms made of materials now lost; they served the function of protecting the deceased and emphasized his social status, which would be continued in the afterlife.

Thousands of such terracotta statuettes, nude and without arms, have been found in the area of the tomb of the emperor Jing (reigned 156–141 BC) and in several kilns of the Han period.

In Beijing, the "knife men" carried on their activity in front of the walls of the Forbidden City and subjected the males, usually of young age, to the punishment of total castration.

The amputated genitals, euphemistically called the "treasure," were preserved, being displayed each time the eunuch rose in rank, and in the end were deposited in the eunuch's coffin so that he could present himself "complete" in the afterlife.

► Statuette of a eunuch, Western Han dynasty, 2nd century BC, from the area of the mausoleum of the emperor Jing, Yangling, Shaanxi, terracotta, slip decoration, pigments, 56.2 cm high, Provincial Institute of Archaeology, Xi'an.

"When Yu made the work of stemming the flood of waters, heaven conferred on him the black jade gui, with which he announced the completion of the work" (Shen Yue)

Controlling water

Terms
Yellow River
(*Huanghe*)
Grand Canal
(*Da Yunhe*)

Related entries
Qin Shi Huangdi,
Wudi, Mandate
of heaven,
Administration,
Transportation

The construction and maintenance of irrigation systems, dikes, and transportation canals were among the emperor's primary responsibilities, and failure in these areas could result in the loss of the mandate of heaven. In 246 BC a hydraulics expert under Qin Shi Huangdi made a canal 150 kilometers long between two rivers, thus fertilizing the arid land of the plain of central Shaanxi with deposits of the canal's muddy waters. Under the Han emperor Wudi, an irrigation canal was built in Shanxi, some of it constructed at a subterranean level. The great challenge of the Yellow River, whose loess-rich water caused terrible floods and repeatedly changed the course of the river in the province of Henan, was taken on in a systematic way by Qin Shi

Huangdi, who had all the local embankments knocked down to erect the first massive dam, later improved and enlarged many times. When the authorities failed to maintain the dams, whether out of negligence or lack of funds, the inevitable result was a terrible flood, with disastrous consequences for the population. Qin Shi Huangdi also built the first navigable canals, primarily to facilitate the movement of troops. The greatest hydraulic undertaking of ancient China was the Grand Canal, begun in the 7th century AD, which made up for the lack of a navigable waterway on the north-south axis.

▶ Model of a well, Western Han dynasty, 1st century AD, glazed terracotta, 31.8 cm high, Fondazione Giovanni Agnelli, Turin.

The first artificial connections between China's two largest rivers, the Yellow and the Yangtze, date to the 5th century BC and were located at the point where a moderate slope made maintenance of the water level possible.

Construction of the system of waterways known to historians as the Grand Canal began in the first years of the 7th century AD and involved an enormous army of peasants performing forced labor, a factor that contributed to the fall of the brief Sui dynasty.

During the Song period the capital Kaifeng was connected to the fertile south with a canal, while the Mongols promoted construction of a canal that created an uninterrupted waterway between the capital Dadu (Beijing) and the south.

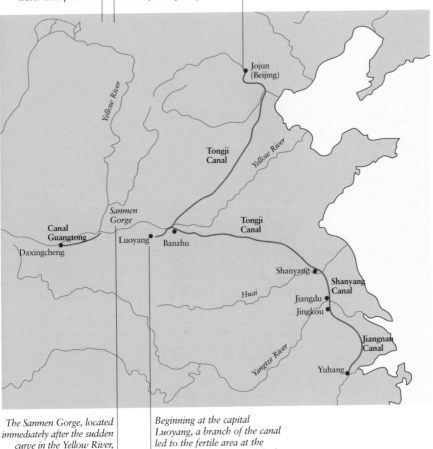

The Sanmen Gorge, located immediately after the sudden curve in the Yellow River, ruled out the possibility of making connections to the river from the west.

Beginning at the capital Luoyang, a branch of the canal led to the fertile area at the mouth of the Yangtze, while the northern branch made it possible to supply troops stationed on the empire's northern frontier.

▲ The Grand Canal in the Sui period.

The Bodai ("Precious Belt") Bridge was first constructed in AD 806, following the intervention of the governor of Suzhou, who donated a valuable jade belt to contribute to its construction.

Almost 317 meters long, the bridge has fifty-three arches. The three central arches are taller to permit the passage of boats, reaching a height of seven meters. Later dynasties undertook various works of reconstruction and modification. The present bridge dates to 1446.

Boats in the past, many of them also the homes of the boatmen, were pulled along by animals on the banks, pushed by poles, or moved by a sternpost.

The Grand Canal was, and still is, highly trafficked by large and small craft. The area of Suzhou is particularly lively, and the city is famous for its canals as well as for its bridges and gardens.

▲ The Bodai Bridge on the Grand Canal, Suzhou, Jiangsu province.

Men were said to have learned the methods of regulating great rivers from Yu, the "Great Engineer," founder of the legendary Xia dynasty (2205–1500 BC).

The first dikes to embank rivers were built about two thousand years ago along the Yellow River and on the sea in the area around Hangzhou and Jiaxing on the southeastern coast.

Beginning in the Ming period, dykes were built not only to prevent flooding but also to narrow the courses of rivers so as to favor the discharge of sand and other sediment.

▲ *Work Regulating the Black River,* woodcut of the Qing period.

In the periods in which the state lost authority and could no longer force tens of thousands of men to work along the waterways, the dikes inevitably gave way after a few years, causing terrible flooding.

"Be an example to subordinates, absolve those who have committed minor offenses, and promote those who are gifted with virtue and talent" (Confucius)

Administration

Terms
Nine ministers (*jiuqing*)

Related entries
Qin Shi Huangdi,
Wudi, Education and
exams

▼ *Scene of Audience*,
Eastern Han dynasty,
2nd century AD, from
Mount Banzi at
Chengdu, brick with
molded decoration,
39.2 x 46 cm, Sichuan
Provincial Museum,
Chengdu.

In order to govern the vast territory of the new imperial china, Qin Shi Huangdi created administrative structures overseen by officials nominated and directly controlled by the central government. Emperor Wudi of the Han made a law prohibiting officials from serving in the region they were from, a law maintained under later dynasties. In periods when the reigning dynasty fell into weakness, however, powerful clans and local families stepped in to take the place of imperial authority, thus eroding the very foundation of the dynasty. The bipartite state system, instituted under the Western Han, remained at the base of later governments, although it underwent numerous modifications: the imperial secretariat served as the legislative organ of the emperor, while the execution of state affairs was in the hands of ministers. Under the Han there were nine ministers, while the Tang had only six, flanked, however, by various central offices. Also part of the government was the censorate, instituted as early as the first emperor, whose inspectors commented on and criticized the actions of other government offices in all the provinces of the country and reported any irregularities to the provincial government or to the capital. The Hanlin Painting Academy had consultative functions, but as the most prestigious Confucian organism, it exercised a notable influence on the central government in certain circumstances.

The topographic map shown here, along with a prefecture map and a military map, were found in Tomb 3 at Mawangdui, demonstrating the high level of administrative organization and cartography in the 2nd century BC.

The map, drawn to a scale of 1:180,000, shows the Xiang River in the area bordering the three southern provinces of Hunan, Guangdong, and Guangxi. Ancient Chinese maps are always oriented to the south.

▲ Topographic map, Western Han dynasty, circa 168 BC, from Tomb 3 at Mawangdui, ink on silk, 96 x 96 cm, Hunan Provincial Museum, Changsha.

Cities are indicated with a square, counties and villages with a circle. It thus appears that in an area covering roughly 30,000 square kilometers, there were eight cities and about fifty communes and villages.

Vassals and public officials received a seal from the ruler that gave them the authority to exercise their functions.

Such seals were made of jade, gold, bronze, or stone, according to the rank of the official. Beginning in the Eastern Han dynasty the color of ink to be used was also regulated.

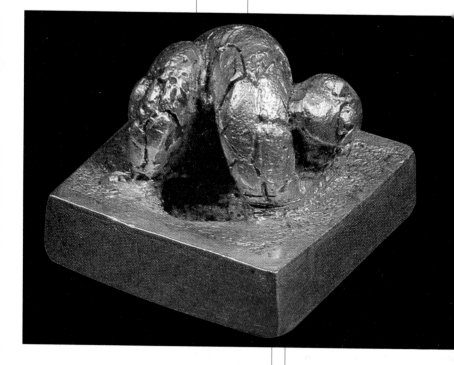

The seal has an unusual grip, shaped like a serpent; on its face, written in small seal script (xiaozhuan), are the characters for "seal of the king of Dian."

Official documents became effective with the application of the seal, usually carried on the belt.

▲ Seal of the king of Dian, Western Han dynasty, end 2nd century BC, from Shizhaishan, Jinning, gold, 2 cm high, Yunnan Provincial Museum, Kunming.

"Take your seal and go back to the countryside: how wise, this man! Young, he dared correct a few wrongs; old, he has become a Confucian man of letters" (Wang Wei)

Officials and literati

The ideal of a great Chinese empire survived through the periods of state disintegration thanks to the unitary culture of the class of public officials, based on the standardization of writing and on the shared study of the Confucian classics, which provided them with a sense of ideological continuity. China's official historiography became the reflection of a monolithic culture, with events reported in conformity with Confucian morality, and only exceptionally was mention made of various figures from outside the bureaucratic structure. Since criticism and suggestions came only from people within the system, they were directed only at certain limited aspects of the social and political apparatus. Confucian ideology dominated all aspects of social life, including artistic expression and rigorously hierarchical personal relationships. Beginning in the Han period, literati and officials used a sophisticated means of communication known as "literary Chinese." This was used not only to draw up edicts and administrative records but also for the elevated genres of literature: compositions in verse or prose, analyses of and commentaries on Confucian classics, and historical research. This hermetic language, understandable only after long study, gave control of the bureaucratic apparatus to a restricted elite up to the threshold of the 20th century. The ideal of the learned man of letters, busy in futile but aesthetically perfect activities, such as reading or arranging flowers, was codified in the Song period.

Terms
Official (*guan*)
Man of letters (*shi*)
Literary Chinese
(*wenyan*)

Related entries
Wudi, Education and exams, Poetry, Confucianism

◀ Model of a civil official, Tang dynasty, 7th century AD, from the tomb of Zheng Rentai at Liquan, Shaanxi, terracotta, slip, pigments, gold leaf, 69 cm high, Shaanxi History Museum, Xi'an.

Eight such figures, identified as civil officials on the basis of their "tools of the trade," were found in one of the side pits of the immense area occupied by the funerary garden of Qin Shinuandi.

Hanging from the right side of these officials are a whetstone and knife with a ring on its pommel that was used to smooth the wooden or bamboo tablets, the ordinary supports on which documents were written, and to rub away errors in orthography.

▶ Model of a civil official, Qin dynasty, 218 BC, from the southwestern area of the mausoleum of Qin Shi Huangdi, terracotta, lacquer, pigments, circa 190 cm high, Museum of Qin Terracotta Warriors and Horses, Lintong.

Every fragment of the statues was restored as soon as it was extracted from the ground. Doing so has made it possible to preserve a good deal of the lacquer that was used as the base coat for the colored pigments and the coloring of the face.

The somewhat simple clothing worn by the figure can be taken as an expression of the first emperor's Legalist views. To Qin Shi Huangdi officials were simply one more category of worker and thus did not enjoy any special rights.

"Burn incense, sip tea, look at paintings, arrange flowers" were the refined but futile activities, along with the exercise of the "four arts" of poetry, painting, table games, and music.

Beside the pallet stands a large screen painted with a scene very similar to that of the image itself, but more traditional in its details: a man of letters is shown sitting on a pallet in his study in front of a painted landscape.

A somewhat elderly man of letters, only half-dressed because of the summer heat, leans back on a pallet in the garden of a house, flyswatter in his right hand, scroll in his left: either a book, calligraphy, or a painting.

Beginning in the Song period the man of letters became a subject, released from official business and intent on enjoying the idle life, studying or taking part in various pastimes.

Liu Guandao, *Whiling Away the Summer*, Yuan dynasty, end 13th century, handscroll, ink and light color on silk, 30.5 x 71.1 cm, The Nelson-Atkins Museum of Art, Kansas City.

*"People at birth are naturally good. Their natures are similar;
their habits become different"* (Three-Character Classic)

Education and exams

Terms
Imperial exams (*keju*)
Local-level exams
(*shengyuan* or *xiucai*)
Provincial-level exams
(*juren*)
State-level exams
(*jinshi*)

Related entries
Wudi, Wu Zetian, Zhu
Xi, Hongwu, Yongle,
Officials and literati

The promotion of Confucianism to state doctrine under the Western Han occurred at the same time as the creation of upper school with consolidated examinations, thus solving the problem of th need for loyal and competent officials able to ensure cultural continuity. During the reign of the Han emperor Wudi, those admitted to the imperial university to take the exam and study the *Fiv Classics* were either the sons of nobles or candidates for a publi career proposed by administrators. The strongest push to give access to the exam to candidates from lower classes came during th Tang period, from the empress Wu Zetian, who in a uniqu episode in Chinese imperial history even permitted women to ris to the ranks of public officialdom. The early dynasties always ha to pay attention to the hereditary positions reserved for the members of powerful clans; the Song finally succeeded in selecting officials primarily by way of public exams, with a program integrating the *Four Books,* selected and annoted by Zhu Xi, with variou more practical materials. The later Yuan dynasty, after years i which the system had bee abolished, gave preference to non-Chinese and the first emper of the Ming, Hong wu, was highly sus picious of overl capable candidates Yongle restored th institution to its basi role, but the rigidity o the system kept it from being brought up to date rendering it anachronistic.

► Vase painted with four moral scenes, detail of teaching, Ming dynasty, Jiajing period, 1522–1566, porcelain with painted underglaze decoration, 32 cm high, Roemer-Museum, Sammlung Ohlmer, Hildesheim.

The sons of well-to-do families began their studies very young with the help of private tutors, while the children of the less wealthy often made use of "public" schools set up by local important people.

The teachers at such schools had often failed the national exams. Unable to qualify for a position in the public administration, inaccessible without that diploma, they were forced to make a living in another way.

The painting depicts a classroom full of children running amok and playing the most fantastic games while the elderly teacher sleeps at his desk, his head resting in his folded arms.

At School, Ming dynasty, 16th century, perhaps a copy of an earlier work, album leaf, ink and color on silk, circa 27.5 cm diam., Metropolitan Museum of Art, Fletcher Fund, A.W. Bahr Collection, New York.

Exam preparation began before birth: in addition to being told to avoid bright colors and flavorful foods, expectant mothers were read selections from the Confucian classics, along with edifying poetry.

The learning system in Chinese schools is still based on mnemonic exercises.

The Three-Character Classic, *compiled in the 13th century and traditionally attributed to the man of letters Wang Yinglin (1223–1296), was used as a textbook until the end of the empire and is still read widely in Taiwan.*

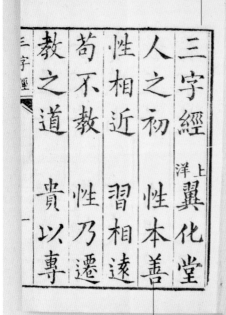

The text is structured in three-syllable lines that compose a complete overview of Confucian tradition in fewer than 1,200 characters.

▲ Example of the *Three-Character Classic (Sanzijing)*, Qing dynasty, early 20th century, book, 23.5 cm high, American Museum of Natural History, New York.

▶ *Book on the Political Strategies of the Warring States* (detail), Western Han dynasty, circa 168 BC, from Tomb 3 at Mawangdui, ink on silk, 24 cm high, Hunan Provincial Museum, Changsha.

"At the time of the Master of Dragons and the Emperor of Fire and the Bird Officials and the Emperor of Men, characters were invented for the first time" (Thousand-Character Classic)

Writing

n the West, the written Chinese language is often referred to as "ideographic," but in fact fewer than 10 percent of Chinese characters have a concrete origin. In *The Written Chinese Language* the lexicographer Xu Shen (died AD 147) grouped the characters on the basis of six formative principles. Pictograms represent concrete images, such as "sun" or "mountain"; a figure can also express a concept, such as "tower" for "high." Simple indicatives suggest simple abstract concepts, like "above/climb" or "center." Compound indicatives unite simple characters to represent an idea; thus "sun" and "moon" can be joined to indicate "luminosity." In these three categories there is no relationship between sound and writing, while phonetic compounds contain an element of phonetic origin together with a radical. The phoneme *yang*, for example, borrowed from the pictogram "sheep," means "ocean" if associated with the semantic radical "water," but becomes "illness" if joined to "heart." This category offers an almost infinite variety of possible combinations: while the written Chinese language has only a somewhat limited range of semantic radicals—today there are a little more than 200—the number of characters amounts to more than 50,000. Borrowed characters and false synonyms, the last two categories named by Xu Shen, are based on the graphic and phonetic relationships among characters and are somewhat rare.

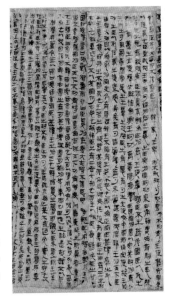

Terms
Character dictionary
(*Shuowen Jiezi*)
Six principles (*liushu*)
Pictograms (*xiangxing*)
Simple indicatives
(*zhishi*)
Compound indicatives
(*huiyi*)
Phonetic compounds
(*xingsheng*)
Borrowed characters
(*jiajie*)
False synonyms
(*zhuanzhu*)

Sun (*ri*)
Mountain (*shan*)
High (*gao*)
Above, climb (*shang*)
Center (*zhong*)
Moon (*yue*)
Luminosity (*ming*)
Sheep (*yang*)
Ocean (*yang*)
Illness (*yang*)

Related entries
Officials and literati,
Education and exams,
Calligraphy

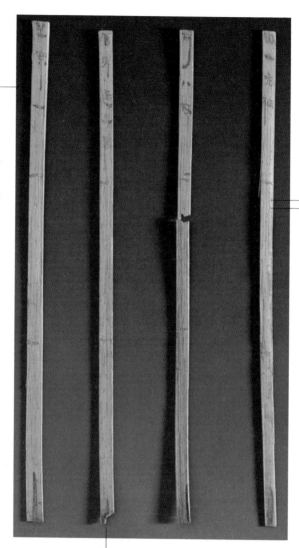

The four strips shown here are part of a group of sixty-six, originally held together by a hemp cord, that formed the complete inventory of the burial items of the district magistrate Sui, who died in 167 BC.

Before the invention of paper, the supports used for writing with brush were silk and bamboo strips (jian).

Beginning at the end of the 2nd century BC, bamboo strips were used for every type of document, public or private.

▲ Inscribed bamboo strips, Western Han dynasty, *ante* 167 BC, from Tombs 167 and 168 at Fenghuangshan, Hubei, bamboo, ink, circa 22 cm long, Municipal Museum, Jingzhou.

In order to use bamboo, it had to be scraped free of the external green membrane, then the wooden surface had to be smoothed, cut in strips, and dried over heat. Tying together individual strips with a cord created true books that were preserved rolled up or folded shut like an accordion.

Each character is composed of a series of conventional strokes that must be written in the correct sequence to assemble a well-proportioned and coherent image.

The great calligrapher Wang Xizhi wrote a book on the eight strokes that compose the character yong ("eternity"), which was the basis for the study and practice of calligraphy.

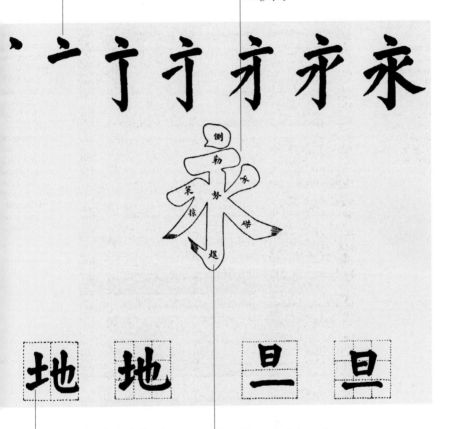

A character can be looked up in a dictionary on the basis of its semantic radical, which is among the 214 radicals listed in the opening pages. Characters containing the same radical are organized on the basis of the number of additional strokes.

In reality, some of the strokes are joined and thus drawn on the paper without lifting the pen. In that way, the number of strokes for this character is reduced to five.

▲ Composition and harmony of Chinese characters.

"On Mount Fanguo, atop the peak, I met Du Fu. . . . I said to him, 'Since our last meeting you have lost too much weight. How long have you been sick from poetry?'" (Li Bai)

Poetry

Terms
*Classic of the Odes
(Shijing)*
Songs of Chu (Chuci)
Descriptive prose (*fu*)
"Music Bureau" poetry
(*yuefu*)
Classical poetry (*shi*)
Lyric poetry (*ci*)

Related entries
Wudi, Li Bai, Su Shi,
Games

Art and literature were seen by Confucians, who selected and adapted about 300 ancient poems for the *Classic of the Odes*, as didactic methods to express feelings in a controlled way and to learn from the ancients by imitating their works. Despite the stylistic variety of Chinese poetry, some elements are common to all of it. The Chinese language is concrete and has few abstract terms; to avoid the expression of sentiments, considered vulgar, it prefers to make use of metaphors and concrete images capable of awakening a poetic perception of reality. Furthermore, since it contrasts a great quantity of written characters with a highly restricted number of phonetic syllables, the language lends itself to word games, such as puns, homophones, and literary puzzles. Reference to masters of the past implies continuous recourse to quotations along with recondite allusions to events from earlier times or to poetry by famous writers. The stock of classical themes, the only ones deemed "worthy," presented a limitation that few poets dared break with. They were equally loath to violate the complex aesthetic and metrical rules of the various styles. The periods of greatest vitality in the evolution of China's poetry occurred during periods of political instability, when weakness in the imperial ideology, Confucianism, made possible the development of expressive forms and criteria based on the aesthetic, rather than the didactic. The prototype of an "alternative" poetry is the *Songs of Chu*, ascribed to the legendary Qu Yuan (4th–3rd centuries BC), which was not "purified" by Confucians and even contains religious and magical elements.

▶ Mi Fu, *Poetry*,
Northern Song dynasty,
early 12th century,
horizontal scroll, ink on
paper, 31.2 x 487 cm,
National Museum,
Tokyo.

When it came into being, during the 2nd century BC, fu designated a very refined poetic genre, rhetorical and full of hyperbole. The fu style adopted over the course of the 11th century referred instead to a type of composition free of moralisms and marked by simplicity.

The Red Cliff, which rises straight out of the Yangtze, was the site of a great naval battle in AD 208 when the fleet of General Cao Cao was destroyed, ending his dreams of uniting China under his rule.

The painting illustrates a famous ode by the man of letters Su Shi entitled the Fu of the Red Cliff (Chibi fu), which describes two excursions he took in the company of a pair of friends.

The poet, confronted by the history of the past, is led to reflect on the vanity of human life while eating with his friends in the boat.

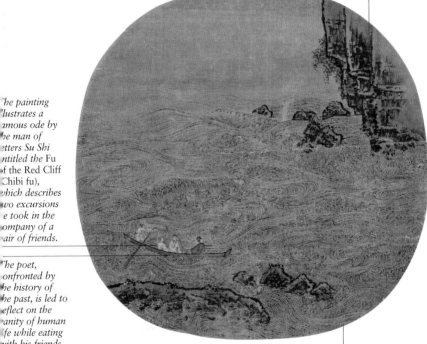

The Fu of the Red Cliff is written in a language free of metric schemes and moderated by the use of rhyme and parallelisms. Perhaps it was precisely the clarity of the composition that made the poem famous, illustrated many times in the history of Chinese painting.

▲ Li Song, The Red Cliff, Southern Song dynasty, 1190–1230, album leaf mounted on a vertical scroll, ink and light color on silk, 24.8 x 26 cm, The Nelson-Atkins Museum of Art, Kansas City.

An anthology of Tang-period poetry contains more than 48,000 compositions, an excellent demonstration of the social importance of poetry in ancient China.

"Classical poetry" (shi), widespread most of all in the Tang period, consists of verses of five or seven characters with a caesura that falls before the last three characters in every line.

The genre of "lyric poetry" (ci), preferred by the poets of the Song period, was written to the melodies of popular songs that today, sadly, can no longer be reconstructed.

The creation of improvised works in verse or prose, inspired by nature, by the moon, by friends, became an extremely popular diversion among literati beginning in the 12th century.

▶ Mountain Landscape: Three Poets and a Servant under a Pine, Ming dynasty, 16th century, vertical scroll, ink and light color on silk, 239 x 94.2 cm, Freer Gallery of Art, Smithsonian Institution, Washington, DC.

"Calligraphy is liberation. A person who wants to write must first free himself of what weighs upon his heart" (Cai Yong)

Calligraphy

Calligraphy is not an abstract art, but adds codified aesthetic values to the semantic indication of the sign along with information about the personality of the creator. The concept of calligraphy as an artistic discipline expressive not only of the creator's talent but also of his soul came into being during the late Han period. Use of the "small seal script" imposed by Qin Shi Huangdi was limited to inscriptions on bronzes and on seals, and the "clerical script" used to write official documents was replaced during the period of disintegration of China by "regular script," simpler and more pleasing in appearance. The expressive forms that make calligraphy the highest art, superior even to painting, were the personal styles, used in daily notes and, most of all, in lengthy missives to friends. The "cursive script" that appeared at the end of the 2nd century was characterized by sinuous strokes joined to one another. The "running-and script," which came into being following the Neo-Confucian movement of the Song period, represented the apex of the search for purified spontaneity; it could be achieved, however, only after long training based on daily exercise and the imitation of works of masters of the past. The artist's freedom is in his ability to control the gesture and in the energy of the strokes he generates.

Small seal script (*xiaozhuan*)
Clerical script (*lishu*)
Regular script (*kaishu*)
Cursive script (*caoshu*)
Running-hand script (*xingshu*)

Related entries
Qin Shi Huangdi, Su Shi, Writing, Confucianism

◀Zhang Xihuang, *Penholder*, Ming dynasty, early 17th century, bamboo, 13.3 cm high, Metropolitan Museum of Art, New York.

Eleven generations of the Wang family were esteemed calligraphers, but Wang Xizhi of the Tang period was elevated to the highest fame.

His works were studied and copied innumerable times by thousands of calligraphers, but today it is believed that not even one authentic work by Wang Xizhi survives.

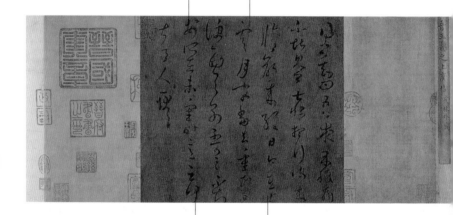

Wang Xizhi excelled in the various calligraphic genres and in particular in the "regular script" (kaishu), "running-hand script" (xingshu), and "cursive script" (caoshu), the style in which this letter is written.

The Tang emperor Taizong (ruled AD 626–649) so admired the calligraphy by Wang Xizhi that he had the twenty-three of his most beautiful letters carved in stone in order to preserve them for eternity.

▲ Copy of the Tang epoch of Wang Xizhi, *Shang Yu Tie*, Jin dynasty, 4th century AD, ink on paper, Shanghai Museum.

The "four treasures"—ink, inkstone, brush, and paper—were the expressive means and the work tools of the officials and literati and were thus usually of excellent quality and elegant design.

The principal ingredients of ink (mu) were pinewood soot, tung-tree oil, and natural glues; to this were often added aromas or precious perfumes, such as musk. The mixture was shaped and pressed in molds; as it dried, the ink hardened. To use it, a small amount was grated on the inkstone and diluted with water.

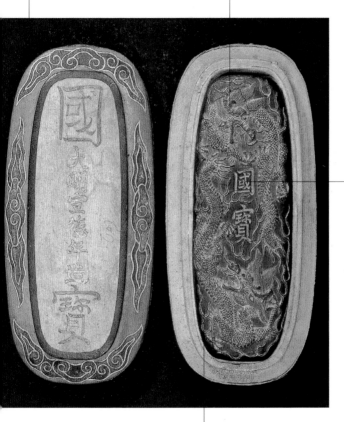

The two characters engraved on the inkstone are "treasure [of]" and "country." This inscription, together with the dragons modeled in the surface of the ink and the yellow velvet of the case, indicate that the object was an imperial gift.

Inkstone and case, Ming ynasty, Xuande period, 426–1435, case: wood, ather, velvet, 21.5 cm long; k: ink, gold leaf, 19 cm long, chlossmuseum, Gotha.

High-quality inks were greatly valued as early as the Han period. The culture of ink reached its height beginning in the 12th century. The names of several Song-period producers are still today synonyms for elegance.

Calligraphy

Zhu Yunming, born into a family of artists like most painters and calligraphers, was one of the "great masters of Suzhou" and specialized in the "modern" calligraphy styles of the cursive and running-hand scripts.

Painting and calligraphy, the two chosen means of expression for the Chinese man of letters, are closely related, and art work was often created within a dialogue with other artists, even across generations.

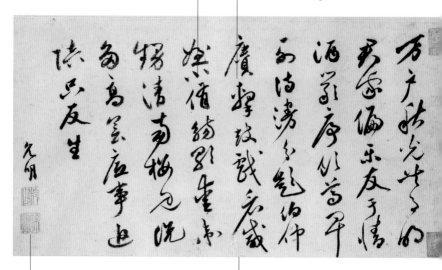

Poetry, signed and confirmed with the application of a seal, was read from top down and from right to left.

Chinese literati expressed their thoughts inspired by a work present on the same sheet, adding their poetry in the calligraphic style deemed appropriate. On occasion these expositions inspired the addition of further annotations.

▲ Zhu Yunming, *Colophon to "Looking at the Mid-Autumn Moon" by Shen Zhou*, Ming dynasty, late 15th–early 16th century, section of horizontal scroll, ink on paper, 25.7 x 49.2 cm, Museum of Fine Arts, Chinese and Japanese Special Fund, Boston.

▶ Detail of a poem by Zhu Yunming, carved in stone, Forest of Steles Museum, Xi'an.

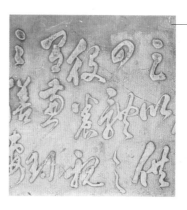

To preserv calligraphy held worthy o immortality emperors had engraved in stone

The distant mountains and the clouds combine their shapes. The distant sky and the water blend their luminosity" (Wang Wei)

Landscape painting

Mountain-water" (*shanshui*), the term that designates Chinese landscape painting, itself expresses the play of opposites that generates and animates the entire universe: the mountain, male element yang, needs the female element yin, symbolized by water, to be complete in a dynamic synthesis. The earliest Chinese landscapes depicted a universal harmony made explicit by nature and served more to validate the social and political order than to produce an accurate image of a landscape. A few original works and several later copies testify to two coexisting trends around the end of the Tang dynasty: "blue and green" painting, based on chromatic splendor and the execution of details, and "broken ink" painting, made with rapid gestures using only ink, a style whose invention is attributed to the painter and man of letters Wang Wei. The brief period of the division of China following the collapse of the Tang dynasty was the setting for the extraordinary development of landscape painting, from the monumental landscapes made most of all in the north to the lyric scenes created in the south. The neo-Confucianism of the Song period drew attention to the individualistic expression of the artist by way of strokes using only ink. In later dynasties, the monochrome landscape became the mirror of the inner life of the literati, given concrete form through the evocation of the work of ancient masters.

Terms
Landscape painting
(*shanshui*)
Blue and green painting
(*qinglü*)
Broken ink painting
(*pomo*)

Related entries
Su Shi, Zhu Xi,
Calligraphy, Gardens,
Feng-shui

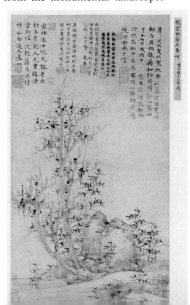

◀ Ni Zan, *Bamboo, Rock, and Tall Tree*, Yuan dynasty, circa 1348, vertical scroll, ink on paper, 67.3 x 36.8 cm, Cleveland Museum of Art.

The white of the snow stood out less starkly in the past, for the silk has darkened over the years.

Jing Hao was an official until the fall of the Tang dynasty in AD 907, when he retired from public life to live in the mountains of Henan, dedicating himself to painting. His innovative techniques in the search for authentic naturalism are documented in the few works attributed to him and are given a theoretical basis in his Record of Brush Methods (Bifa ji).

To protect it from complete disintegration, the work was glued to a canvas support. The restorer retouched several details and accidentally created a small open space in the center of the rocky wall.

▲ Jing Hao, *Travels in Snow-covered Mountains*, Five Dynasties period, first half 10th century, vertical scroll, ink, white tempera, and light color on silk, 136 x 75 cm, The Nelson-Atkins Museum of Art, Kansas City.

The painting was discovered in the 1930s in a tomb located in the province of Shaanxi and was in a very poor state of preservation, with several lacunae in the central area.

Li Tang was admitted to the academy of the emperor Huizong at an advanced age and fled south in 1127, after the fall of the Northern Song dynasty.

He resumed his work at the court academy at Hangzhou and had a great influence on later generations.

The angular "ax-cut" strokes that create the outlines of the mountains are distinguishing characteristics of Li Tang's work and were later the subject of infinite imitation.

The cloud that separates the mountains is not open space but a palpable and material pictorial element.

The space appears real and can be visually traveled along the length of the stream.

The painting, made in 1124, anticipates the new direction of Chinese landscape painting, which moved from grandiose and intimidating images of nature to a more intimate and evocative style.

▲ Li Tang, *Wind in the Pines amid Ten Thousand Valleys*, Northern Song dynasty, 1124, vertical scroll, ink and color on silk, 188.7 x 139.8 cm, National Palace Museum, Taipei.

Each of the three existing sections of the Eight Views *is accompanied by a poem of four verses, followed by a seal that reads "disciple of the three religions."*

No fewer than four monks named Yujian painted in the 13th–14th centuries, during the Song and Yuan dynasties. Since the work is unsigned, attributing it to a precise artist is difficult.

▲ Yujian, *Boats Returning from Afar,* Southern Song dynasty, circa 1250, section of the horizontal scroll called *Eight Views of Xiao and Xiang,* ink on paper, Tokugawa Art Museum, Nagoya.

By identifying the masts of the sailboats and the two figures seated in the small boat, the landscape begins to take form, with its suggestion of water; plants then become recognizable along with distant peaks and rocks in the foreground.

The figure of the monk-painter is a part of the Chinese (and Japanese) world, much like that of the official-painter.

Spontaneity and freshness characterize the painting, which at first glance seems completely abstract.

"He who reviews the past to understand the present can be considered a true master" (Confucius)

Collectors of antiquities

Terms
Catalog of Paintings of the Xuanhe Emperor (Xuanhe huapu)
Four arts of the Chinese scholar (*sishu*): music (*qin*), board games (*qi*), calligraphy (*su*), painting (*hua*)

Related entries
Huizong, Su Shi, Calligraphy, Landscape painting, Games, Music and dance

The past enjoyed such a high level of prestige during the Song period that it awakened scientific interest in archaeology and epigraphy. The first archaeological excavation took place in the district of Anyang (Henan) during the reign of Huizong (1100–1126). There were also the first systematic efforts to classify and date known ancient objects and to identify their original ritual functions. Indeed, most of the names for ritual vessels still in use today date to this period. Thanks to the diffusion of printing, encyclopedias of archaeology and studies of epigraphy were published. The great collections of art, private and imperial, were documented in catalogs, outstanding among them being the famous *Catalog of Paintings of the Xuanhe Emperor*, commissioned by Emperor Huizong. Devotion to the past was also reflected in the private life of the man of letters. The ideal in this period was the man of letters who withdrew from public life to spend his time together with friends delighting in the four traditional arts—music, chess, calligraphy, painting—and dedicating himself to the study of works of the past.

▶ Drawing and description of a *Fu Ding jue* vase, Ming dynasty, Wanli era, 1563–1620, from *Sketches to Investigate Antiquity (Kaogu tu)*, 24.5 x 31 cm, National Library, Taipei.

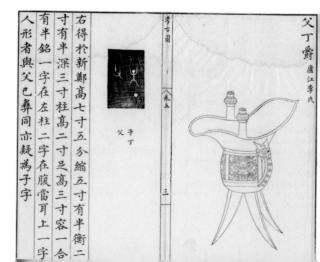

Qiu Ying was a professional painter from Suzhou from the first half of the 16th century. Unlike the painters-literati, who at least in theory painted for amusement, the professional painter lived off his work.

Professional painters were generally looked down upon by the literati, but Qiu Ying's paintings were highly admired, and his works are often completed by calligraphic inscriptions from the hands of intellectual friends.

Three friends sit at a table surrounded by ancient objects in the courtyard of a house, closed off by two large screens. In the background is a garden of bamboo with the typical eroded rock.

Archaic bronze vessels are displayed along the table: a gu and a jue, both known as ritual vases from the Shang period (2nd millennium BC) that were used for wine and grains, and a fang ding, used for grain offerings.

The owner of the house is looking at an album with ancient paintings. On the table are other scrolls of paintings and several books.

▲ Qiu Ying, *Enjoying Ancient Things in the Bamboo Garden*, Ming dynasty, first half 16th century, leaf 1 of an album of 10 leaves entitled *Paintings of Historical Figures and Events*, ink and color on silk, 41.1 x 33.8 cm, Palace Museum, Beijing.

"Perfect: a large rock with a weeping willow on the bank of the river to rinse the cups. If the spring wind does not weaken our spirit, let us go with music" (Wang Wei)

Gardens

Term
Garden, park (*yuanlin*)

Related entries
Landscape painting,
Yin and yang and the
five phases, Feng-shui

Landscape painting and garden design were intimately related disciplines, both being visual representations of universal harmony achieved through the dynamic balance of yin and yang. Rocks and water were the essential elements of both landscape painting and the Chinese garden, integrated with various constructions and with plants. Humans did not so much make use of nature as enter it, putting themselves inside the landscape in the role of the active creator of overall order. Panoramas of great breadth alternated with intimate views to complete the oneiric vision of a complete microcosm. Pavilions, pathways, and bridges were part of the scenery and at the same time were sites from which to enjoy particularly significant views, sometimes framed by a window. Wooden or bamboo lattices diminished the impact of architectural structures on the landscape. Semicircular bridges joined their reflections on water surfaces to create full circles, symbolic of the heavens. Plants were chosen on the basis of visual effect but also with close attention given their literary or historical symbolism. Long-lived plants were cultivated, such as the pine, cypress, plum tree, and bamboo, along with seasonal flowers such as peonies, chrysanthemums, and orchids.

▶ *Painting of a Country Refuge, ante* 1453, section 6 of a horizontal scroll with 10 sections, ink and color on silk mounted on paper, 27.7 cm high, Bernard Berenson Collection of Oriental Art, Villa I Tatti, Florence.

Miniature gardens, known in
the West by the Japanese
name bonsai, offer spaces for
contemplation in which the
mind is free to wander as in
an ideal microcosm.

This model, the prototype
of a genre very widespread
in later periods, was found
near several models of
pavilions and small houses.
Taken all together, they
present an image of the
layout of the gardens of
the Tang period.

irds are perched
top some of the
ocks, while other
ocks are covered
ith moss. The
ense green glaze
hat covers the
ntire rock is
nlivened by brown
nd bluish areas.

Model of a pond with large rock
enjing), Tang dynasty, early 7th
ntury AD, terracotta with "tree-
olor" (sancai) glaze, from
hongpucum, Shaanxi, 18 cm high,
haanxi Provincial Museum, Xi'an.

A tiny pond, surrounded by
a raised border, creates a
miniature landscape together
with the rocky formation
that closes off the back.

Against a background carved with repeated geometric motifs that symbolize the earth, water, and air, emerges a scene in high relief located in a pleasant setting.

Special trees, rocks, and clouds with bizarre shapes, a half-hidden pavilion, and a terrace surrounded by a stone balustrade are among the elements that characterize the literary garden of ancient China.

In the early years of the reign of Yongle, elegant boxes of this kind were often used as diplomatic gifts for Japan.

The sides are decorated with carvings of the flowers of the four seasons: peonies, pomegranate flowers, chrysanthemums, and camellias.

The carved scene—two men, revealed to be immortals, play weiqi *while being observed by a woodcutter who has set down his load of wood—alludes to a story dating to the Liang dynasty.*

▲ Circular box with engraved decoration, Ming dynasty, reign of Yongle, 1403–1424, red lacquer, 13.6 cm diam., National Palace Museum, Taipei.

With the rise of a commercial economy in southern China, the city of Suzhou, located on the Grand Canal, became an important center. The new mercantile elite surrounded itself with luxuries, from exotic or imported objects to collections of antiquities, new kinds of interior furnishings, and also elegant gardens.

The garden is crossed by numerous paths that open onto partial views of panoramic vistas (jing), thus creating the illusion of a limitless world.

The garden's name is an ironic allusion to a poem from the 3rd century AD in which a retired politician says that planting trees and growing vegetables "is the way of ruling for an unsuccessful politician."

In fact a politician who had withdrawn to private life had this garden made, located in the center of the city and thus surrounded by a wall.

The gardens of Suzhou have profited form the city's abundant water: in this case, the water was used to create ponds and even the bend of a "river," which appears endless.

The Humble Administrator's arden (Zhuozheng Yuan) at izhou, Ming dynasty, 510–1515.

Printing

Terms
Inscription on stone drum (*shiguwen*)
Inscription on stone slab (*biwen*)
Buddhist canon (*Tripitaka*)
Daoist canon (*Daozang*)

Related entries
Su Shi, Buddhism, Mogao

As early as the 2nd century AD, the Chinese preserved importan texts by engraving them on cylindrical or flat stones, a techniqu that continued even after the appearance of woodcut printing o paper or silk. The first printed work known today is the text of Buddhist invocation from the 7th century, and the first entire book discovered in the Buddhist caves of Dunhuang, contains the *Dia mond Sutra*: this is a horizontal scroll more than five meters lon with an illustrated frontispiece and a final colophon bearing th name of the author and the date of the composition of the work, A 868. During the Song dynasty no fewer than six editions of th body of Buddhist texts were printed, each of them requiring n fewer than 60,000 wooden blocks, and the edition of the Daoi canon was of similar size. The state academy was responsible fc the publication of the Confucian classics and official histories bu also supervised the printing of dictionaries, rhyming dictionaries encyclopedias, anthologies, and scientific works of all kinds. Som of the most popular books were printed by private individuals, bu only in the 16th century did commercial printing companies com into being in southern China. These printed primarily novels an illustrated manuals in high-quality editions.

▶ Song Boren, *Register of Plum-blossom Portraits*, Southern Song dynasty, mid-13th century, leaf 1 from a woodcut-printed book, 23.1 x 28.6 cm, Shanghai Museum.

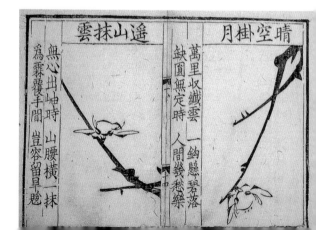

The method of preserving texts of fundamental importance by inscribing them in stone is very ancient and was not abandoned after the invention of printing.

Paper and silk, the primary supports for printing, deteriorate easily, while stone is long-lasting and resistant to wear.

Works of art and texts inscribed in stone can be reproduced with the technique of rubbing: a moistened piece of thin, fibrous paper is placed over the area of the stone with the writing and gently pushed into the letters with a brush; then a soft cotton compress soaked in ink is dabbed over the surface, so that the writing comes out white against a black background.

.ubbing of an inscription
ved in stone.

The oldest paper was made using hemp fiber; these six images from the book by Song Yingxing illustrate the process of making paper from the internal fibers of bamboo canes.

The first three images illustrate (a) cutting the canes and soaking them, (b) boiling the canes in a pot for eight days, and (c) lifting the pulp from a vat using a woven mold.

Archaeological finds date the appearance of paper, the indispensable support for printing, to the 2nd–1st centuries BC, while tradition attributes its invention to an official named Cai Lun, in AD 105.

▲ Song Yingxing, *The Process of Making Paper*, Ming dynasty, 1637, Chapter 13 of *The Exploitations of the Works of Nature (Tiangong Kaiwu)*, woodcut printing.

These images illustrate (d) pressing damp paper sheets to squeeze out moisture and (e–f) finally drying the large paper sheets on a heated wall.

The scroll dates to May 11, 868, as indicated by its colophon: "Reverently made for universal distribution by Wang Jie, on behalf of his two parents, the fifteenth day of the fifth moon of the ninth year of Xiantong."

The scroll, more than five meters long, is composed of seven sheets of paper pasted together.

The blocks used for printing were usually made from pear wood, which allows for very precise and detailed carving.

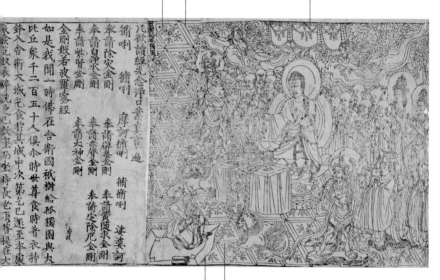

Printing in color, achieved with the superimposition of colored blocks, appeared in China in the 14th century and came into widespread use near the end of the 16th century, when it was used for the accurate reproduction of paintings. Typographical printing, made with movable type, was invented in the 11th century and perfected over the course of the 14th, using a revolving case for the typographical characters.

The quality of the printing, precise even in the details, indicates the technical skills with which this book—the oldest that can be dated with certainty—was made.

Frontispiece of the *Diamond Sutra*, Tang dynasty, AD 868, from Cave 17 at Dunhuang, Gansu, woodcut printing, horizontal roll, 26.5 x 533 cm, British Library, London.

"The Great River flows to the sea, flowers shake the waves, heroes shatter the sands, when all the dreams have dried away, defeat and victory become the same thing" (Luo Guanzhong)

Novels

The evolution of the technique of printing contributed to the diffu sion of literature written in the spoken vernacular, contemptuousl dismissed by orthodox literati as "small talk." As early as the Tan period, the plots of these works repeated the story cycles of tales tol by professional storytellers. These short works, divided in chapter that indicated the duration in days of the story, were so successfu that literati later began to compose complete version of oral stories. The loss of interest in learned litera ture and the temporary suspension of nationa exams during the Yuan dynasty and begin ning of the Ming dynasty contribute to the emancipation of the novel. Th *Romance of the Three Kingdoms* written by the man of letters Luo Guanzhong in the 14th century was the prototype of a new genre against the background of histori cal events numerous tales are recounted involving a host of charac ters, some factual, others invented "Objective" facts are related rathe than the expression of sentiments. Sign of the oral tradition remained, as in th chapter division, each one ending at moment of high tension, or in the manipu lation of the collective imagination, whil the learned background of the authors wa revealed in the abundant quotations, th moralistic asides, and the stereotypical descrip tions, drawn from literary images unrelated t the novel's action.

▶ *Meiping* vase with decoration drawn for the novel *Romance of the West Chamber* (Lady Zheng rebukes Hongnian), Yuan dynasty, 1279–1368, porcelain with underglaze blue decoration, Victoria and Albert Museum, London.

The quality of the four-color printing of this series of illustrations, unfortunately incomplete, is excellent.

The Romance of the West Chamber *is a love story based on the story* Fatal Meeting *by Yuan Zhen (AD 779–831), already made into a theatrical work in the Yuan dynasty (end 13th century).*

The beautiful Yingying is writing a letter to her lover, Zhan Junrui, who has just taken the national exams in the capital.

With the adoption of this frame, the artist creates the illusion of opening a section of a precious vertical scroll.

A messenger waits in the garden near a rock with a bizarre shape, an indispensable element in the luxury gardens of the Ming and Qing periods.

The small handmaid Hongnian is the third main character in the story, after the two lovers. It is she who advises the lovesick student to write a poem to his beloved.

Min Qiji, *Romance of the West Chamber (Xixiangji)*, Ming dynasty, 1640, folio 18 of a series of colored woodcuts, 5 x 32 cm, Museum für Ostasiatische Kunst, Cologne.

> *"Laws consist in making public the edicts of the ruling government and in impressing in hearts the inescapable character of the punishments"* (Han Fei)

Legal system

Terms
Law (*fa*)
Rites (*li*)

Related entries
Qin Shi Huangdi, Li Si

▼ *Capture of a Prisoner*, Tang dynasty, 8th–9th century AD, fragment of a wall painting from the ruins of a Buddhist temple at Kumtura, Chinese Turkistan, circa 36 x 40 cm, Museum für Indische Kunst, Berlin.

Traditional Chinese history blames the short duration of the Qin dynasty on the brutality of the laws in force, established by Legalist thinkers. According to Confucius, social harmony was to be based not on fear of punishment but on shared moral conduct, expressed in rites. In reality, the legal order put in place during the Qin reign remained at the base of judicial practice for two thousand years, as indicated by the fragmentary writings on administrative, civil, and penal law recently discovered in several tombs of officials. The administration of justice was among the responsibilities of local officers who received precise instructions from the central government concerning the ways in which investigations should be conducted and the criteria to follow in reaching a final verdict. Neither lawyers nor public defenders existed. Flogging was applied in cases of reticent witnesses or unjustifiable contradictions in testimony on the part of witnesses or the accused. Punishment included the death penalty, forced labor, mutilation, and fines. The rank and social position of the accused had enormous influence on the seriousness of the penalty, following the Confucian principle of the hierarchy of humans. It was possible to avoid punishment by agreeing to a proportional payment.

A magistrate, dressed in his official robe, is listening to the petitions of four kneeling people, his right hand raised in a gesture of repulsion.

The magistrate, a state functionary responsible for the application of penal and civil laws in a certain district, performed the roles of investigator and judge.

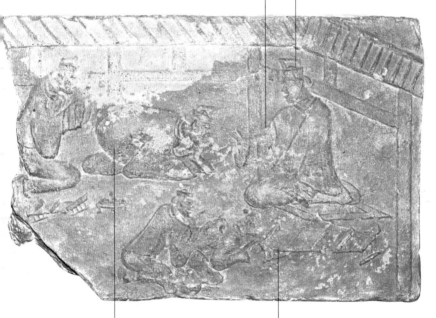

The accused and witnesses had to kneel for the entire duration of their deposition. No one could be condemned without having confessed to his crime.

In cases in which contradictions or doubts arose during the course of an interrogation, the magistrate had the power to have the involved parties tortured.

Request for Mercy, Eastern Han dynasty, 2nd century AD, brick with molded decoration, 45 x 37.5 cm, Sichuan Provincial Museum, Chengdu.

The illustrations were inspired by an apocryphal sutra from AD 903 that portrays the Ten Kings of Hell, who preside over the successive spheres that each soul must overcome on its way to rebirth. The scroll, incomplete, illustrates the Buddhist concept of judgment after death and at the same time offers a vision of legal proceedings during the late Tang period.

Each of the ten king-judges is immediately recognizable by his official robe and characteristic hat; they preside over hearings seated at a table draped with a heavy cloth.

Two wretches, dressed only in loincloths, are handcuffed and wear wooden yokes, still in use early in the 20th century.

Assistants carry documents and protocols, while guards oversee the condemned, weapons at the ready.

▲ *Sutra of the Ten Kings* (detail), Tang dynasty, early 10th century, from Cave 17 at Dunhuang, Gansu, horizontal scroll, 27.8 x 239.9 cm, British Museum, London.

rom Yuan it lies . . . at a distance of about 10,000 li. . . . [The
ople] have wine of grapes and many fine horses. The horses sweat
od and are descended from heavenly horses" (Book of Han)

Horses

1 important element of the army, and also symbolic of its
premacy, the horse, both draft and saddle, was not a domestic
imal but one of the instruments of power in ancient China. Sev-
al sacrificial pits located to the east of the tomb complex of Qin
i Huangdi hold the imperial stables, with skeletons of horses
cing the central tumulus accompanied by terracotta statues.
ie horses of the quadrigas that were part of the ranks of the ter-
cotta army are instead themselves made of clay. These stallions
e strong but small and somewhat stout, while tombs of the
an epoch also include statues of "heavenly horses," fashioned
the model of the famous steeds imported from Central Asia
ginning with Wudi of the Han. An edict of AD 667 restricted the

Term
Heavenly horse
(*tianma*)

Related entries
Qin Shi Huangdi,
Wudi, Taizong,
Domestic animals

ght to ride to officials and
obles, and various imperial oper-
ions of the Tang were aimed at
nproving the breeds through
osses with Turkish or Arabian
oroughbreds and strict instruc-
ons concerning breeding. The
nperial stables held tens of thou-
nds of horses, bred for military
arposes or for the amusement of
obles, who used the horses in
inting or playing polo. The
longols, the nomadic people that
onquered almost the entire
icient world thanks to the speed
id discipline of their cavalry,
aid no mind to the improvement
horse breeds.

◀ Frontlet for a horse
bridle (*danglu*),
Western Han dynasty,
from Luozhuang,
Shandong, gilt bronze,
16.5 x 7.5 cm,
Municipal Museum,
Jinan.

Posed in a loose and elegant synchronized trot, this animal, with its erect tail and mouth open in a neigh, is a portrait of a "heavenly horse," also known as a "blood-sweating horse."

In 110 BC the duke of Wusun married a Chinese princess and sent one thousand horses as a nuptial gift; other horses arrived at the Han court following the conquest of the capital of Ferghana (Dayuan) in 101 BC.

Wudi of the Han desired heavenly horses not only to improve the performance of his army but because he believed they were able to reach the mountains of Kunlun, the paradise of the immortals.

The steed seems to move beneath the eyes of the observer, so dynamic is its pose, balanced on a single hoof, which rests on a base shaped like a swallow in flight.

▲ Model of a running horse, Eastern Han dynasty, late 2nd–early 3rd century AD, from the district of Wuwei, Gansu, bronze, 34.5 x 45 cm, Gansu Provincial Museum, Lanzhou.

The bridle that holds the bit is held by a strap over the muzzle.

The mane is cut short except for a forelock and a strand in front of the saddle that offers a grip to a rider in difficulty.

Without doubt the model portrays a horse from the famous imperial stables, which in the Tang period became one of the symbols of the military and economic supremacy of the Chinese empire.

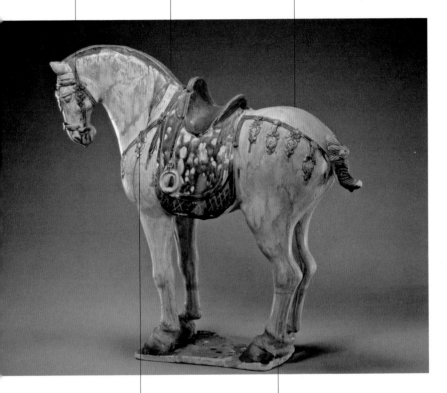

The bridling shows Sassanid influence and reproduces embossed-metal ornaments.

The horse and its trappings were made with the use of molds, but several touches done by hand and the polychrome glaze, applied with intentional casualness, made each specimen special.

Model of a white horse, Tang dynasty, 8th century AD, terracotta with "three-color" (sancai) glaze, 49 cm high, Palace Museum, Beijing.

Li Gonglin was one of the leading promoters of the culture of the literati-officials, which became codified in the Song period. From a learned family, the painter was also a calligrapher, poet, and expert in antiquities.

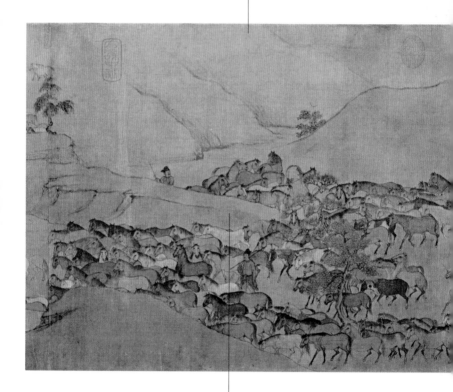

The hints of the landscape serve to create open spaces and to give the image rhythm.

▲ Li Gonglin, *Pasturing Horses, after Wei Yan of the Tang Dynasty* (detail), Northern Song dynasty, early 12th century, handscroll, ink and light color on silk, 46.2 x 430 cm, Palace Museum, Beijing.

The Wei Yan named in the title was a painter of horses of the 8th century. This painting is thus the copy of a work that no longer exists.

Chinese painting, largely codified, was based on the study of masters of the past, but not in the sense of making faithful copies of works; rather, the artist gathered the essence of the earlier work and expressed it by way of his own personal style.

The painter is known for his fluid and sure lines, which express the individuality of subjects using a style he himself created and called "plain drawing" (baimiao): the background colors are left light to express the sense of emptiness.

The style of Ren Renfa drew inspiration from the Tang-period aristocratic tradition of horse painting: the animals are defined in the smallest detail and in their entirety, with intense colors.

The inscription on the painting clarifies its meaning, referring to how the corpulence or the slenderness of officials makes clear their corruption or, on the contrary, their integrity.

Ren Renfa was one of the literati who adapted to the Mongol occupation: a low-level official, he married his daughter to a foreign noble.

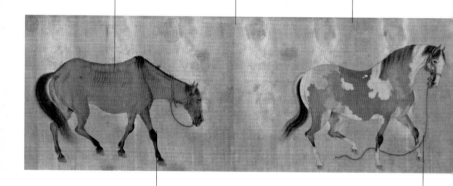

The shading of the colors reproduces chromatic variations in the hide of the animals and does not represent the effects of light and shadow, something that the Chinese have never taken into account.

The bridles of the thin horse hug its neck, while those of the fat horse hang loosely to the ground, indicating the lack of control caused by corruption.

▲ Ren Renfa, *Two Horses*, painted section, Yuan dynasty, early 14th century, horizontal scroll, ink and color on silk, 28.8 x 143.7 cm, Palace Museum, Beijing.

"At fifteen years I was sent to the north to guard the river; at forty I was sent to camp to farm in the west on the frontier"
(Du Fu)

War

The authority of the Confucian sovereign depended on the moral example he offered his people; Chinese historiography thus criticizes martial emperors and disparages the career of arms. Even so, the fortune of a dynasty depended in large measure on its military force, which had to protect the country from the continuous invasions of foreigners to the north while defending the imperial hegemony of the capital. The danger posed by having an excessive concentration of power and troops in the hands of overly autonomous generals was dealt with in various ways over the course of history. The military system of the Western Han was based most of all on forced labor and the recruitment of peasants, but in the 6th century the non-Chinese Wei dynasty instituted permanent settlements of soldier-farmers in the frontier regions. Under the Sui and the Tang, every commander was responsible for one thousand soldier-farmers, who could be mobilized in the event of war. The decline of this system around the end of the Tang period led to one of the most devastating revolts in Chinese history. The Song were primarily occupied with the defense of the capital and tried to reduce the threat of foreign invasion by the payment of exorbitant tributes. The military organization of the Mongols made all social categories equal, while the Ming developed a variation of the soldier-farmer settlement system.

Terms
System of militia-farmers (*Fubing* system)

Related entries
Confucianism, Agriculture

◀ *Battle on Bridge*, Eastern Han dynasty, 2nd century AD, rubbing of a stone bas-relief, from the western wall of Room 1, Wu Liang Shrine, Shandong.

133

Military technology made notable progress during the period of the Warring States, with the introduction of helmets and armor for the infantry.

Breastplates were usually made of leather sections sewn together; rare examples of helmets and armor made with iron plates have been found.

The plaques are overlaid in a "fish-scale" manner to provide flexibility without exposing the body.

In 1998 the loose plaques of 150 suits of armor and more than 50 helmets were found, all heaped in a single pit. It took several years to reconstruct the first examples of the armor.

Weighing about 18 kilograms, such stone armor was too heavy to ever be worn. This was thus an object of substitution conceived for the infantry that would fight for the first emperor in the afterlife.

▲ Armor, Qin dynasty, from pit K9801 in the tomb of Qin Shi Huangdi, limestone plaques, metal thread, Museum of Qin Terracotta Warriors and Horses, Lintong.

The crossbow made its appearance in China around the 4th century BC, roughly one thousand years before its appearance in Europe.

The firing mechanism, the heart of the weapon, is made of bronze and has been preserved more or less intact, whereas the bow and the stock, made of wood, rotted away ages ago.

The sear, held in place by the trigger, has an extension that makes it possible to aim and a short curved part that, together with the nut, held the string in place. The arrow was inserted between the two hooks of the nut.

The mechanism is composed of two pieces, connected by pins: the first fixed the string to the nut, the second turned a ratchet that released the arrow.

Pulling the trigger released the ratchet, held in place within the mechanism, thus turning the nut and releasing the string and the arrow.

▲ Crossbow mechanism, Eastern Han dynasty or Western Jin, 1st–4th century AD, bronze with gold inlay, 18 cm long, Musée Guimet, Paris.

Until the discovery of a suit of armor in a pit belonging to the tomb of Qin Shi Huangdi, it was believed that horse armor had been invented in Central Asia in the 3rd century BC.

This discovery led to the hypothesis that the use of horse armor began with the Sarmatian people and spread west to the Romans and Germans and east to the Chinese.

The horse, with its massive body and short legs, may be a species native to northern China and Mongolia.

▲ Model of a horse and rider, Northern Wei dynasty, AD 386–534, from Caochangpo, Shaanxi, painted terracotta, 37.5 cm high, Shaanxi History Museum, Xi'an.

The statuette was covered by a pale slip decoration and was painted after firing with mineral pigments of which slight traces remain that make the plate armor stand out.

Sulfur and saltpeter, the main ingredients in gunpowder along with carbon, had been used by Chinese alchemists since the Han period.

The earliest indications of the military use of gunpowder date to the early 9th century, and the large-scale use of "fire arrows" and "fire lances" began around the year 1000.

火
龍
出
水

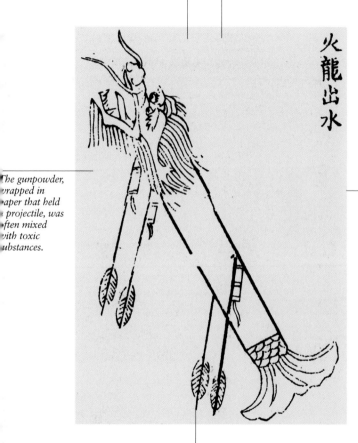

The gunpowder, wrapped in paper that held a projectile, was often mixed with toxic substances.

The first explosives for military use appeared in the 12th century, and the first portable firearm in the world is dated to 1288.

It seems probable that the use of firearms arrived in the West from China, having first passed through the Arab world, where the earliest mention of saltpeter is in a treatise from the 13th century in which it is called "Chinese snow."

▲ Jiao Yu, *Composite Rocket Named "Fire Dragon Rises from Water" (Huolong chu shui),* Ming dynasty, 1412, woodcut illustration from the *Classic of the Fire Dragon (Huolongjing).*

"Old battles were waged by the Great Wall in ancient times, fought by men everyone calls prodigies of mind and heart.... Antiquity now is a yellow dust" (Wang Changling)

Great Wall

Terms
Great Wall
(*Changcheng*)

Related entries
Qin Shi Huangdi,
Hongwu, Foreign
dynasties

The first emperor, Qin Shi Huangdi, promoted construction of a single wall along the northern frontier, constantly in danger because of recurrent invasions of the Xiongnu. This barrier connected several existing forts belonging to kingdoms and cities from the period of the Warring States. Thanks to the work of the troops and the hundreds of thousands of peasants involved in forced labor, in the period of ten years more than 5,000 kilometers of wall had been built, made of earth held inside a timber framework that was later removed. The Han extended this line of defense westward, through the Gobi Desert; signal towers of earth were built at regular intervals, but the route often consisted of a ditch instead of a raised barrier because of the scarcity of raw materials. Works of preservation and enlargement were performed during later dynasties; the Mongols, who themselves came from the steppe, neglected the maintenance of the wall. The rulers of the Ming dynasty built a new wall parallel to the old one but farther south; it was more effective because it ran along the slopes of mountain chains and was more solid because it was made of baked bricks and stone.

▼ Route of the Great
Wall in the Ming
period.

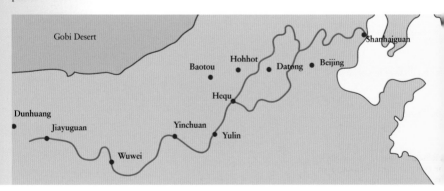

Visible in the distance is one of the watchtowers, part of an efficient system of communication.

About 80 km west of the Dunhuang oasis is the "Jade Gate Pass" (Yumen Guan), a structure of impressive dimensions that represents one of the rare examples of Han-period architecture.

Not far from the Jade Gate Pass are several stretches of the wall, built during that period, that ran alongside the commercial routes to Central Asia for more than 300 km.

The construction system can be easily recognized, composed of an alternation of layers of plants, in this case reeds from a nearby stream, with layers of packed earth.

The gate and the wall were probably built to force commercial caravans to enter the empire by way of a tollhouse.

◢ Remains of the wall built during the Han period, circa 105 BC, near the Yumen Pass, Gansu.

During the brief Sui dynasty (AD 581–618), several large-scale works were undertaken, including the reconstruction of the Great Wall and the construction of the Grand Canal.

Sources speak of more than 1 million peasants forced to work on the Great Wall, with a great number dying during the work.

It is assumed that on the plains, the Ming workers built atop the remains of fortifications from the Sui period, while in the hilly areas they built instead along the crests of mountain chains.

The wall built by the Sui was meant to protect the empire, just reunited after more than three hundred years of division, against the constant invasions of Turkic peoples.

▲ Remains of the Great Wall built in the Ming period, 15th century, near Sanguankou, Ningxia.

After a first period of construction in the second half of the 15th century, beginning in the 16th century public works were undertaken on a large scale that continued until the fall of the Ming dynasty.

By way of the signal towers, built close to one another, news of a sudden attack could reach the capital in a matter of a few hours.

The evolution of military technology, first of all that of firearms, required a type of construction more resistant than simple packed earth.

In the area near the capital the defensive walls were built in stone or baked brick. Their width reached 8 meters at the base, while they rose as much as 9 meters high.

Defenders could move along walkways atop the walls and hurl their weapons through loopholes.

The Great Wall near Beijing, reconstruction on the wall of the Ming period.

"When will the Hun invaders be defeated and an end to the w[ar]
come for our men?" (Li Bai)

Foreign dynasties

Terms
Foreigner (*yi*)
Foreigner from
the Northwestern
Regions (*hu*)

Related entries
Kublai Khan,
Buddhism, Yungang,
Longmen

▶ Crouching lion,
Northern Zhou
dynasty, AD 557–581,
from the outskirts
of Xi'an, Shaanxi,
stone, 25.3 cm high,
Forest of Stone
Tablets Museum,
Xi'an.

China's relationship with the peoples along its northern bord[er]
was always difficult. The mobility of the nomadic tribes favor[ed]
cultural, technological, and commercial exchanges with near[by]
and distant civilizations, but it also posed a continuous threat [to]
the integrity of the country. After the collapse of the Han dynast[y]
various nomadic peoples managed to take control of vast areas [of]
northern China, and several kingdoms rose and fell there over th[e]
course of three centuries. The conquerors adopted typically Ch[i]-
nese customs and traditions and sought to legitimize their power with the help of Buddhism, the religion wit[h]
foreign origins that in that same period managed to penetrate Chinese society to its core[.]
When the Tang dynasty ended in 907, som[e]
tribes, already partially Sinicized, invade[d]
China and founded dynasties modeled o[n]
the Chinese example: the Khitan tribal con-
federation instituted the Liao dynasty (A[D]
916–1125), destroyed by the allie[d]
troops of the Song dynasty and the Ju[r]-
chen nomads who had erected the Ji[n]
dynasty. After this triumph, the Ju[r]-
chen turned against their allies, conquering all of northern China in 112[7]
with the help of Chinese experienced in siege techniques. Th[e]
Jurchen became Sinicized t[o]
the point of losing their language, while the Mongol invaders, who united China unde[r]
their domination in 1271, took cautionar[y]
measures to avoid excessive assimilation.

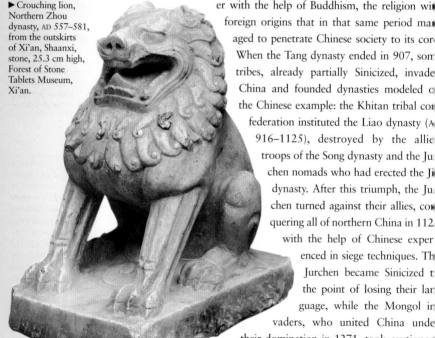

The king wears a large crown made of gold inlaid with turquoise, the same materials of which the incense burner in his left hand is made.

大朝大寶于闐國大聖天明天子

he cartouche entifies this as portrait of the ng of the Khotan sis, son-in-law of e cave painter's tron, Cao Yijin, ho had the walls corated with cred images and mily portraits.

The cloak is decorated with symbols of power: aside from the dragon, the traditional emblem of imperial Chinese authority, symbols of the sun and moon are embroidered on his shoulders.

The Cao family governed the region of Dunhuang from AD 920 for more than one hundred years, consolidating their power with a skillful policy of marriages and maintaining diplomatic relations with the dynasties that followed one another in northern China.

Portrait of the King of hotan, Five Dynasties period, 920, wall painting on the estern wall of Cave 98 at ogao, Dunhuang, Gansu.

These two slabs were part of a stone platform on which the sarcophagus of the deceased rested.

Although they are not symmetrical, the scenes carved on the two slabs go together: two processions are arriving at the gate to a Chinese city.

▲ Bas-relief in two parts in the shape of a gate, Northern Qi dynasty, gray limestone, both 71.5 x 74 cm, Museum für Ostasiatische Kunst, Cologne.

The stone reliefs illustrate the techniques used in the building of the wooden towers (que) that, beginning in the Han period, protected the entrances to sepulchral areas, palaces, and cities.

Clearly visible are the round eyes, exotic dress—cloaks tied with wide belts and edged in pearl—that make clear the Central Asian origin of the members of the two processions, led by two nobles.

*"A nomad with curly hair and green eyes, in the silence of the
night, standing beside a tall palace, played the flute" (Li He)*

Foreigners at the imperial cour

Numerous reports from diplomats, religious men, and merchan
from throughout the world have survived that, with their ma
veling accounts, add to the traditional vision of the customs of th
imperial court offered by official Chinese historiography. In som
periods, Chinese interest in the outside world facil
tated access to the palace by foreigners; the earl
Tang period (circa AD 618–655) was characte
ized by a taste for the exotic, understood as
caprice related to fashion, not as a tru
interest in distant civilizations. The emi
saries that succeeded in obtaining an audienc
at court were indiscriminately considered vassal
their gifts taken as tribute, while any presents th
Chinese gave in return were called "wages." Th
high-sounding titles that were conferred on dele
gates were purely symbolic and only rein
forced Chinese hegemony. With regard t
the welcome given foreigners at the cou
of Kublai Khan, we have the enrapture
testimony of Marco Polo. The Venetia
trader's reception is a clear indicatio
of the Mongolian policy that reserve
special treatment for foreign merchant
Other travelers experienced this, suc
as the Franciscan missionaries Odoric c
Pordenone and Giovanni da Monteco
vino. The Sinocentrism of the Ming epoc
became profitable during the reign of Yongl
who established tributary relationships wit
bordering lands and received ambassado
from distant countries.

► Pitcher in the
shape of a
phoenix, Tang
dynasty, first half 8th
century, terracotta
with "three-color"
(*sancai*) glaze, 32.5 cm
high, Museo di Arte
Orientale, Turin.

After the restoration of the Tang dynasty in AD 705, one of the first acts of the new ruler was the construction of tombs for the various members of the imperial family who had fallen victim to the empress Wu Zetian.

Three of these tombs, built as spacious underground palaces, are famous in particular for their wall paintings, which provide an idea of the "metropolitan" pictorial style of the Tang epoch.

Three Chinese dignitaries, deep in conversation, turn their backs on three foreigners, whether emissaries or hostages. At the time, such people were sent to China by vassal states and lived near the court, invited to take part in important events.

On the walls of the access ramp of the tomb of the hereditary prince Li Zhanguai, who died in AD 684, are scenes of hunting and games followed by other depictions of groups of people.

The three foreigners are presented with a realism that touches the caricatural, dressed in their traditional clothes; the man in the middle seems to come from the Asiatic southeast, while the other two have more "Western" features.

Foreign Embassy, Tang dynasty, 796, wall painting from the tomb of Prince Li Zhanguai, ianling, Shaanxi, 184 cm high, aanxi History Museum, Xi'an.

The dignitary's
military function is
indicated by his type
of hat, the pectoral
that is visible under
his robe, and his left
hand, which originally
grasped a weapon.

Globular eyes, a big
nose, and thick lips
characterize the
features of this
dignitary and clearly
identify him as a
"Western" (Central
Asian) foreigner.

The modeling of this
statuette shows rare
refinement, most of
all in its asymmetrical
pose and very
realistic expression.

The wide sleeve was
painted with precious
mineral pigments in
red, blue, and green
and was bordered
with gold leaf, small
traces of which
remain.

The most elaborate tombs
sometimes contain pairs of officials,
one of which has exotic features.

▲ Model of a military dignitary,
Tang dynasty, 8th century AD,
terracotta, slip decoration,
pigments, and gold leaf, 67 cm high,
Museo di Arte Orientale, Turin.

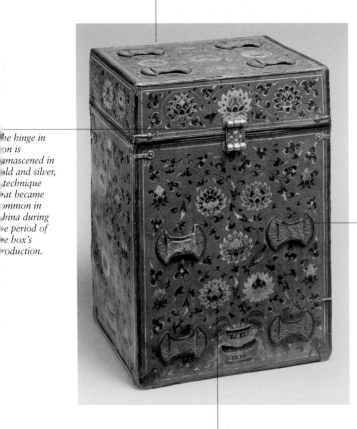

The box was probably given to a Tibetan visitor to the Ming court and may have contained fabrics or porcelain.

he hinge in
on is
amascened in
ld and silver,
technique
at became
ommon in
hina during
e period of
e box's
roduction.

A strap fit through these leather grommets for holding the box during travels.

The large lotus flowers with pointed petals recall the decorative tradition of the minor arts of Nepal, which were introduced to China around the end of the 13th century.

Travel box, Ming dynasty, early 5th century, leather, wood, iron, ld, and pigments, 53.3 cm high, etropolitan Museum of Art, ew York.

"The first people that are known of here are the Seres, so famo[us] for the wool that is found in their forests. After steeping it in water, they comb off a white down" (Pliny the Elder)

Contacts with Europe

Terms
Roman empire
(*Daqin*)

Related entries
Wudi, Foreigners at
the imperial court,
Minor religions

▼ Circular object
engraved with the
letters of an alphabet,
Western Han dynasty,
lead, 5.4 cm diam.,
Shaanxi History
Museum, Xi'an.

Contact between the East and the West began with the expansic[n] of Alexander the Great, in whose wake the first commercial rout[es] were opened through the Hellenistic kingdoms. By way of t[he] explorations of Zhang Qian as well as Chinese military exped[i]tions in Central Asia, the Chinese knew of the existence of t[he] Roman empire. In AD 97, general Ban Chao, who had extende[d] the Chinese empire up to the basin of the Tarim, decided to mak[e] direct contact with Rome and sent an emissary. This emissar[y] made it as far as the Black Sea before turning back, frightened o[ff] by the false information given him by parties that feared the loss [of] their intermediary role. Chinese historiography records the fir[st] visit of a Roman delegation in AD 166, and until AD 284 there we[re] several others. During the cosmopolitan period [of] the Tang (circa AD 620–655), the new pow[er] of the Arabs took hold between Byzan[tium] and Chang'an. The "Wester[n]ers" living in the capital we[re] Sogdians, Persians, Arabs, Ind[i]ans, and Turks, peoples wh[o] could hold high positio[ns] under the government of th[e] Yuan. Most of the Europea[n] missionaries who arrived i[n] China during that perio[d] were Franciscans, while begin[n]ing in the second half of th[e] 16th century there were als[o] Jesuits. Conversions to Christianit[y] were rare, but the scientific knowledg[e] of some Jesuits, such as Matteo Ricci an[d] Adam Schall von Bell, was highly esteemed.

In 1601, after spending twenty years in southern China, the missionary Matteo Ricci, founder of the Catholic missions in China, was finally admitted to the court in Beijing.

The Jesuit, who had learned to read and write Chinese perfectly, greatly admired Confucian culture and was the first to translate the works into Latin, along the way coining the name Confucius *as a romanization of* Kong Fuzi.

The map, of which six examples are known, includes instructions for use.

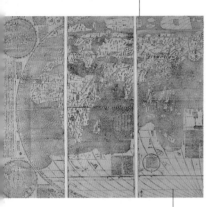 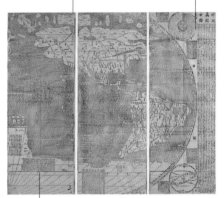

Ricci gained the respect of literati and officials and finally even of the emperor himself with his knowledge of sciences, in particular mathematics, astronomy, and geography.

The concepts of the "systems of terrestrial and celestial world" are illustrated in theoretical explanations that together with the drawing display the development of the geographic science of the period.

Matteo Ricci, *Complete Geographic Map of all the Kingdoms of the World*, Ming Dynasty, 1602, copper-plate engraving on rice paper, Biblioteca Apostolica Vaticana, Rome.

Religion and philosophy

Container decorated with figures
against a landscape, Tang dynasty,
from the crypt of the Famen
Temple pagoda at Fufeng, Shaanxi,
partially gilt silver, 24.7 cm high,
Famen Temple Museum, Fufeng.

"Those six influences are called the yin, the yang, wind, rain, obscurity, and brightness. In separation, they form the seasons. Whe[n] an element is in excess, there ensues calamity" (Chronicle of Zuo)

Yin and yang and the five phase[s]

In the 5th century BC, during the period of the oldest citations, y[in] (shadow) and yang (sun) designated a series of opposing natural ph[e]nomena. By the 3rd century BC, the abstract notion of the dualism [of] yin and yang had appeared, a result of the unity of the primordial li[fe] force and seen as responsible for the cyclical rise and decay of ever[y]thing. Although by nature opposed, yin and yang are not antagonis[tic] but are rather complementary, since their interaction creates t[he] rhythm that animates the universe. Between the 3rd and 2nd centu[ry] BC, the bonds between yin and yang became combined with the fi[ve] phases—wood, fire, earth, metal, and water—understood not as sta[tic] elements but rather as creative energy. Beginning in the Han period, t[he] scheme of the cyclic alternations, born of the dualism of yin and yan[g] and expressed through the succession of the five phases, was applied [to] all phenomenological and temporal phenomena: long lists related t[he] five phases with the seasons, the cardinal points, the planets, and al[so] with the five senses, colors, animals, and the organs and parts of t[he] human body. The *Book of Changes*, the book of divination compil[ed] in the 3rd–2nd centu[ry] BC on the basis of f[ar] older sources, express[ed] the Chinese vision of t[he] relationships betwe[en] the universe and huma[ns] by way of yin and yan[g] and the five phases, [a] theory accepted by [a]Chinese thinkers b[ut] given particular elabor[a]tion by Daoism.

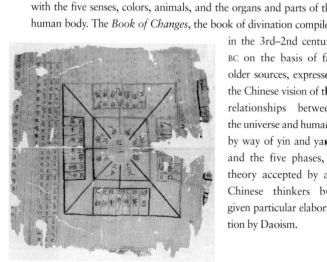

▶ *Book on Yin and
Yang and the Five
Phases* (fragment),
Western Han dynasty,
circa 168 BC, from
Tomb 3 at
Mawangdui, ink on
silk, 24 cm high,
Hunan Provincial
Museum, Changsha.

Divinities associated with long life, prosperity, and happiness are studying the symbol, which presents the flow of life as a natural phenomenon, a result of the opposing actions of yin and yang.

The figures are accompanied by other symbols of immortality, wealth, and long life: the pine tree, the deer, and the fish offered by the boy.

▲ A Group of Daoist Divinities Studying a Scroll with the Yin and Yang Symbol (detail), Qing dynasty, second half 17th century, ink and color on silk, Trustees of the British Museum, London.

By the end of the 6th century AD, the ancient symbols of yin and yang, the white tiger and green dragon, had been replaced by this symbol, which was originally applied to the concept of taiji. Yin and yang arose from the original energy, complementary and inseparable. Each bears a small dot of the color of the other, indicating that each of the two forces contains the seed of the opposite force.

Early in the 3rd century BC, the five phases had replaced the ancient division of the world into four states: the concept of the center had been added to the four cardinal points.

In spring, the period of waxing yang, the force of wood prevails, associated with the green dragon of the east.

Yin grows stronger in the fall, when the phase of metal begins, associated with the white tiger of the west.

▶ Tile antefixes decorated with the four cardinal points, Han dynasty, 206 BC–AD 220, molded terracotta, 13 to 19 cm diam., Shaanxi History Museum, Xi'an.

The depictions of the directions are still tied to the iconography developed in the preceding period, which also agreed with the series of four seasons.

In the summer, yang is at its greatest power, related to fire and the red bird of the south. The period of transition that follows symbolizes the center, the earth, the color yellow, but no specific animal represents it.

Yin dominates the winter, the female element, revealing itself in the "black warrior" of the north, represented by the union of the turtle and the serpent.

> "If there is concern in the ceremonies for the dead and sacrifices are performed for ancestors, then virtue among men will once again be great" (Confucius)

Ancestor worship

Ancestor worship was of fundamental importance among the divinatory practices of ancient China. It was not limited to the ceremonies that attended the death of a family member and the funeral rites of the deceased: at established intervals sacrifice were performed in honor of ancestors. These could take place a the family tomb, in a temple dedicated to ancestors, or on the domestic altar. Ancestors could perform an active role as intermediaries between supernatural powers and the living family, with which they maintained intrinsic ties. In China, the border between life and death was permeable, and a family member's position remained unchanged after death. The deceased was honored in relation to his function within the clan, not for any individual act performed during life. The rites with which the sacrifices for ancestors were performed were prescribed in the smallest details, and the rank of the ancestor in the afterlife and, as a consequence the family's fortune depended on their correct execution. As early a the time of Confucius (6th–5th centuries BC) devotion of ancestors was often displayed in the richness of such sacrificial offerings. Confucius was opposed to this custom putting most importance on the behavior of descendents and on their strict performance of the rites for ancestors, which help consolidate the hierarchical order of Chinese society.

▶ Ancestral tablet, Qing dynasty, 19th century, wood, cloth, pigment, string, 15 cm high, American Museum of Natural History, Asian Ethnographic Collection, New York.

Surrounded by stars, Fuxi and Nüwa embrace, their long extremities intertwining. Nüwa holds a compass, symbolic of the circular Sky.

Fuxi, the first among the mythical Three Sovereigns, holds a carpenter's square, emblematic of the square earth. He was credited with invention of the eight trigrams, which make it possible to enter into contact with the heavens and to regulate the life of all beings.

Depictions of the two divinities began appearing on tombs in the Han era, usually with anthropomorphic trunks and tails like those of a serpent or dragon.

Fuxi and Nüwa, Tang dynasty, from the tombs of Astana, Turfan, Xinjiang, ink and color on hemp, Xinijang Provincial Museum, Urumqi.

Fuxi and his consort Nüwa, who is also his sister, are the supreme ancestors of Chinese civilization.

Together with the founder of the Xia dynasty, named Yu, the last two emperors of the dynasty, Yao and Shun, were often held up by Confucian sages as ideal rulers and moral exemplars.

Chinese mythology includes the "Three August Ones" (San Huang) and the "Five Emperors" (Wu Di), who ruled China in primordial times, before the arrival of the mythical Xia dynasty (2200–1500 BC).

Here are depicted from right to left Fuxi and Nüwa, Zhurong, and Shennong, the divine peasant, followed by the Five Emperors, all crowned, and finally by the founder and last emperor of the Xia dynasty.

▲ The Legendary Sovereigns, Western Han dynasty, 2nd century AD, rubbing of stone bas-relief from the western wall of Room 3, Wu Liang Shrine, Shandong.

The first of the Five Emperors was the Yellow Emperor (Huangdi), considered the founder of Chinese civilization, located by traditional historiography in the area of the middle course of the Yellow River.

In every state sacrifices must be offered to the mountains and rivers. . . . The ruler . . . must see that the official in charge prepares the proper offerings" (Chronicle of Zuo)

Cult of the state

In China sacred power and political authority have always been joined, with supremacy going to the state over religious practice. Since the preimperial period of the Shou, only the "Son of Heaven" had the right to sacrifice to royal ancestors and to the supreme divinity, Heaven. In 219 BC Qin Shi Huangdi made a sacrifice in honor of Heaven and the Earth on Mount Tai, performed six times over the course of China's dynastic history, with the last dating to AD 1008 (Northern Song dynasty). In 113 BC Wudi of the Han added an imperial rite dedicated to the "Supreme One" to emphasize the unity of the emperor with the central power. The emperor had a new Hall of Light erected on Mount Tai in 109 BC in honor of all the divinities of the universe. Its architecture, modeled on that of the Zhou epoch, was meant to reflect ancient cosmology: the body of the building had a square plan, like the earth, while the roof was circular, like the sky. During the Han period the rites celebrated on Mount Tai expressed the exclusive communication between the ruler and the heavens; beginning in the Tang period the journey and the celebration of the sacrifices were transformed into an exhibition of imperial authority. Emperor Hongwu of the Ming began the tradition of honoring heaven during the winter solstice, while during the summer solstice the divinities of the earth were venerated.

Terms
Son of Heaven (*tianzi*)
Supreme One (*ianyi*)
Sacrifice to Heaven
(*Feng*)
Sacrifice to the Earth
(*Shan*)
Hall of Light (*Ming Tang*)

Related entries
Qin Shi Huangdi,
Wudi, Wu Zetian,
Hongwu, Sacred
mountains

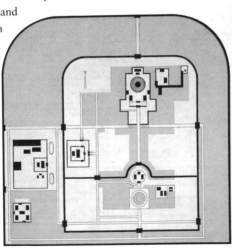

◀ Plan of the Temple of Heaven at Beijing.

161

The ancient ceremonies of the emperors, the sacrifices dedicated to Heaven (Feng) and to Earth (Shan), were performed at the top and at the bottom of Mount Tai. In AD 666 Emperor Gaozong officiated at the sacrifices together with his wife, transforming the rite, which had originally been seen as confirmation of the secret union between ruler and divinity, into a public spectacle celebrated with officials and foreign emissaries.

Wu Zetian, proclaiming herself empress, was the only Chinese ruler to honor Mount Song, going there ten times and changing its name to "Divine Mountain."

The text, made for the public, lists the ruler's virtues and the graces received from the divinity, which the emperor returned with offerings of jade, silk, and choice foods.

The emperor Xuanzong restored the ancient ritual on Mount Tai and wrote with his own hand a dedication to the Queen Mother of the Earth, faithfully repeated on these stone tablets.

▲ Stone tablet inscribed with the Shan sacrifices of Emperor Xuanzong, Tang dynasty, dated to AD 725, engraved marble, 29.2 x 39.8 cm, National Palace Museum, Taipei.

Constructed in the image of the palace of worship erected by the first emperor of the Ming dynasty at Nanjing, the Temple of Heaven was built in Beijing along with the Forbidden City on the initiative of the emperor Yongle.

The temple complex was located to the south of the palace, just outside the wall. During the celebration of rites of the cult of state, the emperor with the entire court paraded along a large avenue to reach this destination.

In 1530 the "circular hill" was added, with its numerous references to numerology. This is where the emperor performed solemn sacrifices on the day of the winter solstice.

In the "Hall of Prayers for Good Harvests," covered by three concentric roofs, the emperor celebrated sacrifices to propitiate a good harvest on the fifteenth day of the first lunar month.

The four pillars of the inner roof represent the four seasons, while the middle and outer rows have 12 pillars each, symbolic of the twelve months of the year and the twelve hours of the day.

After a night passed in the "temple of abstinence," the emperor walked barefoot along the central axis of the temple complex.

The Temple of Heaven (*Tiantan*), Ming dynasty, 1421–1426 and 1530, detail of the temple for sacrifices to the earth, Beijing.

"The Master took four subjects for his teaching: culture, conduct, conscientiousness, and good faith" (Confucius)

Confucianism

Confucianism was originally a pragmatic moral teaching based on the collection and commentary of ancient writings promoted by Confucius (Kongzi, 551–479 BC) and his disciples. Master Kong made reference to models from the past to present a code of ethical-moral values that he saw as the basis of the social order. The "rites" are the exterior manifestation of the rules that strengthen the structure of the collectivity, arranged in a rigid hierarchy: humans are not defined through their personalities but through the observance of rites, meaning through the maintenance of behavior in terms of one's position within society. The virtuous man, who also possesses the quality of "benevolence," has the right and also the duty to rule; his subjects are expected to display "filial piety." Beginning with Wudi of the Han dynasty, Confucianism became the state doctrine, and the canonical classics, the result of the systematic arrangement of the entire literary production of earlier ages in accordance with the criteria of rational dignity, formed the cornerstones of Chinese culture for the next two thousand years. The official worship of Confucius began in AD 59 with the introduction of sacrifices in his honor and that of the duke of Zhou, obligatory in all schools. Beginning in the 5th century temples were dedicated to the master and to other important historical figures.

▶ Ma Yuan, *Portrait of Confucius* (detail), Southern Song dynasty, late 12th–early 13th century, ink and color on silk, 27.7 x 23.2 cm, Palace Museum, Beijing.

The city of Qufu was the capital of the kingdom of Lu and the birthplace of Confucius. Tradition relates that already in 478 BC, one year after the death of the great philosopher, a small temple was erected in his honor. In 195 BC the first imperial sacrifices in honor of Confucius were celebrated, and this even before Confucianism had been made the state doctrine.

The temple complex is quite vast and faces south with an arrangement along a median axis.

Located beside the temple is the historical residence of the Kong family, which dates to the 1st century BC, when the descendents of the "Master Kong" were given noble titles and holdings.

The entire structure has been enlarged and reworked many times. In the Ming epoch the official responsible for the district lived there.

The temple of Confucius
Qufu, Shandgong.

The fragment documents the promotion of the standardization of the Confucian classics carried out by the state during the Han period.

Under the direction of the secretary of the imperial archive, Cai Yong (AD 133–192), a group of calligraphic experts wrote out the texts in red ink on stone slabs that were then engraved by stonecutters.

The Han period established the custom of immortalizing an event, person, or text by way of monumental inscriptions on stone steles (bei).

The texts we written on t front and ba of forty-s stone stel about 2.30 high usin "clerical scrip (lishu), which the Han peric was replacin the "small se script" impose by Qin S Huanga

The Xiping Classics on Stone, held in an area of the imperial university of Luoyang, were destroyed a few years after completion of the work. Beginning in the Song dynasty the fragments were eagerly sought by collectors.

▲ Fragment of the Xiping Classics on Stone (*Xiping Shijing*), Eastern Han dynasty, AD 175–183, stone, 15 cm high, Luoyang Municipal Museum, Henan.

The master said, 'The dao is so great that it has no end, and so small that nothing escapes it. For this reason it is omnipresent in all beings" (Zhuangzi)

Daoism

The *dao*, conventionally translated as the "way" or "principle," is a common idea in ancient Chinese schools of thought. To Confucians, the *dao* represents virtuous conduct, while the various trends grouped under the name *Daoism* see the *dao* as the origin of perpetual universal transformation, ineffable by nature, since the reality with which one might seek to classify it is itself fatally transient, falsified in the moment in which it is uttered. The *Classic of the Way and Its Power*, attributed to Lao Tzu (5th century BC) and compiled several centuries later, and the *Zhuangzi*, ascribed to Master Chuang (4th century BC) but containing far older texts, seek to dissuade the disciple from logical reasoning by way of absurd associations and paradoxical phrases. Freeing the mind and letting oneself move spontaneously with the flow of life, without judging or forcing events, following the concept of "non-doing," makes it possible to enter the harmony of universal life in continuous change. Daoism is heir to the cosmological speculations of many magical-religious practices of ancient China, including the quest for immortality. Following the disintegration of the Chinese empire in the 3rd century AD, Daoism responded to the growing religious needs of the people and the spread of Buddhism by dividing into sects, each with its own canons and dogmas.

Terms
Classic of the Way and Its Power (Dao De Jing)
Master Chuang (*Zhuangzi*)
Non-doing (*wu wei*)
Transformation (*hua*)
Daoist canon (*Daozang*)

Related entries
Landscape painting, Yin and yang and the five phases, Sacred mountains, The quest for immortality

▼ *Interrogating a Spirit*, Qing dynasty, 1730, wall painting in the Lingbao palace, Xiyun temple, Dunhuang, Gansu.

The sphere in the figure's right hand may represent a peach of immortality.

The iconography of the Han period described the immortals (xian) as hybrids with a human bearing, but the nose and beak of a bird, wings on the back, and a skirt of feathers.

The unusual cove with its fine worked conic shape, reproduce the "mountain the immortals (Kunlun), locate at the far wester end of the worl

This ritual va with its typic cylindrical shap and feet in th shape of crouchin bears, was create to hold wine mad of fermente cereal grain

Modeled in light high-relief are three series of mountain chains populated by fantastic animals, all of it engraved with the rhythm and density typical of the Han-period style: no area of the surface is left empty.

▲ Vase with immortal on lid, Western Han dynasty, first half 1st century AD, bronze, 32 cm high, Museo di Arte Orientale, Turin.

The Queen Mother of the West (Xiwangmu) appears in Han-period tombs, often depicted together with her husband, the King Father of the East (Dongwanggong).

The Queen Mother of the West, who also rules the paradise of the immortals, is seated on a throne in the shape of a dragon and tigers and is surrounded by the faithful.

The periodic union of this pair of cosmic protectors, as well as that of others, such as Fuxi and Nüwa, leads to the rebirth of the heavens and nature.

The wolf with nine tails is an auspicious creature.

The three-footed crow is symbolic of the sun.

The dancing frog is symbolic of rebirth and together with the rabbit personifies the moon.

▲ The Queen Mother of the West (*Xiwangmu*), Eastern Han dynasty, second half 2nd century AD, brick with molded decoration, 46.5 x 40 cm, Sichuan Provincial Museum, Chengdu.

Ma Lin descended from a family of literati-painters. Her father, Ma Yuan, was one of the leading landscape artists in the history of Chinese art, famous for his "one-corner" compositions: the center is empty, the subject relegated to one side of the work.

The Daoist pantheon, which was consolidated in the Tang period, recognized two categories of divinities, the "celestial masters" and the immortals.

The Three Functionaries record the actions of humans and determine the duration of their lives and their destinies after death. The functionary of heaven travels among the clouds on a carriage drawn by a goat.

The "Three Pure Ones," sometime also includin Lao Tzu, an the Thre Functionarie came into bein spontaneous from primordia energy an are among th first being

The functiona in charge the earth followed b bureaucra charged wit recording th deeds an misdeeds humans and preceded b threatenin soldiers wh punis malefactor

The functionary of waters rides a dragon, symbolic of rain.

▲ Ma Lin, *The Three Functionaries (Sanyuan) Make a Tour of Inspection,* Southern Song dynasty, 13th century, ink and color on silk, 174.2 x 122.9 cm, National Palace Museum, Taipei.

Thanks to esoteric methods of purification and self-discipline, some humans could become immortal and obtain a position within the celestial hierarchy.

The eight small panels, not covered by the glaze thanks to the careful application of wax during the second firing, were made in molds.

The glaze characteristic of the kilns of Longquan was highly appreciated for its translucence and for qualities that recall jade; the Chinese believed that the glaze was able to indicate the presence of poison in food.

Intermediaries between the heavens and earth, the immortals live in a transcendental state. The Eight Immortals, whose worship began in the 14th century, are very popular eccentric figures.

Octagonal vase decorated with the Eight Immortals, Yuan dynasty, 14th century, stoneware with celadon glaze, 43.2 cm high, from the Longquan kilns, Zhejiang, British Museum, London.

Wares from the kilns of Longquan were exported in large quantities and were highly sought after in the Orient and in Europe, where the term celadon was coined, taken from the hero of the French writer Honoré d'Urfé's bucolic romance Astrée (1610).

The subject, somewhat common in the Song period, has been enriched by the addition of a detail, a butterfly that makes reference to a famous dream of the great Daoist thinker Zhuangzi.

Zhuangzi dreamed he was a butterfly and on awakening was uncertain if he was Zhuangzi dreaming of being a butterfly or if, instead, he was a butterfly dreaming of being Zhuangzi.

Legend narrates that Lao Tzu who worked in the royal archives, grew tired of the court and decided to retire to private life.

Riding a water buffalo, Lao Tzu ("Old Master") reached the far border of China where he composed his Classic of the Way and Its Power at the request of the gatekeeper before fainting in the desert.

Such paradoxes were very popular with the Daoists and also the followers of Chan (Zen) Buddhism, who used them to liberate the mind from preconceptions and the limits of conventional logic.

▲ Zhang Lu, *Lao Tzu Riding a Water Buffalo*, Ming dynasty, mid-16th century, vertical scroll, ink and light color on paper, 101.5 x 55.3 cm, National Palace Museum, Taipei.

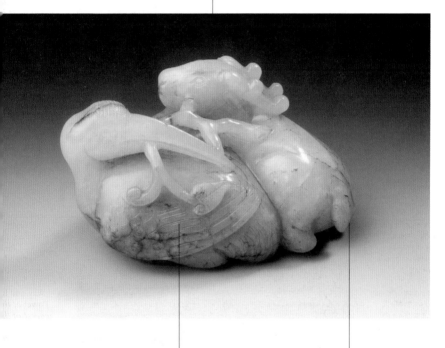

The crane and deer, both symbolic of long life, are positioned on a large acanthus leaf.

The deer also expresses the promise of wealth, a result of the harmony between the sounds of the words deer *and* earnings, *both of which are pronounced* lu.

Crane and deer on acanthus leaf, Ming dynasty, nephrite, Museum of East Asian Art, Bath.

The divinity of Long Life was being worshipped as early as the first emperor, while the other two stellar divinities did not appear in the Daoist iconography until the 15th century.

The complex pantheon of Daoist divinities includes personifications of ancient sciences, along with divinities of the constellations, the stars, and the calendar.

The politica instabilit following th collapse of th Han dynasty i AD 220 and th progressiv spread o Buddhisr in China led t the birth o religiou Daoism, whic. met the nee for dogmas an precise rules

Beginning i the 5th centur AD, the Classi of the Way an Its Power wa flanked by th Daoist cano (Daozang which contair revelations an teachings, rites descriptions o sacred sites anthologies and sel education texts

▲ The Three Stellar Divinities of Good Fortune, Retribution, and Long Life, Ming dynasty, 1454, vertical scroll, ink, colors, and gold leaf on silk, 140 x 78 cm, Musée Guimet, Paris.

Various ancient myths located the abode of the Queen Mother of the West in the Sanwei Mountains on the northwestern border of ancient China.

*The structure, which includes, aside from the temple, the Queen Mother Tower (*Wangmu Lou*) and the Venerable Sovereign Hall (*Laojun Tang*), reflects Daoism's rejection of right angles.*

The roof gutters are usually so curved that they bend upward.

The windows of Daoist constructions are never quadrangular but rather circular or polygonal.

The base wall undulates, and the corners are curved.

West Cloud Temple (*Xiyun uan*), Qing dynasty, 1730, unhuang, Gansu.

*"Must the desire to return be profound? The world and I: emp[ty]
space" (Wang Wei)*

Buddhism

Terms
Buddha (*Dafo*)
Bodhisattva (*pusa*)
Arhat (*Luohan*)

Related entries
Xuanzang, Wu Zetian,
Foreign dynasties,
Images of the Buddha

The weakness of Confucian doctrine following the fall of t[he]
empire in AD 220 made it possible for Buddhism, which ha[d]
appeared in China over the course of the 1st century AD, to ta[ke]
hold in Chinese society. Its interior analysis, chastity, and negatio[n]
of reality were all principles in sharp contrast to the social order an[d]
filial piety that were the foundations of Confucian teaching. Durin[g]
the three centuries that preceded the reunification of the empir[e,]
Buddhism, founded by Prince Siddhartha in the 5th century BC [in]
northern India, underwent several transformations that made po[s]-
sible its integration in Chinese thought, such as addition of the fun[c]-
tions of prayer for the protection of the sovereign and for decease[d]
family members. The Mahayana school (or vehicle) worships [a]
series of reincarnations of the Buddha, asid[e]
from the Bodhisattvas, the enlightened on[es]
that choose to remain on earth to help ot[h]-
ers, and the arhats who have reached sa[l]-
vation. It was this school, more open an[d]
less ascetic than the Hinayana, that sprea[d]
in China. In the north, Buddhism receive[d]
financing for the construction of tem[]-
ples and monasteries in exchang[e]
for glorification of the sovereig[n.]
Under Empress Wu Zetian, Bud[]-
dhism briefly rose to the status [of]
state religion, only to then suffe[r]
harsh persecutions durin[g]
the troubled times of th[e]
late Tang dynasty, whe[n]
xenophobia turned th[e]
Chinese against all fo[r]-
eign religions.

▶ Buddha Sakyamuni,
Eastern Jin dynasty,
AD 338, gilt bronze,
39.4 cm high, Asian
Art Museum, Avery
Brundage
Collection, San
Francisco.

Fearing the approach of the end of the world, the monk Jingwan decided to preserve Buddhist texts by engraving them on stone and burying them in caves, a project that continued for more than five centuries and reached truly astonishing dimensions.

About 15,000 stone slabs were engraved with Buddhist sutras. The first 5,000 slabs were preserved in caves carved near the summit of a mountain and sealed to preserve their precious deposits.

The Cave of the Roar of Thunder, consecrated by Jingwan in AD 616 with the burial of a relic of the Buddha, contains the first 147 stone slabs and is still the only accessible space.

The other 10,000 slabs were produced over an astonishingly short span of time, from 1093 to 1180, a result of the organization of the work, including the standardization of the size of the slabs, which made possible a kind of mass production.

Stone library of the Cloud Dwelling Monastery (*Yunju Si*), Cave of the Roar of Thunder (*Leiyin dong*), Sui and Tang Dynasties, AD 618–639, Yunju Si District, Beijing.

Stone library of the monastery of the Cloud Dwelling Monastery (*Yunju Si*), pit with about 10,000 slabs of engraved stone, Song and Liao dynasties, 1093–1180, Southern pagoda of the Yunju Si District, Beijing.

Many Buddhist votive steles, decorated on their front with images of the Buddha and Bodhisattvas, were erected in temples, monasteries, and caves.

Two Bodhisattvas, far smaller than the Buddha to emphasize his greatness, stand at the sides of an open cavity carved to resemble a niche in a cave temple.

One of the oldest subjects presents the historical Buddha, Sakyamuni, seated in front of a leaf-shaped mandorla.

The Northern Wei dynasty, founded by Toba peoples from the northern steppe, was among the leading promoters of Buddhist sculpture.

The miniature Buddhas surrounding the figures are "manifestation body Buddhas" (huafo), while the Atlas figures supporting the structures are demons overcome by the Buddha.

▲ Stele of the Buddha Sakyamuni, Northern Wei dynasty, high-relief in stone, circa 60 x 56 cm, Forest of Stone Tablets Museum, Xi'an.

arly in the 12th century,
uring a period of great political
stability, the fragments of
undreds of sculptures were
uried near the Buddhist temple
 Longxing, of which no trace
 as remained. Purely by
ccident, the deposit was
cently discovered.

he Buddhist iconography calls
or simplicity in the depiction of
e Buddha, usually shown
earing a long cloak and bearing
ecific "signs" (lakshana), while
e Bodhisattvas are decorated
ith diadems, precious robes,
stoons, and jewels.

he cloak that hides and does
ot reveal the body, typical of
e original Chinese tradition,
as been replaced by tight-
tting robes that highlight the
ape of the body.

he rediscovery of this statuary
roup provided precious
formation on the polychromy
 Buddhist sculpture, for most
 the finds reveal abundant
aces of pigments and gold leaf.

Most of the
sculptures date to
the Northern Wei
and Northern Qi
dynasties. Unlike
the Wei, the Qi
did not absorb
Chinese culture,
and the Buddhist
sculpture of that
period took as its
model the Gupta
style from India.

Standing Bodhisattva, Northern
i dynasty, AD 550–577, from
ingzhou, Shandong, limestone,
36 cm high, Qingzhou Municipal
1useum, Shandong.

The Mahayana school served the desire of believers to establish a close relationship with the holy one, resulting in a multitude of Buddhas and Bodhisattvas, each possessing an aspect of his nature.

The depiction Guanyin wi "a thousan arms and ey originated Tanti iconograph The hands ho many Buddhi symbols, fro beads medicine via

Painted to the sides of the head are the sun and the moon.

The depiction of Guanyin was radically transformed over the course of the 13th century, with the male image of the figure being replaced by that of a woman dressed in white with fully human features.

Known in Chi as Guanyr Avalokitesva is one of th manifestatio of Amitabh the Buddha the "Pu Land," ti paradise th had replaced tl abstract idea emptine (nirvana

The patron of the work had himself depicted down here in the act of worshipping the Bodhisattva.

▲ *The Bodhisattva Avalokitesvara with the Thousand Arms and Thousand Eyes*, Northern Song dynasty, dated AD 981, from Cave 17 at Dunhuang, Gansu, ink and color on silk, 189.4 x 124 cm, Musée Guimet, Paris.

The Chinese pagoda has two different origins: one is the guard towers of the Han period, built entirely of wood, and the other is the classical Indian Buddhist stupa, made in stone or baked bricks.

Every floor has a false bottom that makes it possible to slightly reduce its diameter, at the same time increasing the height of the floors with the insertion of projecting beams.

The octagonal plan, of foreign derivation, was first adopted in the 8th century and made possible an improved distribution of weight without having to make use of central pillars.

One of the few wooden constructions that has been preserved to today is this pagoda, built on the orders of a ruler of the non-Chinese Liao dynasty (916–1125) in the Pingcheng capital, today Datong.

▲ Wooden Pagoda of Yingxian, Shanxi, Liao dynasty, 1058, 67.3 m high, and elevation of the pagoda.

Three monks are worshiping the Buddha riding a lion, the favorite animal of Buddhism.

A small group of monks is shown studying the sacred scriptures.

The landscape elements are made with delicate shadings of ink, while the figures are delineated with a great variety of lines and wear colorful clothing.

Eighteen men arrive on Mount Lu from every direction to build the Donglin monastery and spread the teachings.

The painter and man of letters Li Gonglin is credited with several important innovations in Buddhist iconography, including the conventional depiction of the Bodhisattva Guanyin as a woman seated on a rock.

▲ Li Gonglin, *Returning Home*, Northern Song dynasty, end 11th century, ink and color on silk, 92 x 53.8 cm, Nanjing Museum, Jiangsu.

The artist signed this work with an inscription, "In the eleventh month of the year bingzi painted with the method of Wu Daozi by Ding Yunpeng from the eastern sea."

Damo appears wrapped in a long cloak bordered with lotus flowers; his features reveal his foreign provenance.

Buddhist tradition holds that the Indian prince Bodhidharma, Damo in Chinese, arrived in southern China in AD 520 and founded the Chan sect, best known by its Japanese name, Zen.

In contrast to the Pure Land school's prospect of universal salvation invoking the name of the Buddha Amitabha, Damo led his followers in search of individual enlightenment, intuited and without words.

Ding Yunpeng, *Damo Crossing the Yangtze River*, Ming dynasty, 1576, ink and color on paper, 130 x 70 cm, Museum für Volkerkunde, Leipzig.

Finding no support at the court of the Southern Liang, Damo moved north to the court of the Northern Wei at Luoyang. Along the way he crossed the Yangtze River on a reed.

"The paths differ but reach the same end" (Treatise of White and Black)

Syncretism

Terms
The three doctrines are one (*sanjao heyi*)
Three schools (*sanjiao*)

Related entries
Foreign dynasties, Confucianism, Daoism, Buddhism

Buddhism's success in China between the 3rd and 6th centuries provoked a variety of responses among China's literati. Daoists and Confucians united against what they looked upon as a barbarous religion, but at the same time the first voices were raised holding that "the three doctrines are one." The foreign dynasties, rulers of northern China or—in the case of the Yuan—rulers of all China, reinforced the trend toward syncretism, which also served the dynasties' need to justify foreign domination. To confirm the supremacy of Confucianism, the Song emperor Huizong emitted a decree in 1106 against the habit of putting Buddha, Lao Tzu, and Confucius on the same altar. Neo-Confucianism proposed a reform of Confucian thought, enriched, sometimes unwittingly, with metaphysical concepts from Buddhism and Daoism. Beginning in the mid-16th century a synthesis called the three schools was proposed in which spiritual cultivation and principles of reciprocity were given more weight than doctrinal issues. Some followers dedicated themselves to introspective practices or to occult methods to achieve enlightenment, while the common people responded to a variety of different religious leaders. The three schools did not constitute a true doctrinal alternative and was without both clergy and written canons.

▶ *The Three Religions*, Ming dynasty, late 15th–early 16th century, vertical scroll, ink and color on silk, 146.7 x 73.7 cm, The Nelson-Atkins Museum of Art, Kansas City.

"Every religion on earth has its religious teaching, [so that] all living beings can be mysteriously led to salvation" (Imperial decree of Taizong, AD 638)

Minor religions

The monotheistic religions from western Asia differed in substantial ways from the three great Oriental schools of thought present in ancient China, which originally did not include the concept of faith but taught a route toward salvation. Nestorian Christianity, Manichaeism, Zoroastrianism, and, beginning at the end of the 7th century, Islam arrived in northern China by way of the Silk Route, like Buddhism had. Most entered the country between the 3rd and the 6th centuries AD, a period in China's history when the empire was in disarray. During the reign of Taizong, a period characterized by great religious tolerance, foreign religions were permitted the free profession of their faith; as a consequence, religious communities and temples arose in the Chang'an capital and throughout Chinese territory. Nestorianism was rooted among the merchants of Sogdiana and western Turkistan, while Zoroastrianism was the primary religion of the Persians. Manichaeism, an eclectic religion blending elements from Christianity, Zoroastrianism, and Buddhism, was adopted as the ideology of various secret societies of the Song period. Under the Yuan, Islam was still primarily a religion of foreigners, but it later became part of Chinese society, most of all in the north, where the mixing of Muslims and Han Chinese led to creation of the Hui population.

◀ *Palm Sunday*, Tang dynasty, fragment of a wall painting from Khocho, Gaochang, Xinjiang, Museum für Indische Kunst, Berlin.

Terms
Manichaeism (*mingjiao*)
Nestorianism (*bosi jiao*)
Islam (*hui jiao*)
Zoroastrianism (*huotian* jiao)

Related entries
Taizong, Kublai Khan, Foreign dynasties, Kaifeng, Images of the Buddha

The outline of the stele is from traditional Chinese iconography, as are the serpents twisting around the cartouche at the top bearing the title.

The so-called Nestorian Stele (or Nestorian Stone) bears the "memorial of the propagation in China of the luminous religion from Daqin," a history of the Church of the East in China.

The stele was discovered in 1623 in the area of Xi'an, to the great joy of the Jesuit missionaries in China, and the entire text was first published in 1625 by a Chinese Christian.

The text begins with an account of the arrival of Persian priests in Chang'an in AD 635 and continues with an account of the difficulties suffered by the Christian community up to the date of the raising of the stele, in 781.

▲ Rubbing of the Nestorian Stele with its Christian inscription, limestone block, Tang dynasty, AD 781, 279 cm high, Forest of Stone Tablets Museum, Xi'an.

The inscription is in Chinese in regular script (kaishu). Part of the colophon and the list of church members engraved at the side is written in Syriac, the literary language of the Assyrian Church of the East.

Early in the 8th century, Arab emissaries of the Muslim faith were admitted to audiences at the Tang court, although they refused to prostrate themselves before the emperor. The new faith was granted the same rights enjoyed by other religions; this made possible the foundation of a Muslim community in the capital Chang'an.

The architectural style of the Xi'an mosque is from the Chinese tradition, with a series of courts and pavilions built in wood, while the decoration, rigorously aniconic, illustrates passages of the Koran with Arabic writing.

During the Mongol domination, the Muslim community, favored by the foreign-led government, spread throughout China and became installed most of all in the western provinces of Gansu, Ningxia, and Yunnan.

Following the defeat in the Battle of the Talas River in 751, the Chinese lost their authority in Central Asia to the Arabs, whose faith began to replace Buddhism and Manichaeism.

Mosque of Xi'an,
ng dynasty, AD 742.

"Venerated in rites like the three ancient leaders, the five sacred mountains stand over the four directions: in the center is Mount Song" (Han Yu)

Sacred mountains

According to ancient Chinese cosmology, five high mountains, o at each of the four points of the compass and the fifth at the center the earth, support the vault of the sky. Myths and legends made the the abodes of eminent divinities, powerful spirits, and immort sages able to locate rare medicinal plants and to concoct long-l elixirs. The emperors performed their most solemn sacrifices the summit of Mount Tai (province of Shandong), which was n only home to various divinities but was itself by nature divine. Son time around the beginning of the 5th century AD, the primary heirs the archaic myths, the Daoists, made the "Five Sacred Mountain part of their doctrine. Even so, temples and monasteries belonging other beliefs were located along the slopes and on the peaks mountains or even mountain chains. A mountain made the ide location for Daoist or Buddhist hermits, who found there, as the forest, the necessary tranquility for their meditative practic

Some hermitages we transformed into famo monasteries where litera and poets took refuge search of inspiration a peace. As the Daoists ha their five mountains, t Buddhists chose "Fo Great Mountains," ea of them dedicated to Bodhisattva. The mo famous of these is Wut Shan (province of Shanz dedicated to Manjus Bodhisattva of wisdom.

▶ Hengshan monastery, Shanxi province, Northern Wei dynasty, 6th century AD.

Wild beasts and armed men move among the smoky clouds and towering peaks of the mountain, finely modeled and damascened in gold thread.

Incense and mountains are closely related to the visions of immortality of the Han period, which reached their height during the reign of Wudi (141–87 BC).

The Chinese of the time located the paradise of the immortals on Penglai, an island in the eastern sea imagined as a cosmic mountain.

e incense rner is a ndamental m of Daoist ual since the oke of ense purifies e space and, ing to the sky, nals to vinities the rformance of itual.

Incense burner in the shape a mountain peak (*boshanlu*), estern Han dynasty, *ante* 113 , from the tomb of Prince Liu eng at Mancheng, Hebei, onze damascened with gold, cm high, Hebei Provincial useum, Shijiazhuang.

The island, washed by the waves, stands on a base composed of three dragons.

189

More than seven thousand stairs lead to the peak of Mount Tai, and walls along the length of the route are crowded with poems and various other compositions engraved in the stone.

Mount Tai (Taishan) plays a central role in ancient Chinese mythology, adopted by Daoism.

Chinese cosmology saw Mount Tai as the eastern pillar of the vault of the sky, supported to the west by Mount Hua (Shaanxi province), to the north by Heng Shan Bei (Shanxi) to the south by Heng Shan Nan (Hunan), while at the center stood Mount Song (Henan).

The most important state sacrifices were celebrated on the peak and at the foot of Mount Tai.

Numerous temples, and not only Daoist, were erected on the summit of Mount Tai.

▲ Mount Tai in the province of Shandong.

The animate world

nt or animal, natural force or work of art, mythical hero or
irit of a dead relative, everything in China possessed a soul and
is capable of assisting humans if offered gifts. At the same time
ese spirits were equally able to injure humans and might do so
revenge an offense or an unauthorized intrusion, whether
tentional or accidental. Behind popular worship in China there
is always the concept of reciprocity, which is also found at the
se of social relationships: in exchange for offerings, whether
cks of incense, food, or drinks, a divinity is obliged to concede
favors to the petitioner. On the occasion of the numerous
nual festivities, such as the celebration of the new year or that
the dead, family rites were celebrated, dedicated to the divini-
s of the hearth or to the souls of the dead. The most solemn fes-
ities sometimes required the mediation of an expert, in ancient
nes the figure of a shaman and, beginning in the Song dynasty,

Buddhist or Daoist
onk. Under the Ming,
e state cults included
remonies dedicated to
e sun, the moon, the
d of literature, and to
ennong, the mythical
iperor-farmer, while
e officials in districts
rticipated in local
lts, which had arisen
the Tang period and
re dedicated to pro-
ctive divinities and
cal heroes.

Terms
Spirit, divinity (*shen*)
Demon (*gui*)
Protective divinity of a
city (*cheng huang*)

Related entries
Festivals, Daoism,
The five relationships

▼ Vase in the shape of a
cocoon with painted
decoration, Side A,
Western Han dynasty,
late 2nd–early 1st
century BC, terracotta
painted with mineral
pigments, 43 cm high,
Fondazione Giovanni
Agnelli, Turin.

The pictorial art of the Han preferred the depiction of divinities, mythical figures, and ferocious wild beasts both fantastic and real inserted in a dynamic composition without interruption.

The subjects are connected by clouds, volutes, and spirals that express the primordial energy that was the origin of all the manifestations of the world.

The dynamism and swirling movement of the design are based on the decoration of lacquers from the same period; indeed, works in terracotta represented an economical alternative to lacquer.

Loose brushstrokes depict combat between a charging bull and a warrior who has drawn two swords and planted his feet in preparation for the impending impact of the beast.

▲ Vase in the shape of a cocoon with painted decoration, Side B.

At the upper center of the painting is depicted the god of the earth with the branching horns, identifiable thanks to his name, Shè, written under his armpit.

In the Songs of Chu (Chuci), a compendium of poetry assembled early in the 3rd century BC, the "lord of the earth" appears wearing a "sharp horn," a reference that supports the hypothesis that this figure represents the god of the earth.

The god is flanked by other divinities showing off their powers; being of lower order they are depicted smaller.

Between the legs of the god of the earth is a black dragon with a yellow head holding a sphere or disk. The meaning of the gesture is obscure and unfortunately this figure is not accompanied by an explanatory inscription.

Painting of the god of the earth, Western Han dynasty, circa 168 BC, from Tomb 3 at Mawangdui, ink and color on silk, 43.5 x 45 cm, Hunan Provincial Museum, Changsha.

The temple of Zhongyue was instituted as a site of Daoist worship during the Qin dynasty in the 3rd century BC.

According to legend, the temple was completely rebuilt during the Song epoch, and the pieces of statues too damaged to be reused were enclosed in a "Depository of Ancient Spirits."

The mold from which this figure was cast was assembled from sections of dried or baked clay made in separate molds, resulting in a series of horizontal mold marks that were once covered by a preparatory layer that was then painted or lacquered.

Four larger-than-life iron statues were cast in 1064 to protect the four sides of small temple (the "Depository") that is today empty.

Cast iron had been known in China since sometime after the 6th century BC; beginning in the Han period most of the tools were made in iron, while weapons were usually forged.

▲ Guardian of the "Depository of Ancient Spirits," Song dynasty, casting of 1064, iron, circa 260 cm high, Zhongyue temple, Dengfeng district, Henan.

The Chinese dragon is powerful and dynamic, symbolic of the male creative force (yang) and omnipresent in cosmological thinking and mythology.

There are many categories of dragon with differing powers, shapes, and colors; the black Celestial Dragon (tianlong), presented here, expressed the energy unleashed during a storm.

It is said that Chen Rong, drunk and screaming at the top of his voice, would soak his cap in ink and rub or smear it across the surface of a painting, then finish off the details with a few quick strokes of his brush.

Chen Rong was the leading painter of dragons and, like many eccentric figures associated with Daoism and Chan Buddhism, he got drunk to reach the state of euphoria necessary to be creative.

Chen Rong, *Black Dragon*, Southern Song dynasty, 13th century, ink on silk, 34.3 x 50 cm, Palace Museum, Beijing.

On orders from the mythical emperor Yao, Hou Yi used his skills as an archer to shoot down nine of the ten suns that threatened to extinguish all forms of life on Earth. Located on the ridge of a house's roof, Hou Yi would protect the house from fires.

The "Celestial Archer" Hou Yi, identifiable by his quiver attached to the side of his horse, by his armature, and by his helmet, raises his hands to protect himself from the blinding light.

▲ Two roof tiles decorated with celestial deities, Hou Yi and Zhu Rong, Ming dynasty, 16th–17th century, terracotta with three-color glaze (*sancai*), 32 cm high. Graf-Luxburg-Museum, Schloss Aschach.

Such decorated tiles, amulets, and "dragon walls" placed inside the entrances of homes served the function of protecting the buildings from malignant spirits.

Zhu Rong, "celestial deity of fire," served a similar purpose. His right hand probably originally held his distinguishing element, a sword.

During the Ming period, the state sought to control folk religions by associating natural forces with concrete personalities that were then inserted in an orderly hierarchical pantheon that also included heroes and local divinities.

The spiraling clouds beneath the saddles indicate that the horsemen were part of the ranks of the Celestial Emperor; at the same time they also provided further stability to the statuettes.

"An old man sells magic charms from a hole in the wall: he writes magical formulas to bless silkworms and other magical formulas to protect the grain" (Lu You)

Exorcists and magicians

Term
Necromancer (*fangshi*)

Related entries
Writing, Daoism, The animate world, Miracles and omens, Feng-shui, Healers and drugs, The quest for immortality

▶ Statuette of necromancer (*fangshi*), Eastern Han dynasty, 1st–2nd century AD, terracotta, Victoria and Albert Museum, London.

Necromancers (called literally "men of the method") were experts at astrology, the invocation of spirits, the exorcism of demons, divination, and the cure of illnesses. They exercised much influence at the Qin and Han courts, and a few of them, specializing in one of the various disciplines, managed to amass considerable wealth. Particularly popular were those who claimed to possess methods for becoming immortal. Because of their lack of classical culture and their close relationship with the occult world, necromancers were scorned by the Confucian literati, and around the end of the Han period they began to lose credibility. Much ancient proto-scientific and magical knowledge was absorbed by Daoism, and although some schools condemned esoteric practices, they were employed by Daoist priests. Writing, considered sacred, was the most effective means of communicating with the world of the spirits: magical formulas, whose writing in classical Chinese was ascribed to the divinities themselves, were used as talismans and were also used by priests to invoke spirits, while hexagrams and numerological schemes, enclosed in amulets, symbolized the power of the cosmic order. The ashes of such talismans, mixed in water, were often prescribed to the ill.

One of the principal methods for expelling evil demons was the invocation of various martial divinities from the celestial office known as the "Thunder Department" (Leibu).

Beginning in the Southern Song period, texts circulated attributed to the "Thunder Department" that instructed Daoist beginners in how to make use of the officials of the department in exorcisms.

A portrait is being displayed to attract the attention of the divinity in charge of the department.

The family waits in front of their house for the conclusion of the rite, performed to keep away illness, disgrace, and misfortune.

Powders, magical potions, and incense helped the magician come in contact with the martial spirits.

Ceremony of Expulsion of Malefic Demons from a House, Ming dynasty, 16th century, hanging scroll, 190.8 x 104.1 cm, Freer Gallery of Art, Smithsonian Institution, Washington, DC.

"The white horse with the vermilion tail appears when the ruler promotes the good and the virtuous" (Shen Yue)

Miracles and omens

Terms
Book of Changes (I Ching)
Eight Trigrams (*bagua*)

Related entries
Signs from the heavens,
Mandate of heaven,
Yin and Yang and the
five phases, Daoism

▼ Reverse of a mirror
decorated with the
Eight Trigrams, Tang
dynasty, from the city
of Xi'an, Shaanxi,
silver, 16 cm diam.,
Shaanxi History
Museum, Xi'an.

The interpretation of premonitory signs to indicate the path to take and to foresee the future was among the most important undertakings of ancient China. On the one hand there were the astronomers astrologers, charged with recording and interpreting the movements of stars and natural forces; on the other hand there were diviners, who with the assistance of various means came into communication with the divine world to obtain responses to precise questions. Given that the responses were often of primary importance to the fortune of the ruling dynasty, the court specialists were expected to keep what they knew to themselves. The oldest known method of divination consisted in the decoding of cracks produced by fire on turtle shells. Over the course of the 1st millennium BC this practice was replaced by a new means of divination, expressed in the famous *Book of Changes*, which is based on reckoning done with yarrow stalks. There are whole stalks, belonging to the principle of yang, and stalks broken in half, belonging to yin. These are arranged variously to form three lines one over the next thus obtaining eight possible trigrams, whose grouping in pairs leads to sixty-four hexagrams. The *Book of Changes* interprets every line of every hexagram with an occult formula which is used as the basis for a prediction. The book is not, however, simple treatise of oracles, but collects in itself the entire Chinese cosmological concept.

As demonstrated by the numerous finds in tombs containing circular stone plates, the bi disk had a fundamental role in the rites and cult of the dead for several Neolithic Chinese cultures.

Such disks were still being buried in tombs during the Han period and still served an important ritual role, based in part on their antiquity.

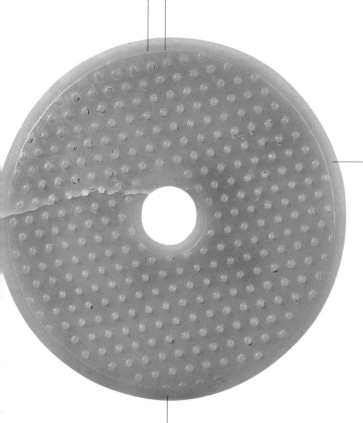

Although their original meaning has been lost, bi disks were part of rituals throughout the entire Bronze Age.

In some Shang, Zhou, and Han period tombs, numerous bi disks, sometimes arranged in long necklaces, cover the body of the deceased.

Bi disk, Eastern Han dynasty, ephrite, exterior diam. 17.4 cm, aanxi History Museum, Xi'an.

The Daoist temple complex on Mount Kongtong, in the province of Gansu, dates to before the Tang epoch and included a temple dedicated to consultation of the dao.

The temple was restored by the Northern Song emperor Huizong shortly before the conquest of northern China by the Jurchen nomads who founded the Jin dynasty.

The Daoist painter and monk Yang Shichang, a contemporary of Emperor Huizong and friend of the man of letters Su Shi, signed this work, also adding his seal.

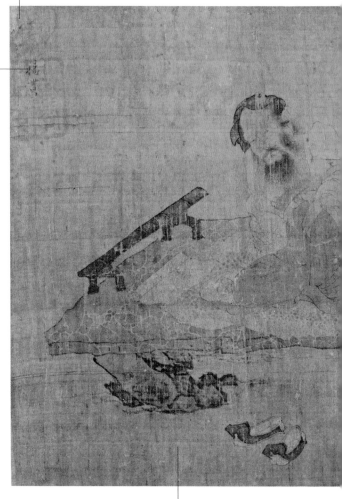

▲ Yang Shichang, *Kongtong Consults the Dao*, Jin dynasty, early 12th century, ink and color on silk, 28.2 x 49.5 cm, Palace Museum, Beijing.

A bearded immortal with a passive expression is resting on a rock slab covered in part by an animal hide.

Having come to ask advice of the great dao, *an emperor humbly kneels, holding in both hands the traditional* hu *tablet, which his functionaries had to hold when appearing before him.*

Two circles with a central square, representations of two copper coins, are engraved on the bottom of the inkstone.

The Eight Trigrams are engraved in the first circle, which overlaps the second, which contains the characters of the Twelve Terrestrial Branches of the Chinese calendar.

Commentary from Emperor Qianlong of the Qing (18th century) is inscribed around the two circles.

The indications contained in the Book of Changes reflect changes provoked by the complementary actions of yin and yang; as a result the prediction deduced changes with every new reading.

The two intertwined circles represent the essence of the efforts of the ancient Chinese to define the transformations of the universe.

▲ Inkstone, Song dynasty, stone, 21.6 x 13.8 cm, National Palace Museum, Taipei.

If the wind shakes the willow branches, or if the wind bends
the grass . . . it will mean trouble . . . it will bring decay and
sickness" (Water Dragon Classic)

Feng-shui

Feng-shui, literally "wind and water," is the art of geomancy, which seeks to discover the interactions between the universe and humans and to apply this knowledge to the environment, selecting the most suitable sites for the construction of buildings and tombs. Geomancy dates to the preimperial period and was so widespread in the Han epoch that the skeptic Wang Chong (circa AD 27–97) dismissed it as folk religion. Water courses and the location of mountains determined the placement of constructions, facing south and closed to the north. Two schools came into being in the Song epoch, the "school of the compass" and the "school of the form." The school of the compass perfected the use of the feng-shui compass, which consists of a disk with a magnetic needle at the center; the external concentric circles contain the Eight Trigrams, the five phases, and the symbols of the Chinese duodecimal calendar, the "Celestial Stems" and the "Terrestrial Branches," as well as other astronomical and cosmological indicators. The followers of the school of the form were more tied to the concrete qualities of the landscape, closely examined by the expert to find the hidden currents in the earth, defined as the "dragon veins," which must not be damaged by the construction. The building was thus integrated with its environment instead of dominating it, with preference given, most of all looking south, to curves and arches instead of sharp angles.

Terms
Geomancy (*feng-shui*)
Feng-shui compass
(*luopan*)

Related entries
Telling time, Yin and yang and the five phases, Daoism, Miracles and omens, Architecture

▼ Feng-shui compass (*luopan*), Qing dynasty, 19th century, wood, leather, paper, lacquer, copper, magnet, glass, 20.5 cm diam., Roemer-Museum, Hildesheim.

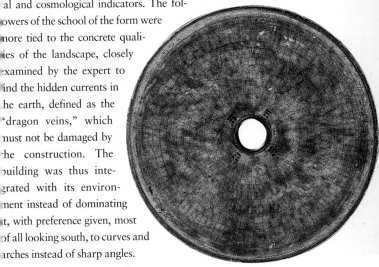

Daily life

◄ Plate decorated with historiated
cene (detail), Ming dynasty, 1489,
ngraved polychrome lacquer, 19
m diam., British Museum, London.

> *"Let the ruler be ruler, the minister minister; let the father be father, and the son son"* (Confucius)

The five relationships

The orderly structure of the Confucian state, inserted in turn within the natural universal harmony, was maintained by respect for the social hierarchy. A human achieved fulfillment in keeping with his social position and within the limits of his rank and was supposed to give his utmost to favor the proper functioning of society. There was nothing different or personalized about the education given the individual; indeed, to grow, each citizen had to participate in a continuous dialog with other citizens within the structure imposed by human relationships. These ties were distinguished by the principle of reciprocity, also present in relationships with the divine world: it was the responsibility of a superior to teach and morally guide an inferior, who in turn would treat the superior with deference. The "benevolence" of one and the "filial piety" of the other are expressed within the sphere of the "five relationships" identified as the state ideology during the period in which the Han emperor Wudi adopted Confucianism. In order of importance, these are the relationship between a ruler and subject, father and son, husband and wife, older brother and younger brother, and between friends. Confucius taught that one should serenely accept the injustice of domineering parents, the cruelty of husbands, the despotism of older brothers, and the inequality of people in the eyes of the law, making a legal response to injustice almost impossible.

▶ Jar with molded
decoration of four
stories of filial piety,
Tang dynasty, 8th
century, from the
tomb of Qi Biming at
Xianyang, Shaanxi,
terracotta with
"three-color" (*sancai*)
glaze, 50.8 cm high,
Shaanxi History
Museum, Xi'an.

The open expression of feelings was considered vulgar, and the learned man communicated them through allusions, allegories, citations, and metaphors.

Lian, the phoneme of the word lotus, is a homophone of the terms love and to join in matrimony). The lotus was thus one of the symbols of conjugal union.

The flower and fruit of the lotus allude to the birth of a child. The lotus flower is also symbolic of the female sex.

Mandarin ducks remain faithful to their companions and thus became symbolic of the enduring cohabitation of the couple.

Zhang Zhong, *Dry Lotus and Pair of Mandarin Ducks*, Yuan Dynasty, 14th century, ink and color on paper, 96.4 x 46 cm, National Palace Museum, Taipei.

The relief is divided in horizontal sections and according to some scholars presents a metaphor of the ideal society based on Confucian principles.

Women live on the upper floor of the noble residence, gathered around the consort of the main character.

On the roof of the palace is a pair of phoenixes, symbolic of immortality, but also of virtuous government.

The tree is perhaps the mythical fusang, *which grows at the farthest east, the point at which the sun rises.*

The central figure, larger in size than the figures bowing down to him, could be a ruler or the proprietor of the tomb on which the reliefs were carved.

▲ *Scene of Homage*, Eastern Han dynasty, 2nd century, rubbing of a stone bas-relief, from the southern wall of Room 2, Wu Liang Shrine, Shandong.

"Filial indeed is Min Ziqian! Other people say nothing of him
[di]fferent from the report of his parents and brothers"
([C]onfucius)

Family

[F]amily was the keystone of the Confucian social system and the
[n]atural fulcrum of the cult of ancestors. As an integral part of the
[fa]mily, ancestors were present in the home: their names were
[in]scribed on wooden tablets placed on the domestic altar. Large
[fa]milies had an ancestral temple located outside the city walls
[w]here the records of ancestors were preserved and where rites were
[ce]lebrated on the occasion of official festivals. The firstborn of the
[p]rincipal line was the head of the family, the succession was patri-
[li]neal. The institution of family names, meaning the name of a clan
[p]assed from father to son, dates to the 3rd century BC and origi-
[n]ated in exogamy: in ancient China the conjugal union between
[pe]ople of the same family name was prohibited, but there was no
[o]pposition to matrimony between matrilineal relatives. On the day
[o]f the wedding, the bride became a member of her husband's
[fa]mily in all senses. She did not live just with her husband and
[c]hildren since the ideal cohab-
[it]ation of Confucians called
[fo]r all the living members of
[th]e family to be together. The
[w]ork of men took place pri-
[m]arily outside the home,
[w]hile women lived within the
[d]omestic walls, enclosed in
[th]e rigid hierarchical system.
[T]he main wife of the head of
[th]e family exercised limitless
[p]ower over the concubines,
[si]sters-in-law, and daughters-
[i]n-law, all of them eager to
[g]ive birth to male children and
[t]hus improve their position.

Terms
Family (*jia*)

Related entries
Ancestor worship, The
five relationships,
Women

▼ *Palace Ladies Bathing*
and Dressing Children,
Southern Song dynasty,
12th–13th century,
album leaf, ink and color
on silk, 23.1 x 24.5 cm,
Freer Gallery of Art,
Smithsonian Institution,
Washington, DC.

These games take place in a classical literary garden of the period, complete with bizarre rock formations, willows, and a pond with lotus flowers.

The work was presumably made on the occasion of the celebrations that marked the thirtieth and hundredth days after the birth of a male child or on the day of his first birthday.

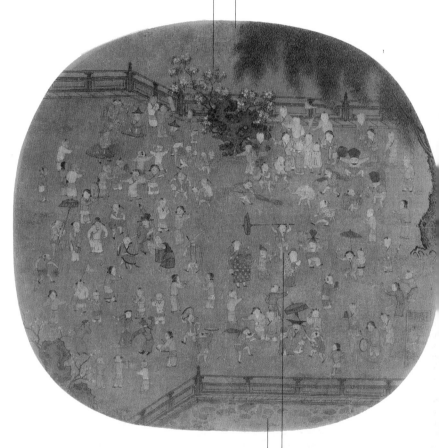

▲ One Hundred Children at Play, Southern Song dynasty, 12th–13th century, album leaf, ink and color on silk, 28.8 x 31.3 cm, Cleveland Museum of Art.

Subjects of this genre became somewhat widespread in the Southern Song period, when the defeat and southward withdrawal of the dynasty led to closer attention to family matters and intimate settings.

The children, most of them dressed as adults, are portrayed with meticulous care even in the smallest detail, without any overlapping.

During the Ming period the growing financial prosperity across broader levels of the population awakened a trend toward individualism that expressed itself through the genre of portraiture, until then reserved for emperors.

Individual attention is paid to the group's facial features, while the heavy ceremonial robes hide most of their bodies. They are arranged following the rigid hierarchical order in force even within a family.

The head of the household is positioned at the center of the composition; the long, well-tended fingernails on the hand that extends from the sleeve indicate that he has no need to earn his bread with physical labor.

The ceremonial clothes, the brocades, and the diadems of the women display the family's wealth, while the absence of badges of rank on the clothes of the men suggests that none of them was ever part of public administration.

▲ Family Portrait, Ming dynasty, 16th century, vertical scroll, ink and color on silk, 128.3 x 84.5 cm, Metropolitan Museum, New York.

"Your beauty was never outdone by any woman, and nothing more than the tale of your beauty was enough to make a man abandon everything" (Tao Yuanming)

Women

Terms
Book of Han (Hanshu)
Lessons for Women (Nüjie)

Related entries
Confucianism, The five relationships

The life of a woman revolved around the needs of men. The range of action for wives and concubines did not extend beyond the domestic hearth. This was true most of all among the well-to-do classes, whose girls, from the age of seven, were taught secrets to make themselves attractive to a future husband as well as useful to a future mother-in-law: how to cook, how to embroider, how to sew. The daughter of a good family also learned how to read, write, and sometimes even paint and play an instrument. Women were excluded from the system of exams because they were held unable to understand the nature of the Confucian classics, but some women, facilitated by their family background, were able to overcome the wall of social conventions. Ban Zhao (AD 45–116), coauthor of the *Book of Han*, not only completed that work following her brother's death, but also wrote *Lessons for Women*, one of the texts that was later part of the cultural baggage of every girl born to a good family. Another prodigious woman was the poet Li Qingzhao (1084–1141), born to a family of writers. Women did not take part in the social life of the men of their family: wives did not accompany husbands to celebrations outside the home or to banquets where young courtesans were charged with seeing to their well-being. There were houses of pleasure in every city, all of them fully legal and under the sanitary control of the state.

▶ Statuette of a woman in a seated position, Tang dynasty, late 7th–early 8th century, from the Wang family tomb on the eastern edge of Xi'an, Shaanxi, terracotta with "three-color" (*sancai*) glaze and traces of pigment, 47.5 cm high, Shaanxi History Museum, Xi'an.

The box is composed of two parts and closes with a lid. Gloves and a silk shawl were kept in the upper part, while the lower was used for articles for the care of beauty.

The boxes contained face powder made of lead power, lipsticks, and ointments; when found, the box also contained a brush for the face powder, combs, a hairpiece, and a hairpin.

The bottom of the container is of solid wood, while sides and lid are made of hemp covered by many layers of lacquer.

The box, wrapped in a strip of embroidered silk, was deposited in the tomb of the marchioness of Dai, along with other cosmetics.

Cosmetic boxes, Western Han
nasty, circa 168 BC, from Tomb
t Mawangdui, Hunan, wood
d lacquered hemp, 20.8 cm
h, 35.2 cm diam., Hunan
ovincial Museum, Changsha.

This necklace was among the splendid works of jewelry buried with the young daughter of a high official of the brief Sui dynasty.

Aside from jewelry, the tomb contained bowls and jars of gold, stone, and glass that had been deposited together with various toys showing clear signs of use that belonged to the young girl.

The clasp adorned by a bl. opal in which th minuscule ima, of a deer w. engrave

Twenty-eig spheres, as lar, as grapes, ea set with ten se pearls, a connected gold filigre

At the center of necklace shine. large flame of surrounded pearls and fram by two elemer that enclose sm half-spheres of bl glass, imported the time from distant Sassar empi

▲ Necklace of precious stones, Sui dynasty, late 6th century, from the tomb of Li Jingxun at Xi'an, gold filigree and granulation, sapphires, opals, pearls, and glass, 23.4 x 9 cm, Museum of Chinese History, Beijing.

The emancipation of Chinese women at the political and private level reached its most advanced level during the Tang period, when the conditions even permitted the foundation of the first and only female dynasty.

...spite the ...mplaints ...esented at court ...various ...nfucian ...nservatives, ...men were even ...owed to travel ...tside their ...mestic setting.

...e dress is ...aped under a ...v-cut bodice ...ot enough to ...eal the woman's ...st, showing a ...te that is ...mewhat unusual ...the history of ...inese art.

...tatuette of a horsewoman, ...ng dynasty, second half 7th ...tury, from the tomb of Zheng ...ntai in the Liquan district, ...aanxi, terracotta, slip glaze, ...neral pigments, 37 cm high, ...aanxi History Museum, Xi'an.

The statuette was found in one of the satellite tombs of the mausoleum of the Tang emperor Taizong and belonged to a high official.

Prescriptions concerning style addressed not only the cut, color, and material of clothes but also gestures and even the body types of women.

The large sleeves and the applications might indicate that this is a dancer, a popular subject during the Tang period, along with orchestras, which were often composed only of women.

Hairdressing u. an art in itself a. required hours preparation; t. style was call "double rir looking at t immortals

Since the textu sources a imprec. concerning t. function certain clothin it is often diffic. to precis. establish the r. of a figur.

▲ Statuette of a dancer or young woman, Tang dynasty, late 7th–early 8th century, from the Zhangwu district, Shaanxi, terracotta, slip decoration, mineral pigments, 37.8 cm high, Shaanxi History Museum, Xi'an.

During the Tang period imperial tombs and those of the aristocracy swarmed with funerary statuettes, among them a notable quantity of women, busy in various amusements.

The hairstyle is called the "fallen off the horse" look, following a legendary fall from a horse by Yang Guifei, the favorite of the emperor Xuanzong (reigned 712–756), who found her loose, disheveled look quite appealing.

round 740, a new sthetic taste posed on women e need to gain eight; tombs are minated by atuettes of omen with fleshy ces, although en delicate pressions, and bust bodies.

The woman's pose is made dynamic by the slight relocation of the central axis of her body, a characteristic element in the naturalistic representations of the Tang period.

Statuette of a court lady, ng dynasty, mid-8th century, rracotta, slip decoration, gments, 48.5 cm high, Museo Arte Orientale, Turin.

The outline of the box is based on the shape of a five-petaled flower.

The absence of a maker's mark, obligatory for an artisan operating in the imperial workshops, suggests that this was made in a private, highly skilled shop.

The embossed decorative motifs have been perfected with refined internal chasing and applied gilding.

The decorative subjects are dominated by pairs of phoenixes, depicted on the convex faces of the sides and also on the small raised lid that closes a supplementary box.

There are two compartments in the box, also in silver. The remains of two silver tweezers and a teaspoon for cleaning ears testify to the box's function.

▲ Cosmetics container, Tang dynasty, second half 9th century AD, partially gilt silver, 26 cm high, 22.2 cm diam., Museum für Ostasiatische Kunst, Cologne.

Imperial portraiture during the Song period called for a semiprofile stance and demanded impeccable execution, with attention given the smallest detail.

As a sign of her imperial authority, the empress wears a diadem decorated with nine dragons; other dragons appear on the border of her robe with its large sleeves, made of a blue fabric decorated with phoenixes.

Pearls frame the face and neckline of the empress and are applied to her cheeks and forehead in what looks like the modern technique of piercing.

The empress's pale and ungainly face seems to reflect a certain degree of realism, in contrast to the open and curious face of the attendant to the right, holding a vase, whose unexpected stance breaks the formal order of the depiction.

Cao was the principal wife of Emperor Renzong (reigned 1023–1063) and was the omnipotent regent during the short reign of his successor, Yingzong (reigned 1064–1068).

Empress Cao, Consort of Renzong, Northern Song dynasty, th century, vertical scroll, ink and lor on silk, 172.1 x 165.3 cm, ational Palace Museum, Taipei.

Mirrors first appeared in the 2nd millennium BC, and during the Spring and Autumn period (770–476 BC), the form and decoration of the mirror were established in a way that remained substantially unchanged until the introduction of the glass mirror in the 18th century.

The Chinese mirror was made of cast bronze; the face was highly polished while the rear was decorated.

During the Tang period, brides often hung a mirror over the marriage bed to drive off malignant spirits; such mirrors could also be auspicious, most of all if decorated with pairs of monogamous animals like the phoenix.

On the rear was a perforated pommel through which a strap could be passed that was used to hold the mirror, which otherwise rested on a special stand.

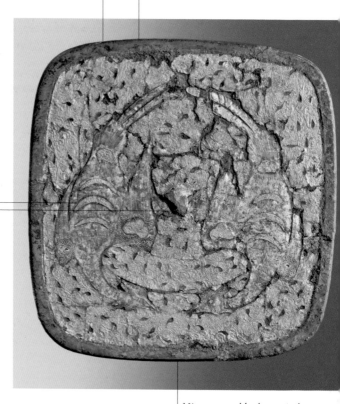

Mirrors served both practical and spiritual uses. They could reflect the features of the human face and could also capture the image of demons, which, once visible, lost their power.

▲ Rear of mirror, Song or Liao dynasty, 11th–12th century, bronze and gold leaf, 17.5 cm long, Musée Guimet, Paris.

The custom of binding feet began in the 10th century and in time affected all women, regardless of their social class, enduring until early in the 20th century.

Many hypotheses have been put forward to explain the spread of this custom, which was painful for young women and an enormous difficulty for older women.

Footbinding restricted women's mobility; most elite women stayed at home, where they formed bonds with female relatives and were charged with managing important matters of the household.

It was impossible for a girl with normally grown feet to find a husband; the interdictions emitted by the Qing dynasty fell on deaf ears, and the custom was not abolished until the early 20th century.

◄ Shoe for a bound foot, Qing dynasty, late 19th century, embroidered satin, 12.2 cm length of sole, Museum für Ostasiatische Kunst, Cologne.

"Ten thousand dou of superb wine, sliced carp and juicy shrimp, turtle in sauce, and roast bear paw" (Cao Zhi)

Culinary arts

Related entries
Yin and yang and the
five phases, Healers
and drugs

▼ Model of an oven
and a seated woman,
Tang dynasty, from the
tomb of Zheng Rentai,
Liquan district,
Shaanxi, partially
glazed terracotta,
pigments, figure 10 cm
high, Zhaoling
Museum, Shaanxi.

Eating is part of the natural cycle of the universe and is thus integrated within the system of yin and yang and the five phases. Chinese cooking recognized two large categories of food, "hot" and "cold," determined not on the basis of their temperature at the moment of consumption but on intrinsic qualities. A balanced meal had to contain plates belonging to both categories, given that an imbalance could cause damage to the organism, the human microcosm. Equally fundamental was harmony among the five aromas—acidic, bitter, sweet, spicy, and salty—as well as the color and the consistency of the food. Continuous imbalance could lead to a variety of ills, which could be cured through the use of foods belonging to the opposite genre of those that had brought on the symptoms: thus, a case of fever was treated with "cold" foods, bitter or acidic, which lowered the temperature and calmed the mind, while "hot" foods, spicy and salty, stimulated circulation and awakened the organism. Grains prevailed in northern China, whereas the cooking of the south was based on rice, usually accompanied by one or more vegetables. Meat, generally pork or beef, was eaten on the festive occasions or during ceremonies, although Buddhist and Daoist monks did not eat it at all. Milk and milk products were completely absent from Chinese cooking.

The figure was made using two two-section molds, one for the head and the other for the body, and the mold marks are still visible on the sides.

The cook is a somewhat common subject in Sichuan tombs from the end of the Han period, when wealthier families hoped to extend the pleasure of life to the afterlife.

The cook may have held some sort of tool made of a perishable material, since his hands are now empty.

In contrast to the figure of the cook, sketched in a somewhat schematic way, the foods were modeled by hand and finished with quick but precise detailing.

▲ Statuette of a cook, Eastern Han dynasty, second half 2nd century AD, from the Zhong district at Chengdu, Sichuan, terracotta, 43 cm high, Sichuan Provincial Museum, Chengdu.

The use of herbal infusions dates to the early Bronze Age. Until the end of the 3rd century AD, *such decoctions were used primarily for medicinal purposes or as ritual offerings. In the period of disunity, between* AD 220 *and 581, the custom of drinking tea on occasions of get-togethers and festivals spread among the well to do.*

The Classic of Tea, *by Lu Yu, dates to the 8th century. This compendium describes the varieties and methods of cultivation, processing, and preparation; furnishes a list of the utensils; and explains the circumstances and the best ways of tasting tea.*

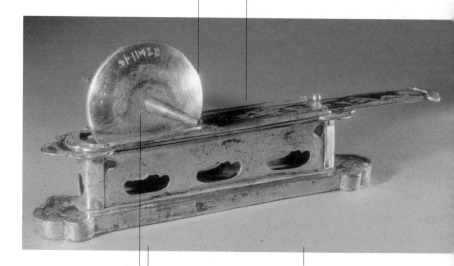

To grind the dried leaves, often pressed into the shape of rolls, the disk was moved into position and operated by the heavy lever along the track.

The place where this was found, a crypt in the Buddhist temple at Famen, and the material it is made of, partially gilt silver, suggest that this tool was used during certain religious ceremonies or on the occasion of imperial visits.

During later dynasties tea became a part of the everyday life of all Chinese, while still preserving its role in private or public rituals.

▲ Tea grinder, Tang dynasty, AD 869, from the crypt of the Famen Temple pagoda, Shaanxi, silver with gilt decoration, 27.4 cm long, Famen Museum, Shaanxi.

In a corner of the garden, shielded by a wind screen, three brothers are preparing a meal.

Baozi, *which are buns stuffed with beef or pork cooked on a grill,* probably first appeared between the 3rd and 5th centuries AD along with mantou, *steam-cooked bread.*

Another stuffed food with an ancient tradition is jiaozi, *a sort of filled pasta like ravioli, that was steamed, boiled in water, or braised and could contain sweet or savory fillings.*

The social hierarchy makes its way even into compositions of an intimate nature: the servant, although more or less the same age as the youngest brother, is depicted as physically smaller.

▲ *Preparing Baozi Together,* Yuan dynasty, vertical scroll, ink and color on silk, 158.9 x 103.3 cm, National Place Museum, Taipei.

> *"Under the pines I ask the disciple. He says, 'The master has gone for medicinal herbs. He is hidden among the mountains, in the deep clouds. Where . . . I do not know'"* (Jia Dao)

Healers and drugs

The system of universal correspondences explicated by yin and yang and the five phases that was elaborated and perfected during the Han period included medical science. The human body was seen as a reflection of the universe since it was an exact reflection of all the aspects of natural phenomena as well as those of the human world. The discovery of a collection of medical writings dating to 168 BC, discovered in 1973 in a tomb at Mawangdui (Hunan), has confirmed that by that period medicine was already inserted within the dualistic cosmogony. Along with instructions on ways to prolong life with physical exercise and with sexual practices and instructions for preparing potions based on natural ingredients, the manuscript also includes magical therapeutic formulas. The medical and pharmacological treatises that have survived from the period beginning in the 2nd

century AD concentrate on scientific questions that include diagnoses reached on the basis of pulse and therapies involving acupuncture and the use of natural substances from vegetable, animal, and mineral kingdoms. Magical practices and exorcist rites continued to be part of popular medicine, exercised by Daoist or Buddhist monks and also by certain folk characters, most of all women, capable of communicating with spirits to diagnose and cure illness.

▶ *Herb Collector*, Liao dynasty, ink and color on paper, 54 x 34.6 cm, Museum of the Lianbei District, Shanxi.

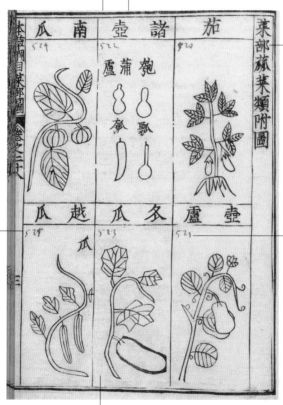

Li Shizhen (1518–1593) was the grandson of an itinerant healer; his father had a career within the Confucian school and was an official of the imperial academy of medicine who wrote various specialized works.

This encyclopedic work, the result of thirty years of research in the field, consultation of ancient texts, and travels throughout southern China, was first published in 1596, three years after its author's death.

The handwritten Arabic numerals are by Christian Menzel (1622–1701), personal physician to the elector-prince of Brandenburg, who analyzed the Compendium to include it in work of his own that, unfortunately, remained unfinished.

Almost 1,900 drugs of vegetable, animal, and mineral origin are described in detail in the pages of the book, which also include precise therapeutic instructions.

Following the numerical sequence of the manuscript, the plants depicted are eggplant, a squash variety, various unidentified gourd-shaped fruits, another squash variety, the pumpkin, and the cucumber.

Li Shizhen, *Compendium of Materia Medica (Bencao Gangmu),* chapter 30, Section 28, "On plants shaped like squash," Ming dynasty, Japanese edition of 1637, printed on paper bound with cotton thread, 8 x 19 cm, Staatsbibliothek Preussischer Kulturbesitz, Berlin.

Most potions were composed of numerous substances that together would heal an illness without causing toxic side effects or imbalances in the organism.

> *"I no longer want poisonous medicines to be given [to my people] but for them to be cured with metal needles that direct energy"* (Yellow Emperor's Classic of Internal Medicine)

Acupuncture and moxibustion

Chinese tradition traces the origin of many scientific disciplines and works to mythical figures, as is the case with medical science, which is traced back to the Yellow Emperor. The *Yellow Emperor's Classic of Internal Medicine*, difficult to date because of its heterogeneous composition and the manipulations made to it over time, illustrates the twelve "meridians" of the body along which "vital energy" flows. With the help of precise applications of heat (moxibustion) and the insertion of needles at certain points (acupuncture), energy can be stimulated, that being the basis and the material stuff of life itself. The *Classic of Difficult Cases*, an organic text that the historian Sima Qian (91 BC) ascribed to a doctor of the 5th or 6th century BC, also names the meridians as well as "needles" and "stones" with which to cure blood. These works, well known since at least the Han period, dominated later research along with the two canonical texts that examine cures obtained using natural substances. Later literary production in terms of medical sciences presents a somewhat coherent view as a result of the fundamental conviction of the ancient Chinese that the point of departure, the past, represented the height of all wisdom. Beginning in the Song period printing facilitated the diffusion of medical knowledge: diagrams of the meridians with the points of application existed along with rare models made of bronze.

▶ The designation of the points of acupuncture on the human body, Ming dynasty, circa 1400, ink on paper, Bibliothèque Nationale, Paris.

Acupuncture and moxibustion act on the meridians, which, beginning with six internal organs—liver, spleen, heart, lungs, kidneys, pericardium—lead to the limbs.

Every limb has three meridians of a yin nature that channel energy and blood to the extremities and three meridians of a yang essence that channel to the organs.

Moxibustion, unlike acupuncture, does not penetrate the meridian but stimulates it with the external application of medical substances.

Two family members hold the patient while the itinerant healer applies a substance; an assistant is at hand, ready with a bandage.

Itinerant healers, although scorned by traditional Confucian doctors, were experts in the cure of illnesses by way of a wide variety of procedures, from natural medicines to minor operations, as well as magical formulas.

Attributed to Li Tang, *Moxibustion*, Southern Song Dynasty, 12th century, ink and color on silk, 68.8 x 58.7 cm, National Palace Museum, Taipei.

"The people neglect the natural rhythm and order of the universe, fail to regulate their style of life and alimentary regimen, and sleep in an improper way" (Yellow Emperor's Classic of Internal Medicine)

Physical exercise

Terms
Care of life
(*yangsheng*)
Vital energy (*qi*)
Master Guan (*Guanzi*)
Soul (*shen*)
Essence of soul (*jing*)
Enlightenment of the
spirit (*shenming*)
Guide and pull
(*daoyin*)

Related entries
Sima Qian, Yin and
yang and the five
phases, Healers and
drugs, The quest for
immortality

Care of life is the generic term that describes the practice designed to give vigor to both body and spirit, from breathing exercises to personal hygiene to sexual activity, from daily diet to the taking of drugs, from gymnastics to martial arts. Exercise is good for the "vital energy" that flows through the body in the channels of the meridians. According to Mencius (4th century BC), morality, the seed of goodness innate in everyone, can be cultivated by nourishing "vital energy" with breathing techniques. Breathing techniques also have a chapter in *Master Guan*, a heterogeneous text compiled between the 4th and 1st centuries BC that advises the promotion of harmony among the three vital essences—vital energy, the soul, and the highest manifestation of the soul—to eventually achieve "enlightenment of the spirit." Han-period texts look on all the methods as being equally beneficial, but by the early 2nd century AD medical science was showing preference for some, such as therapeutic gymnastics, called "guide and pull," or appropriate diets, used as means of prevention or for the early diagnoses of illness. Daoism promoted various other techniques, including sexual practices, to provide the male element with the female, and the administration of drugs which not only ensured physical well-being but served to collaborate with and help preserve the body, rendering it immortal.

▶ *Explanatory Designs
of Daoyin* (detail),
Western Han dynasty,
168 BC, from Tomb 3
at Mawangdui, ink and
color on silk, 50 x 100
cm, Hunan Provincial
Museum, Changsha.

"As a youth I learned to fence; I fenced better than anyone. My spirit was as high as the clouds" (Yuan Zhi)

Martial arts

The martial arts are included within the practices dedicated to the "care of life." Their existence is documented beginning in the 7th century AD, when thirteen monks of the Shaolin monastery battled alongside the first emperor of the Tang dynasty. The Shaolin temple (Henan), founded in AD 495, was one of the first centers of the translation of Buddhist writings. Bodhidharma, the legendary founder of the school of Chan Buddhism, was said to have created a school of martial arts here in AD 530. Given the scarcity of sources, the temple's development cannot be exactly reconstructed, but by the time of the Ming dynasty Shaolin was a famous center for defensive techniques that combined combat methods with breathing exercises, meditative practices, and rigid discipline. By the end of the Ming period the school was famous, known most of all for fighting using a staff, and had spread to southern China, where in 1553 a group of Shaolin monks helped drive off incursions of Japanese pirates from the eastern coast. A different fighting technique was developed by the *Tai Chi Chuan (Taijiquan)* school, which is a "soft style" of martial art, performed using internal power: the *Classic of the Fist* by the Ming general Qi Jiguang, which seeks to increase knowledge of "vital energy" before training the body, was the forerunner of an art that was to see its full development during the last dynasty.

Terms
Martial arts (*wushu*)
Classic of the Fist
(*Quanjing*)

Related entries
Yin and yang and the
five phases, Buddhism,
Physical exercise

◄ Commemorative
stupas of the abbots of
the Shaolin temple at
the foot of Mount Song,
Henan, Ming dynasty.

> *"These palaces and temples form a dense labyrinth; panoramic towers loom over the emptiness in an astonishing way"*
> (Thousand-Character Classic)

Architecture

Terms
Construction methods
(Yingzao fashi)

Related entries
Court, Gardens,
Feng-shui, Beijing

▶ Model of a guard tower, Eastern Han dynasty, 1st century AD, terracotta with lead glaze, 90 cm high, Lindenmuseum, Stuttgart.

Timber having been the construction material of the ancient Chinese, few traces remain of structures dating to before the Ming dynasty. Since the principles of construction methods and building aesthetics were handed down from generation to generation without substantial changes, the conservation of buildings was not seen as a necessity. The wooden structures of houses and palaces followed a module system combining columns and beams that could be repeated many times. The columns stood on stone bases that in turn stood on platforms made of rammed earth faced with bricks or stones. In this way the columns did not rot and were given a certain degree of elasticity in case of earthquakes. The beams were dovetailed at the tops of the columns, and the walls created by this framework were filled with a mixture of earth and straw. To keep rain off walls, the Chinese roof had projecting eaves supported by trusses. The run-off of water was provided by steep roofs; palaces and temples usually had roofs with four slopes, while the roofs of homes had two. The notable weight of the glazed terracotta tiles on roofs was supported by brackets atop the columns composed of a series of beams and supports of decreasing width. The upper end of the truss supported the long axis that supported the ridge of the roof.

By the beginning of the 9th century AD, architectural painting had been recognized as an autonomous genre. The first paintings in this genre depict architectural elements with figures; later on, palaces and temples were inserted in a landscape.

The effect of perspective results from the dimensions of the palaces decreasing toward the top of the painting, and three-dimensionality is depicted in parallel perspective, drawn with the help of a ruler.

Clearly visible is the stone paving that covers the lower terracing, supported on long poles driven into the water and marked off by a balustrade that seems to be partially walled in and is finished with a wooden railing.

The stone bridge has the semicircular span typical of Chinese bridges. The tradition of stone bridges is ancient in China, both arched and with trusses.

▲ *Palace Landscape*, Northern Song dynasty, 11th century, album leaf, ink, color, and gold leaf on silk, 33 x 40.6 cm, Cleveland Museum of Art.

While a building's structure could vary only in terms of the number of modules employed, its decoration could vary widely.

Decorative elements were endowed with magical powers and are thus often a key to a building's specific function.

▶ ▲ Jinci Daoist memorial temple complex, central temple dedicated to the Saintly Mother (*Shengmu*), Taiyuan, Shanxi, Northern Song dynasty, 1023–1031, and decorative detail of a pillar of the temple dedicated to the Saintly Mother.

The temple complex at Jinci is one of the rare sites of ancestor worship, with origins that are said to date to the period of the Western Zhou.

Built between 1023 and 1031, the hall (Shengmudian) dedicated to the Saintly Mother is among the most ancient wooden structures in China.

The steep, widely projecting eaves are supported by a standardized system of brackets.

The building measures seven bays in width and six in depth. A portico runs around the internal structure and is inserted in the front façade, setting back the internal columns the width of one unit.

In the Ming and Qing epochs the size and structure of the bracket depended not only on the type of building but also on the rank of the owner.

The complex systems of brackets developed from simple U-shaped brackets attached to the top of support columns.

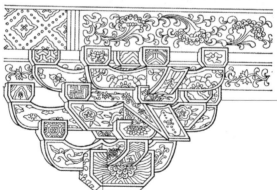

The manual State Building Standards (Yingzao Fashi) prepared in 1103 by Li Jie, head of the state construction department, presented the ancient rules of construction for the first time.

Every component, from the columns of the portico to the tie beams, from the horizontal beams to the brackets, was modular, uniform in length and diameter, and could thus be prefabricated before construction work began; this also made it easy to replace pieces.

▲ Bracket of the Hall of the Supreme Principle (*Taiji dian*) in the Forbidden City at Beijing, Ming dynasty, 15th century, and drawing of a bracket from the volume *State Building Standards (Yingzao Fashi)*, Song dynasty, 1103.

*"[The furniture] made in ancient times, although the length and
width were not standardized, was invariably elegant and
delightful" (Wen Zhengheng)*

Furniture

Most of the surviving ancient furniture in China dates to the last
two dynasties, but images provide a good notion of the earlier
development of styles. Linear and spare in terms of structure,
enriched with ornamental or geometrical decorative inserts that
were sometimes quite complex, all of the pieces were made with
great care. The decorations include inserts of carved wood or
mother-of-pearl; marble with naturalistic veining was sometimes
set in the backs of chairs, in the tops of tables, or within decorative panels fixed to walls. In some instances wood was varnished
in black or red lacquer, but quite often it was left natural, with
the original coloration and genuine veining appearing on the
surface, smoothed and polished to shine. The wood is always of
the best quality, the variety chosen reflecting the circumstance of
its use: toilette boxes are made with a perfumed wood, tables
and chairs with hard and robust wood. The individual parts of a
piece of furniture are dovetailed so as to match perfectly, making
the use of nails or screws superfluous and limiting accessory
materials to natural glues used in minimal quantities. There was
a wide assortment of models including pieces of large size, such
as beds and mirrors, as well as picnic baskets and perfume cases.

Related entries
Architecture

◄Trestle painting table,
Ming dynasty, circa
1550–1640, *huanghuali*
wood, 81.3 cm high,
Museum für Ostasiatische
Kunst, Cologne.

The first stools appeared between the 4th and 5th centuries AD, chairs and tables already existed by the Tang period, and in the course of the two Song dynasties almost all the rest of the classical models of Chinese furniture came into existence.

This type of armchair, called a "meditation" chair in the Ming period, appears in paintings of the time as an item of furniture typical of literati.

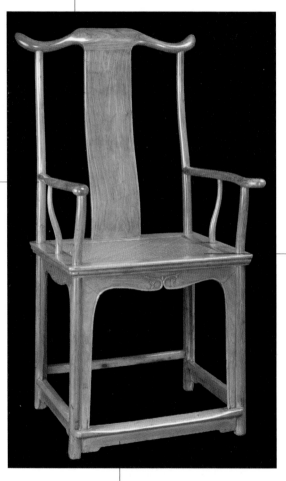

The seat is made of interwoven jute fiber reinforced underneath by palm fibers.

Chair seats were originally made somewhat wide to make possible sitting cross-legged; beginning in the Ming dynasty, however, chairs often were fitted instead with a low footrest.

▲ Armchair, Ming dynasty, first half 17th century, *huanghuali* wood, 119.4 cm high, Museum für Ostasiatische Kunst, Cologne.

In the southern village a young cattlehand stands barefoot atop
an ox. Wind from the river blows through the holes in his cloak,
rain off the mountains pours through his cracked hat" (Lu You)

Agriculture

Cultivation of the land is the heart of Chinese civilization, and agricultural policy has always been a determinant of the success of the
ruling house and the prosperity of the country. Over the course of
history, Chinese governments have adopted various measures to
distribute the land among a great number of small and medium
peasants, primarily to maintain state control over the land. In that
way the state was assured fiscal earnings and labor, in large part a
direct result of the harvest and the forced labor of peasants. At the
same time it also thus opposed the accumulation of land and power
in the hands of small owners. The plain of central China, annually
flooded by the Yellow River, was the site of the first large-scale agricultural society, with millet and wheat as its main harvests, followed by vegetables and fruit (persimmons, pears, apples). The use
of iron tools that spread in the Han period permitted the breaking
up of fields until then not tillable; hydraulic techniques facilitated
the processing of these products. The course of the 9th–10th
centuries AD saw the intensive exploitation of the lower valley
of the Yangtze, with
the cultivation of rice
in methodically irri-
gated terraced fields,
as well as the planting
of cotton in the south-
eastern coastal areas.
Corn, potatoes, and
peanuts were imported
from the Americas
beginning in the 16th
century and were soon
added to the tradi-
tional foodstuffs.

Terms
Yellow River
(*Huanghe*)
Yangtze River
(*Changjiang*)

Related entries
Administration,
Controlling water,
Domestic animals,
Technology and
industries

▼ Wall painting of
plowing a field, Five
Dynasties period, AD
907–960, Cave 61,
western wall
(detail), at Mogao,
Dunhuang, Gansu.

By the end of the Eastern Han the rich landowners of the Sichuan were independent from the central government, and the statues like this that appear in their tombs were images of peasants working for landowners, not for the state.

The invention of agricultural tools was attributed to the divine peasant Shennong, the most important of the eight popular divinities and the third of the Three August Ones, renowned for having taught the Chinese the art of cultivating fields.

The shovel, scoop, and long knife hanging from the side of the statue make possible its identification, while the sword, fixed to a pectoral pommel, suggests that this man also served an auxiliary function in the owner's armed militia.

In the twelfth lunar month the emperor performed sacrifices of thanksgiving to Shennong and to Houji, the god of fruits of the earth, as well as to useful animals such as birds, certain insects, cats, and tigers.

▲ Model of a peasant, Eastern Han dynasty, second half 2nd century, terracotta, pigments, 112 cm high, Fondazione Giovanni Agnelli, Turin.

The peasant wears straw sandals and a simple shirt under a tunic colored only along the edges, a result of imperial decrees forbidding peasants from dying cloth.

Rice has been cultivated in southern China for more than seven thousand years, and during the Shang and Zhou periods (mid-2nd millennium–5th century BC) its cultivation spread to areas of the Yellow River in the central provinces (Henan and Hebei).

By the time of the Song period most of the Chinese people lived on rice, cultivated in the Yangtze delta, an area that had originally been swampy but that had been drained and provided with an efficient hydraulic system.

楊威耕穫圖

The division of the fields into small holdings that facilitated the control of irrigation was attributed to an expert of the Han period.

The man at the center, the only figure dressed in a long cloak and also the only one not busy at work, is the owner of the rice fields.

Running counterclockwise, the work illustrates the annual phases in the cultivation of rice, beginning at the bottom with seeding and moving on to transplanting, flooding the fields, harvesting, and plowing.

Plow and Harvest, Southern Song dynasty, album leaf, ink and light color on silk, 24.8 x 25.7 cm, Palace Museum, Beijing.

"Horse, ox, sheep, chicken, dog, pig. These six animals are those which people raise" (Three-Character Classic)

Domestic animals

Terms
Domestic animals
(*jiachu*)

Related entries
Court, Horses,
Agriculture, Silk,
Acrobatics and the
circus, Chang'an
(Tang)

By the early 1st century BC, the raising of domestic animals—pigs, cattle, chickens, waterfowl—was so highly developed that it satisfied the nutritional and sacrificial needs of the people of central-northern China. To the south the nutritional range had always been broader and included monkeys, dogs, and snakes; people in coastal areas lived primarily off fish. Rabbits were not eaten, being the sacred inhabitant of the moon. Certain animal species were indispensable members of the work force: as early as the Han period, buffalos and horses were being used to plow fields and collect harvests, dogs were doing duty as guards, and cormorants (prevented from swallowing the fish they caught) facilitated fishing. By the end of the 1st millennium AD, elephants were being used in what is now Yunnan to transport people and goods, while the pack animal used for treks across the Gobi Desert had always been the camel. According to their traits, the various animals served curative functions in China's rich *materia medica:* from the earthworm used to fight fevers to the dog's liver, a curative for dysentery. Since the Han period the court and ordinary people alike had taken delight in birds, dogs, cats, crickets, and grasshoppers, and circus spectacles as well as animal combats were much loved.

▶ Model of a cow,
Han dynasty, 1st
century BC–1st century
AD, glazed terracotta,
21 cm long,
Fondazione Giovanni
Agnelli, Turin.

Ordinary people rarely had occasion to eat meat, a costly food normally reserved for well-to-do families.

Since pigs are omnivorous, living off domestic garbage and human excrement, it was not rare to construct latrines directly over sties.

Pork is still the most widespread meat in China today; in the past it was especially important for festive occasions and important gatherings.

Model of sty with pig, astern Han dynasty, 2nd ntury AD, glazed terracotta, 1.5 cm high, Fondazione iovanni Agnelli, Turin.

Models of pig sties with latrines were among the symbols of wealth and fortune tied to the agricultural world that accompanied the landowner to the tomb to provide well-being in the afterlife.

The pictorial genre known as "feathers and furs," meticulous and attentive to detail, came into being over the course of the 12th century, following the neo-Confucian style of investigating nature in its smallest details.

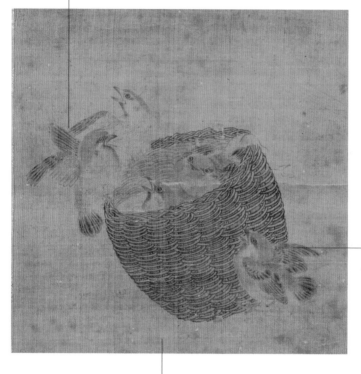

Aside from plow and saddle animals, the Chinese raise animals for culinary purposes, such as sparrows, and others for sheer delight, such as crickets.

Such apparently humble subjects offer an intimate view of nature while teaching the viewer to be aware of even the simplest of phenomena.

▲ Attributed to Song Ruozhi, *Young Sparrows in a Nest*, Southern Song dynasty, 13th century, ink and light color on paper, 21.7 x 22.5 cm, National Museum, Tokyo.

In contrast with the so-called investigation of things of the Southern Song, various 15th-century artists sought to transcend reality and go beyond the mere "copy of truth."

Shen Zhou, active in the second half of the 15th century, was the leading exponent of the artists in Suzhou, a city of great social mobility and artistic vivacity.

In the inscription that accompanies this work the painter writes that he sought to "steal the secrets of creation."

The artist sought to capture the essential traits of the feline—softness, elegance, sense of humor, cunning—with only a few calligraphic strokes requiring no chromatic accents.

Shen Zhou, *Cat* (detail), Ming Dynasty, 1494, from the album *Life Studies* of 16 leaves, dated 1494, ink on paper, each leaf 34.7 x 55.4 cm, National Palace Museum, Taipei.

"Ten thousand things are produced and reproduced; variations and transformations are thus infinite" (Zhou Dunyi)

Technology and industries

The division of labor and mass production are two aspects of Chinese civilization, vividly demonstrated by the terracotta army of the first emperor. This development was in large part a result of China's precocious technological progress, particularly dynamic from the 4th to the 1st centuries BC and then during the Song period (10th–13th centuries). In the saltworks and iron foundries of the Han epoch, put under state control by Wudi in 119 BC, the entire production process took place, from extraction to the finished product, with the participation of hundreds of workers. The invention of the winch, aside from benefiting agriculture, facilitated the exploitation of water and salt resources by way of deep wells. The use of continuous bellows made possible production of hard and strong crockery, similar to stoneware. The common people wore clothing of hemp and ramie (fiber from a plant of the nettle family), spun and woven at home; silk, made for exportation but also worn by officials and nobles, was worked in establishments with thousands of workers. Later, with the country's agricultural center moving to the middle of the Yangtze valley and following the withdrawal of the Song to Hangzhou, southern China became the site of many plants for processing agricultural products (tea, sugarcane, silk, cotton) along with large factories for the manufacture of porcelain, lacquer, paper and books. There were also enormous shipbuilding yards.

▶ Song Yingxing,
Pottery Wheels,
woodblock illustration
from *The Exploitations
of the Works of Nature
(Tiangong kaiwu)*,
Ming dynasty, 1637.

Saggars appeared around the middle of the Tang period. These containers made of refractory clay were used to hold ceramics during firing in the kiln to protect them from impurities and from variations in temperature.

Many decorated vases were fired twice, the first time at a high temperature that compacted the material, still unglazed and now called biscuit, and a second time, during which the vase was decorated with a glaze.

The precocious advances China made in ceramic technology, which led to the mass production of porcelain about a thousand years earlier than in Europe, owe a great deal to developments in kilns.

The kiln in the shape of a dragon, developed in southern China and up to 80 meters in length, permitted the firing of large quantities of ceramics at the same time and at high temperatures under reducing conditions, meaning with restricted oxygen.

Such kilns were composed of a series of connected chambers following the slope of a hillside, with the firebox at the bottom of the hill and the chimney located at the top.

Dragon kiln (longyao), woodblock illustration from The Exploitations of the Works of Nature (Tiangong kaiwu), Ming dynasty, 1637.

In the north, coal was used to fire kilns, and the kilns consisted of a single chamber divided from the firebox by a wall.

The first practical guides to sericulture date to the Han period, at which time production was organized at an industrial level.

To form the cocoon, the silkworm weaves a filament about 3,000 meters long over a period of 2–4 days. Having removed the floss, 700–900 meters of high-quality thread remain.

▲ Lian Kai (attrib.), *Sericulture* (second section), Southern Song dynasty, early 13th century, horizontal scroll, ink and light color on silk, 26.5 x 98.5 cm, Cleveland Museum of Art.

Silkworms need constant climatic conditions and, according to the manuals, require an atmosphere of tranquility and serenity, transmitted by the "mothers" overseeing the "brood."

In the 30- to 35-day period of growth, the silkworms eat large quantities of white mulberry leaves. The mats they are spread on must be repeatedly cleaned.

The production of silk was one of the few activities in the hands of women, from the raising of the silkworms to the working of the fabric. The annual silk-growing season began with a large ceremony attended by the empress.

"The greatly extolled Varnish of China is nothing but simple bitumen, which the Chinese call Cì" (A. Guidotti)

Lacquer

The lacquer of southeastern Asia is made from the latex of the "lacquer tree" (*Toxicodendron vernicifluum*), a plant originally from southern China, in cultivation since the 4th century BC. The latex is obtained by tapping the trees, making an incision in the bark and collecting the viscous liquid, which is then purified through repeated heating and filtering. The final substance gummy and brown, contains a high percentage of urushiol and is resistant to water, acids, alkalines, and alcohol but is sensitive to changes in temperature. Since lacquer remains fluid until it dries, it must be applied to a support, usually wood. The first objects covered in a thin layer of lacquer date to the Neolithic age, but large-scale production began during the period of the Warring States (475–221 BC). Polychrome motifs obtained with pigments mixed in linseed oil were painted on a background of lacquer, colored black with soot or red with cinnabar. The fantastic and bizarre pictorial style of the Han period has been handed down to us by way of containers and vases in painted lacquer. Beginning in the Tang period the layers of lacquer were multiplied to reach thicknesses of 5 to 6 mm. This led to the creation of new, highly demanding decorative techniques, which were perfected during later dynasties: from inlaid stone, ivory, or mother-of-pearl to engraving and the application of gold.

▶ Box with compartments, Yuan dynasty, engraved red lacquer, 19.2 x 19.2 cm, Lee Family Collection, Tokyo.

The cover, made from turned wood, is topped by three semicircular rings.

During the Warring States and Western Han periods, decoration was painted in red on black, sometimes enriched with yellow (trisulphide of arsenic) or brown (iron oxide).

Rare examples have been found of lacquer used as an alternative to bronze in the manufacture of ritual vessels; these are identical in shape but made of lacquered wood, as with this tripod made to hold food offerings.

Stylized motifs of feathers, dragons, and clouds that alternate with volutes and spirals are typical of the decorated lacquerwares of this period.

The body of the vase is composed of a single piece of turned wood into which the rectangular handles and feet were inserted.

The number of sacred vases that could accompany the deceased was determined by ritual rules: a set of seven tripods, as in this case, was reserved for members of the nobility, but only imperial tombs could contain nine.

▲ Tripod, Western Han dynasty, circa 168 BC, from Tomb 1 at Mawangdui, Hunan, lacquered wood, 28 cm high, 23 cm diam., Hunan Provincial Museum, Changsha.

The technique of engraving lacquer, developed in China beginning in the late 8th century AD, requires a great deal of time, since from seventy to one hundred layers of lacquer are required to achieve the workable thickness of 2–4 millimeters.

Each layer must dry for at least 24 hours in a damp and warm climate and then be polished before the application of the next layer.

"Carved red lacquer" (tihong) and "carved black" (tihei) are the two techniques characteristic of Chinese engraved lacquers, today integrated in the style known in the West by the Japanese name guri, which refers to carving through different-colored layers of lacquer.

The soft, delicate carving makes the volumes stand out, facilitating the reading of the scene, which is surrounded by symbols of long life, turtles and lingzhi mushrooms.

Along with lacquers engraved with geometric motifs, there are lacquers with figural subjects, such as this eight-lobed tray with its Buddhist-inspired image of the goddess Guanyin (Avalokitesvara).

The outer panels are decorated inside and outside with lotus leaves.

▲ Eight-lobed vase, Ming dynasty, Hongwu period, 1368–1398, engraved red lacquer, 34.87 cm diam., Lee Family Collection, Tokyo.

"The Seres make precious clothes, decorated with designs, the colors of which resemble the flowers of the field with a fineness that competes with the work of the spider" (Dionysius Periegetes)

Silk

Xi Lingshi, the mythical wife of the Yellow Emperor, is said to have taught the Chinese around the middle of the 3rd century BC the cultivation of silkworms (*Bombyx mori*) and the use of the filaments of the cocoon, an activity that traditionally belonged to women. The production of both woven and raw silk already had reached industrial levels by the time of the Han period. Most of the silk that reached the city of Rome around the 1st century BC had been donated to tributary states, which then put it on the market. The methods of silk making were kept secret for centuries, but by the 3rd century AD the first cultivations had appeared in Japan, followed in the 4th century by India and then Syria, although sericulture reached Europe only in the 10th century. Skeins of silk were dyed with vegetal colorants, combined with mordants. The Han produced damasks woven of different colored threads, translucent gauze, and brocades sometimes interwoven with gold thread; the fabrics were sometimes embroidered, or were painted with mineral pigments. The motifs are geometric, often lozenges, or figural, such as dragons, tigers, birds, trees, and flowers. The silk tapestry appeared in the Tang period but reached its greatest splendor in later dynasties. The Tang made decorations using wooden dies and also knew the batik method for printing fabrics, while the application of cut-piece decorations was popular in the Ming period.

Terms
Yellow Emperor
(*Huangdi*)
Silk (*si*)
Silkworm (*can*)
Cocoon (*canjian*)
Velvet (*sirong*)
Thread (*siji*)
Damask (*ling*)
Brocade (*jin*)
Gauze (*sha*)
Tapestry (*kesi*)

Related entries
The five relationships,
Technology and
industries, Afterlife

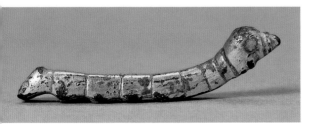

◄ Silkworm (*Bombyx mori*), Western Han dynasty, Shiquan district, Shaanxi, gilt bronze, 5.6 cm long, Forest of Stone Tablets Museum, Xi'an.

In later periods, heavy silk cloaks displayed the wearer's emblems, embroidered on the chest.

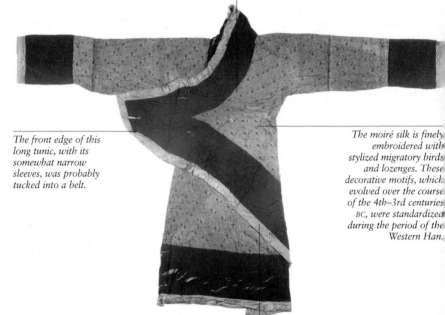

The front edge of this long tunic, with its somewhat narrow sleeves, was probably tucked into a belt.

The moiré silk is finely embroidered with stylized migratory birds and lozenges. These decorative motifs, which evolved over the course of the 4th–3rd centuries BC, were standardized during the period of the Western Han.

The tunic in embroidered silk gauze is trimmed in flat silk bordered in turn with brocade and lined with cotton silk.

▲ Silk tunic, Western Han dynasty, circa 168 BC, from Tomb 1 at Mawangdui, Hunan, embroidered silk, 150 cm long, Hunan Provincial Museum, Changsha.

The technique of "engraved silk," here simplified in a "silk tapestry," was perfected in the Song period and made possible the rendering of the most delicate shadings.

The warp thread of these tapestries did not pass selvedge to selvedge but turned back at the areas of the decoration, which was then later added using threads of a tonality, thickness, and consistency different from the background fabric.

▲ Zhu Kerou, *Camellias*, Southern Song dynasty, 12th century, silk tapestry (*kesi*) mounted like an album leaf, 25.6 x 25.3 cm, Liaoning Provincial Museum, Shenyang.

The procedure was used to immortalize certain works by painters of the imperial Song academy, and the tapestries reproducing such works were themselves considered works of art in all senses.

> *"The Chinese have a fine clay of which they make drinking vessels as fine as glass; one can see the liquid contained in them"*
> *(Suleiman al-Tajir)*

Ceramics

Terms
Terracotta (*tao*)
Stoneware (*ci* or *yingtao*)
Porcelain (*ci*)
Glaze (*you*)

Related entries
Hongwu, Yongle,
Technology and
industries, Afterlife,
Virtual companions,
Tomb guardians,
Hangzhou

▼ Globular jar, Western
Han dynasty, late
2nd–1st century BC,
terracotta with olive-
green glaze, 17 cm high,
Fondazione Giovanni
Agnelli, Turin.

Chinese ceramics present an infinity of qualities, shapes, colors, and decorations, including pieces made as luxury goods, others that served as objects of daily life, and those destined for use as burial offerings. The art of pottery has been part of Chinese civilization since its origins, but it was never the expression of individual inspiration and was always instead the fruit of the organization of labor in a series of specialized fields. Vases were often worked on fast wheels whose invention dated back to the Neolithic period; figural pieces were instead produced in molds, two section or composite, a usage that began in the 3rd century BC. The ceramics of northern China were made of a sedimentary clay and were distinguished by their wide variety of forms, glazes, and decorations; in the 7th century AD the kilns of Xing (Hebei) produced ware of a whiteness, thinness, and hardness that many scholars see as the world's first porcelain. Finer raw materials were available in the south of China, making possible the production of translucent porcelain beginning in the 10th century and further improved during the Yuan domination, with an increase in the percentage of kaolinite, a hydrous aluminum silicate that is the chief element in kaolin. Glazes, whether monochrome or multicolor, are an essential element of Chinese ceramics. They can cover the entire vessel or only part.

This plate may be a product of the kilns grouped under the name of Xing in the province of Hebei, where translucent white porcelain with a thin and compact body was produced on imperial orders.

Initially, the potters often had to hide chromatic and paste imperfections with a white slip decoration, but this was made superfluous when they mastered the use of secondary kaolins as their raw material.

While the ceramic production of northern China culminated in white porcelain, beginning in the 3rd century AD the workshops of Yue (Zhejiang) began making ceramics with a gray body covered with an olive-green translucent glaze.

The beauty of the plate results from the purity of its form, inspired by the works of Middle Eastern silversmiths, the thinness of its body, and the perfect application of the transparent glaze.

▲ Five-lobed plate, Tang dynasty, from Huoshaobi, Shaanxi, white porcelaneous stoneware with transparent glaze, border 13.8 cm diam., Institute for the Protection of Cultural Relics, Xi'an.

Since antiquity the north and south of China contributed to the evolution of ceramic production with certain characteristics that were united in a common effort only beginning in the 11th century AD.

"Three-color" (sancai) ceramics are an outgrowth of the traditional use of lead glazes, which appeared in northern China in the 3rd–2nd centuries BC in imitation of the shininess of bronzes.

Cobalt came in general from the Middle East, which was also the source of inspiration for the numerous shapes and decorations of these ceramics, produced during the period of great splendor and cosmopolitanism achieved by the Tang dynasty.

The colors could be brushed on, dripped, or even sprayed, a technique that gave the decoration a casual sense of lightness.

The production of "three-color" ceramics seems to have originated in the 7th century AD on the basis of earlier types and saw its culmination in the first half of the 8th century, after which it rapidly declined.

Although called "three color," the chromatic range of such glazes was often limited to one or two colors, usually green, amber, or cream, and in truth the palette also extended to yellow as well as purple black and cobalt blue.

▲ Tripod jar, Tang dynasty, first half 8th century AD, white terracotta with "three-color" (*sancai*) glaze, 13.4 cm high, border 12.2 cm diam., Museo di Arte Orientale, Turin.

Floral and leaf motifs bordered by fretwork or by other recurrent geometric elements prevail over such figural subjects as birds and fish.

Around the end of the Tang dynasty (10th century AD), the Ding potters in Hebei produced a quality of white porcelain destined to replace Xing ware.

The most common types of Ding ware are bowls and plates, the rims of which were often bound in copper or silver because that area was free of glaze as a result of being fired upside down in the kiln.

In the first phase of production, Ding ware was often given hand-carved decoration, but by the beginning of the 11th century, decorations made with molded patterns began to prevail.

Bowl (pan) with molded decorations, Northern Song dynasty, 12th century, white porcelain with cream color glaze, rim bound in copper, 15.6 cm diam., Porzellansammlung, Dresden.

Black-glazed porcelain appeared in the Tang period, was perfected in the bowls of the Song period, and was favored in particular by the followers of Chan Buddhism (Japanese Zen) in the performance of the tea ceremony.

The Song period was distinguished by a multitude of porcelains of different typologies that have in common the desire for essential forms, with simple and linear shapes and monochrome glazes with a few spontaneous chromatic effects.

So realistic is the leaf-shaped decoration on this cup from Jizhou that some scholars believe it may be an actual applied leaf, but how the application was achieved or what chemical treatments were involved are questions that remain unresolved.

The most famous tea bowls were those of Jian'an (Fujian), whose production included the glaze known as "hare's fur" because of its fine streaking in various shades of brown, and those of Jizhou (Jiangxi), distinguished by their apparently accidental decorations.

▲ Tea bowl, Southern Song dynasty, porcelain with black glaze and leaf decoration, rim 14.3 cm diam., Museum of Fine Arts, Boston.

The Jingdezhen kilns, under imperial patronage beginning in 1004, had a fundamental role in the development of the last great innovation in the field of ceramic techniques, underglaze decoration.

The kilns at Jingdezhen produced a pure, fine, white, translucent porcelain, the ideal background for painted decoration, which began over the course of the Yuan dynasty using two pigments, cobalt blue and copper red.

The decoration was painted on the dried but not yet fired body; this had to be done quickly because of the absorbent nature of the ceramic surface.

Sealed by the glaze and fired at high temperature, the decorations became permanent.

Vase, Ming dynasty, Yongle era, 1403–1424, white and blue porcelain with underglaze blue decoration produced in kilns at Jingdezhen, 44 cm high, Palace Museum, Beijing.

At first, porcelains decorated in white and blue, which were exported in large quantities to the Middle East and Southeast Asia, were considered vulgar by the learned class in China, still enamored of monochrome decoration.

Only over the course of the first decades of the 15th century did the court begin to appreciate these wares, which later became characteristic of all of China's ceramic production.

The large-scale exportation of Chinese porcelain to Europe began in the 16th century, centuries after the opening of the market to the Middle East and Southeast Asia.

After a first high-temperature firing (circa 1350ºC), colored glaze was applied to the plate, which a second, lower-temperature firing (circa 800ºC) stabilized.

"Swatow ceramics" were made in the late Ming period, destined for the Southeast Asian market. They are named for the port, Shantou, from which they were exported.

Most of all in southern China, in areas around major ports, kilns turned out large quantities of porcelain using techniques and decorations matched to the tastes of the countries for which they were intended.

▲ Plate, Ming dynasty, late 16th–first half 17th century, enameled porcelain, 42.8 cm diam., Idemitsu Museum, Tokyo.

Zigong said, 'If you possessed a beautiful piece of jade, would you hide it away in a locked box or would you try to sell it at a good price?' The Master replied, 'Oh, I would sell it!'" (Confucius)

Jade

Jade's high esteem in ancient China was matched only by that of bronze; its characteristics—shininess, transparency, coloration, internal veining, hardness, and pure sound when struck—endowed it with great symbolic and magical authority that endured over the centuries. Numerous archaic shapes whose original meaning was lost over time, such as *bi* disks and *cong* cylinders, which had appeared in the middle of the 3rd millennium BC in the culture of Liangzhou, were imitated in later periods, in part for apotropaic reasons, in part because the past has always been taken as a model in China. Indeed, interest in jade on the part of collector-literati in the 10th century led to a rapid increase in production. The term *jade* referred to a group of precious stones and colored stones that were not necessarily related at the mineralogical level. The "true" Chinese jade is nephrite, imported from time immemorial from Chinese Turkistan, while jadeite was introduced to China only beginning in the 18th century. Nephrite, which can assume different colorations according to the impurities in the stone, is harder than iron, even than steel; thus it was not carved but smoothed with a series of abrasive powders of quartz, garnet, and corundum.

◀ Bowl with handles in the shape of Daoist immortals, Yuan dynasty, white jade (nephrite), border 10.3 cm diam., Cleveland Museum of Art.

Jade

During the period of disorder that marked the end of the first dynasty, one of the Qin generals formed the independent state in southern China known as Nan Yue, with its capital at Panyu in today's Canton.

In 1983, construction workers discovered the tomb of the second king of Nan Yue, Zhao Mo, who had been buried in 122 BC.

At the center of the tomb was a chamber in which lay the deceased ruler wrapped entirely in a jade shroud, while the side rooms held the bodies of fifteen people who had been forced to accompany their ruler in his tomb.

This pierced-work two-ring disk was found near the ruler's head.

A dragon is enclosed in the inner ring, its tail and front legs extending beyond the ring, the legs holding a phoenix with a long tail.

▲ Double ring with dragon and phoenix, Western Han dynasty, kingdom of Nan Yue, 122 BC, from the tomb of Zhao Mo, ruler of Nan Yue, at Guangzhou, jade, 10.6 cm diam., Museum of the Nan Yue King of the Western Han, Guangzhou.

"In the eastern suburbs a rich old man has amassed wealth in
the five cities . . . by day business, by night he counts his wealth,
and day and night he finds no peace" (Bai Juyi)

Commerce

In the hierarchy of the "productive classes" established by the
Confucians, peasants occupied the highest level, while merchants were relegated to the lowest. China's rulers always looked
upon buying and selling as a social risk and sought to maintain
tight control over internal traffic; for a long time any commerce
with foreigners was associated with the exchange of tribute. The
reopening of the commercial routes to Central Asia in the Tang
period led to a large-scale increase in commercial activities,
which were restricted to special market areas in the administrative centers. Toward the end of the Tang dynasty, the government's need to find new sources of income resulted in the partial
liberalization of the domestic market. A great commercial revo-
lution was put in motion with the relocation of China's political
and agricultural center to the south in the 11th century; the volume, variety, and quality of goods increased enormously. Private
exchanges were greater than the state market, and the process of
urbanization transformed the administrative centers into commercial centers, the residences of leading merchants and
landowners. The increase in agricultural productivity under
Hongwu of the Ming dynasty reinforced this trend, and merchants, by then directing a network of enterprises and banks,
came to enjoy a certain level of social prestige.

Related entries
Wudi, Hongwu,
Yongle, Agriculture,
Technology and
industries, Silk

◀ Four bronze weights,
three of them datable.
From left to right: Qin
dynasty, 221–206 BC;
period of Wang Mang,
AD 9–24; Northern
Dynasties, AD 386–581,
7.7 kg, 126 g, 280 g,
Shaanxi History
Museum, Xi'an.

Several wall paintings in the Mogao caves at Dunhuang use scenes based on real-life events to illustrate Buddhist precepts.

The enti
southern w
of Cave 45
dedicated to t
mercy
Bodhisatt
Guanyin: t
invocation
her name
sufficient
burst the chai
of prisoners ar
to make
possible
travel unscathe
through regio
infested l
bandit

The armed man could be a bandit but also a customs official on the Chinese border, in charge of collecting duties.

The sce
presents a gro
of beard
merchan
probab
Sogdians, w
have set do
their goods ar
are lifting the
hands in
imploring gest
in front of
armed man wi
a long swor

The subject of the scene is open to discussion, but it offers a view of the difficult life, full of obstacles, faced by merchants in ancient China.

▲ Traveling Merchants, Tang dynasty, 8th century AD, detail of the southern wall of Cave 45 at Mogao, Dunhuang, Gansu.

With commercial activity concentrated in administrative centers, the countryside depended on traveling peddlers.

To the joy of women and children, these itinerant vendors carried on their backs an infinity of small, useful, and delightful items, from tools to medicinal herbs, from pots and pans to talismans, from toys to talking birds.

The vendor has hurriedly set down his pole, loaded at both ends, to retrieve a small snake in the hands of five very excited little boys.

During the Song period, scenes of the daily life of ordinary people became a genre of painting embraced by several painters at the imperial academy, resulting in rare views of the habits and customs of ordinary Chinese.

Li Song, *The Knickknack Peddler*, Southern Song dynasty, 212, album leaf, ink and light color on silk, 24.2 x 26 cm, Cleveland Museum of Art.

"Along these roads the Great Khan's messengers have only to go twenty-five miles and there find a posting station, a spacious hostel for lodging with splendid beds with coverlets of silk" (Marco Polo)

Transportation

Creation of a network of transportation was a necessity in term of maintaining the unity of the empire. The system of "fast roads" that extended from Xianyang, capital of the first emperor, into a the provinces had an overall length estimated to be 7,000 kilom ters. The Han amplified the road network, which by the end of t 2nd century AD had reached an extension of about 35,400 kilom ters. The highways on the plain were as wide as 23 meters and ha three lanes, the middle one paved and reserved for couriers and o ficials. Way-stations for changing horses were located at regula intervals. With the expansion of power under Emperor Wudi the Han, commercial and cultural exchanges with Central As began along the Silk Routes, brought to new life during the Tan period. In many parts of China rivers presented the fastest an most economical means of transportation, as Qin Shi Huang had already understood. The Grand Canal, which beginning the 6th century created a north-south axis, was elongated an amplified in the Song period to conne the South Sea with the Yellow Rive The transfer of the political and eco nomic center southward favore overseas commerce; progress mapmaking and nautical tech nology—such as the compas in use beginning in the 11t century—made China th world's greatest maritim power, a position it held un til the early Ming period.

▶ Model of a pack camel, Tang dynasty, from the tomb of Zheng Rentai, Liquan district, Shaanxi, terracotta, glaze, pigments, 48 cm high, Shaanxi History Museum, Xi'an.

A small inn, located in a mountainous landscape and frozen by the cold, offers refuge to travelers.

A cart drawn by five oxen has almost arrived at the area in front of the inn, where four camels are already resting.

A sort of sled moves over the snow, drawn by a large ox and pushed by a man using all his strength.

▲ Transportation in the East, Southern Song dynasty, vertical scroll, ink and light color on silk, 109 x 49.5 cm, Palace Museum, Beijing.

Long-distance transportation in China had to overcome major difficulties because of the variety of climatic and geographical conditions, from the hot and humid swamps and tropical forests of the south to the snowy mountains and arid deserts of the north.

Nautical technology was highly evolved and specialized: the navigable waters of ancient China were plied by several hundred different types of watercraft.

In the absence of wind the boat was propelled by poles or was hauled along from the riverbank by way of long bamboo hawsers.

The painting may well give an accurate view of the quantity of river traffic in ancient China: as far as the eye can see, there are the masts of boats, from those anchored in the foreground to those on the far side of the central island.

The basic material of the Chinese sails was bamboo, woven together and unfolded like a fan. Unlike the sails on a Western boat, the sails of a Chinese boat are furled downward.

Merchant ships like this, which navigated the Grand Canal, could hold up to 140 tons of grain.

▲ Transportation of Grain, Southern Song dynasty, vertical scroll, ink and color on silk, 95.4 x 48.1 cm, National Palace Museum, Taipei.

The helm is in the stern, while the anchors—usually two—drop from the prow.

"Only in money do I take no delight. While you live it does not come on its own. And when you die you cannot take it with you" (Yuan Mei)

Money

At the time of the foundation of the Chinese empire, various bronze coins were in circulation, issued by different kingdoms and thus varying in size and shape. In 336 BC the Qin kingdom began issuing the "half-ounce" coins that after unification rose to become the standard exchange unit for the entire empire. Its shape, circular with a square hole in the middle, making it possible to string the coins on a cord, remained unchanged up to the opening decades of the 20th century. Wudi of the Han introduced the "five-grain" coin, which was replaced only 700 years later with the "new beginning" copper coin, in circulation until the end of the empire. Alongside these small-size coins there were also gold bars in various shapes, in use until the Western Han, and silk was also used as an exchange good in important transactions. Beginning at the end of the 8th century, silk was combined with silver, produced and distributed outside of state control. During the same period "flying money" appeared, this being certificates of credit, covered by money held on deposit by leading merchants. This system was amplified under the Song: at first the state took part in the production of acts of credit, but it issued these in the form of regular paper money. The government never managed to prevent abuses and counterfeiting, and paper money fell out of use in the 16th century because of persistent inflation.

Terms
Coin (*qian*)
"Half-ounce" coin
(*banliang*)
"Five-grain" coin
(*wuzhu*)
"New beginning"
coin (*kaiyuan*)

Related entries
Qin Shi Huangdi, Li Si,
Commerce

▼ *Wuzhu* ("five-grain")
coin, Western Han
dynasty, copper, 2.6 cm
diam., Shaanxi History
Museum, Shaanxi.

This is one of two halves of a mold for producing forty coins. With the two parts sealed shut, liquid copper was poured through the opening at the top, spreading out along the central canal.

The "half-ounce" coin, also called the "four-grain," was introduced by Qin Shi Huangdi as part of his campaign to standardize the empire's weights and measures and remained in circulation until 118 BC, when Wudi introduced the "five-grain" coin.

Such molds for casting coins were made of ceramic, metal, or (as this one) stone.

In ancient China coins were not minted but cast in two-part molds.

After casting, the metal connecting the coins removed for reuse, along with the metal from the central canal.

▲ Mold for casting coins of the "half-ounce" type (banliang), Western Han dynasty, ante 118 BC, stone, 17.3 cm high, Shandong Provincial Museum, Jinan.

The paper, made of fibers from mulberry bark, bears printing on one side only.

Standing out at the center is the indication of the value of "1 guan," the term to indicate a string of 1,000 copper coins.

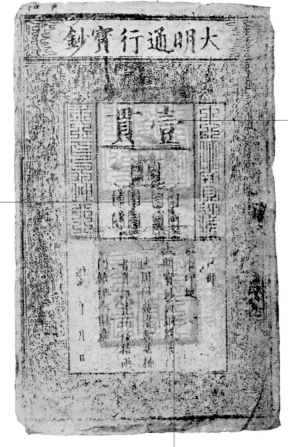

Ten strings of 100 coins each indicate the value of the banknote to the illiterate.

A message from the imperial treasury: "User of counterfeits will be beheaded. Informer will be rewarded 250 ounces of silver in addition to confiscated property of convicted."

▲ Banknote of 1 *guan*, Ming dynasty, Hongwu era, 1368–1398, printed paper, 34 x 22 cm, Kestner-Museum, Hannover.

"It is difficult for a man who always has a full stomach to put his mind to some use. Are there not players of [liu]bo and weiqi? Even playing these games is better than being idle" (Confucius)

Games

▼ Game of *liubo*, Western Han dynasty, circa 168 BC, from Tomb 3 at Mawangdui, Changsha, Hunan, lacquered wood, ivory, 45 x 45 x 17 cm, Hunan Provincial Museum, Changsha.

Among board games, *liubo* and *weiqi*, created in China, both originally contained divinatory factors related to elements of astrology. *Liubo* disappeared somewhat suddenly after the 3rd century AD, whereas *weiqi*, known in the West by its Japanese name, *go*, became a game of military strategy. The game of *xiangqi* is similar to chess and may have originated from the same Indian source. An indigenous game, documented in China as early as the 10th century, is the "seven boards of skill," in which the player combines seven geometric shapes like puzzle pieces to create a great quantity of figures. Numerous amusements accompanied the banquets of the Chinese aristocracy, from the ancient hunts to games of soccer, played as early as the Han period. The Tang court was fond of the exotic game of polo, but also played games of Chinese origin, such as flying kites, which dated to the Zhou dynasty and originally had military purposes. Beginning in the Song dynasty cultural hobbies spread among the literati: alone or with friends they delighted in creating a perfect aesthetic environment, playing instruments and board games, writing poetry and painting, challenging one another with complex "riddles," rebuses, and enigmas whose solution often required a solid classical background, such as, for example, the Lantern Riddles related to the Lantern Festival.

A taste for the exotic and the desire to move in the open air made polo one of the favorite games at the Tang court, also participated in by women, as indicated by various statuettes of polo players from the period.

For uniforms, the teams wore different colored tunics.

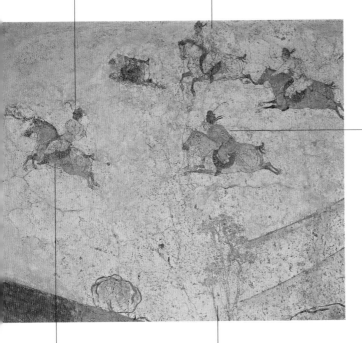

The game of polo, of Iranian origin, reached China by way of the people of the steppe, accustomed to spending their lives in the saddle.

The detail shows four of the twenty riders who took part in the game. The first rider is turning to strike the ball with a mallet, curved at the end to form a semicircle.

The rock and tree indicate that the scene is taking place outdoors, but at the same time these elements are predecessors of the genre of landscape painting, destined to reach its highest levels under the Song.

▲ Wall painting of a polo game (detail), Tang dynasty, AD 706 or 711, from the eastern wall of the access ramp of the tomb of Prince Li Xian at Qianling, Shaanxi, Shaanxi History Museum, Xi'an.

The archer's head, which still bears traces of pigments applied after the firing, was modeled in white clay and later applied to the body.

The extended arm, bent body, and eyes directed skyward to take aim at a bird in flight indicate that the archer is about to let loose an arrow from his bow, both of which have been lost since they were made of perishable materials.

Hunting was already part of the iconography of the Han period and remained a popular subject until the Tang.

The marbled design of the statuette was achieved by combining two clays of different colors (white and brown).

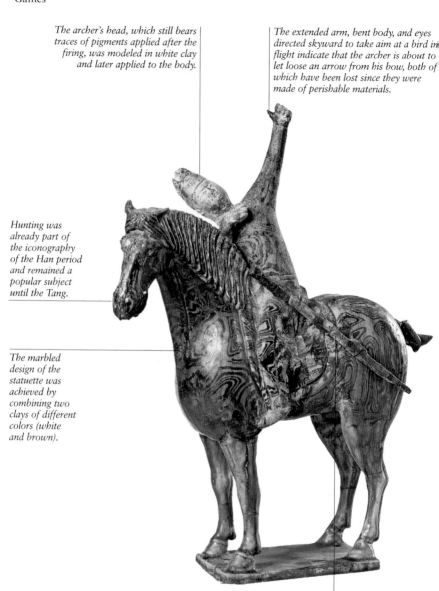

▲ Model of a hunter, Tang dynasty, circa AD 706, from the tomb of Prince Li Zhongrun (known as Yi De), at Qianling, Shaanxi, marbled terracotta, 36.2 cm high, History Museum, Shaanxi.

After the first firing at somewhat high temperature, the body was covered with a lead glaze, in part amber, in part green, as seen on the sword hanging from the rider's left side.

The bowl illustrates the favorite pastimes of the Chinese elite beginning with the Song dynasty: two people enjoy a walk in the lyrical setting of a garden (other side), while four men are busy with a table game.

The players' features are indicated with a few almost caricatural strokes. One expresses his joy at a successful move, while the others seem to indicate variations of displeasure.

This may be the ancient game of weiqi, mentioned in the Chronicle of Zuo (Zuo Zhuan), which dates to the 6th century BC.

Table games have always been an aspect of Chinese culture, sometimes praised for their didactic aspects, as in learning the basic concepts of tactics, and sometimes scorned as frivolous wastes of time.

▲ Bowl, Ming dynasty, first half 6th century, porcelain decorated with overglaze colored enamel, 2.2 cm diam., produced in the kilns of Jingdezhen, Jiangsu, Idemitsu Museum, Tokyo.

"The big string rumbles like a storm while the smaller ones moan in a long whisper" (Bai Juyi)

Music and dance

To Confucius, the keys to safeguarding the social and political order were "rites" and "music," the latter appreciated for its beauty, but also for its "beneficial" influence on humans. The Confucian classics, compiled in the Han period on the basis of the traditions of the past, are the points of departure for the musical theories of the following 2,000 years. The *Book of Changes* includes music in the cosmogony of yin and yang and the five phases, while according to the *Record of Rites*, music gives expression to harmony between the heavens and earth. The *Book of Songs* includes a list of musical instruments organized according to the eight materials they were made from: gourd, bamboo, wood, silk (lute), earth (terracotta), bronze, stone, and hide (the drum). Tonality is at the center of the Chinese musical system, and each sound is articulated adagio and isolated from the others so as to reveal timbre and tone. Each dynasty chose its "foundation tone," from which descended another twelve notes, put in relation to the pentatonic (five-tone) scale. In fact, the base of ritual music was the five-tone scale, while secular music also used the heptatonic scale.

The Han emperor Wudi instituted an administrative office to record popular songs, but since it was limited to the transcription of texts, the melodies have been lost. There were various ways to annotate the sounds of musical works, but no way to transcribe the rhythm.

▶ Octagonal bowl with high-relief decoration of musicians and dancers, Tang dynasty, 7th–early 8th century AD, from Hejiacun, Shaanxi, partially gilt silver, 6.6 cm high, 7.2 cm diam., Shaanxi History Museum, Xi'an.

Suspended in long rows from the ring at the top, the bells formed carillons, grouped according to size.

The writing yue fu *("music department") confers an official role on the bell, found in the area nicknamed the "banquet palace" of the immense funerary garden of Qin Shi Huangdi.*

Solemn compositions based on the harp, rhythmic percussion of carillons were characteristic of the Zhou epoch and accompanied banquets and sacred ceremonies.

Chinese bells are without inner ringers and are struck from the outside in the lower area: according to the site of the percussions, central or lateral, they give two distinct notes.

▲ Bell of the *zhong* type, Qin dynasty, from the area of the tomb of Qin Shi Huangdi at Lintong, bronze damascened in gold and silver, 12.8 cm high, Museum of Qin Terracotta Warriors and Horses, Lintong.

Music and dance

Zhou Fang, a painter who specialized in depictions of court life, presents three women in the intimacy of the palace's inner garden. One is tuning a qin, while a servant holds the box with the extra strings.

The qin, a sort of zither with silk strings that were plucked with the tips of the fingers or with a pick, was the most prestigious instrument of ancient China; its invention was attributed to the mythical Fuxi in the 3rd millennium BC.

Over the course of the 3rd–4th centuries AD, the qin assumed its definitive form, defined by the Chinese in terms that refer to the ancient cosmology: the upper panel of the body was symbolic of the heavens, the one beneath alluded instead to the earth.

In ancient times the instrument was played resting on the knees, but beginning in the Song dynasty tables appeared with projections on which to rest the instrument during use.

For Ming-dynasty literati, the qin *was a fundamental tool of self-education to be used preferably in an isolated place, either alone or in the company of intimate friends.*

▲ Copy from the 12th-century of Zhou Fang, *Court Ladies Tuning a Qin and Drinking Tea*, Tang dynasty, second half 8th century AD, horizontal scroll, ink and color on silk, 28 x 75.3 cm, The Nelson-Atkins Museum of Art, Kansas City.

Seven musicians surround a singer who stands at the center of a platform mounted on the back of a camel and covered by a heavy, brightly colored carpet.

To the side of a harpist sits a player of the cylindrical oboe (bili), flanked by a player of a pear-shaped lute (ruan).

"Western" music, most especially the lyrics and songs from Kucha in Central Asia, were very popular in the 8th century AD.

Groups of musicians composed of men and women, Chinese and foreign, often took part in festivals and public processions.

▲ Statuette of a camel with singer and musicians, Tang dynasty, early 8th century AD, from Zhongpucun, Xi'an, Shaanxi, glazed terracotta, 58 cm high, Shaanxi History Museum, Xi'an.

"A great lion is led into the Great Khan's presence; as soon as it sees him it flings itself down before him with every appearance of humility and seems to acknowledge him as lord" (Marco Polo)

Acrobatics and the circus

The fascination of acrobats, tumblers, and similar performers dates to China's preimperial age: a source from the Warring States period relates how the Chu army defeated the soldiers of the Song kingdom because they had been distracted by the performance of a highly talented juggler. During the Han period, acrobatics were part of the "hundred entertainments" and combined indigenous traditions with those drawn from Central Asia. Wall paintings, bas reliefs, and funerary objects with tightrope walkers, meant to extend the pleasures of life to the afterlife, are somewhat common in the tombs of the 1st–2nd centuries AD. Among the performers are found magicians and conjurers, dancers and acrobats, fire-eaters and weight lifters, tumblers and jugglers, often accompanied by musicians. During the Tang dynasty, the shows from Central Asia again enjoyed great fame, and troupes of acrobats and actors performed in market squares and the homes of the elite. At court, the passion for shows reached its height under Emperor Xuanzong (reigned AD 712–756), who had a special fondness for trained-animal acts, from speaking parrots to dancing horses, of which a few splendid models in colored terracotta have survived.

Terms
The hundred entertainments (*baixi*)
Acrobatics (*zaji*)

Related entries
Wudi, Virtual companions

◀ Brick decorated with bas-relief of circus scene, Eastern Han dynasty, from the Peng district, Sichuan, terracotta, 28 x 47 cm, Sichuan Provincial Museum, Chengdu.

During the Tang era, musicians, singers, dancers, magicians, and actors from Central Asia flocked to the capital of Chang'an, where many of them found steady work and a livelihood at the court or in the palaces of the elite.

The long sleeves accentuate the movements in keeping with the tradition of Chinese dance, while the belts and most of all the headdresses recall costumes of Iranian provenance.

The three taller actors are performing a rhythmic dance that probably acts as a backdrop to the declamations of the dwarf in the foreground.

Various burial statuettes indicate that dwarves often performed the role of storyteller or jester.

▲ Models of four actors or acrobats, Tang dynasty, first half 8th century, terracotta, pigments, slip decoration, maximum height 25 cm, Museo di Arte Orientale, Turin.

"I saw next a man in front of a door, arms wide, and he bellows, 'Come on!' . . . He says, 'Come late and we'll be full, nothing but standing room only'" (Du Renjie)

Theater

Spoken theater did not exist in ancient China, which over the course of its history knew instead various genres of musical theater, in which the music was accompanied by recitations and dance. Acrobatic exhibitions and monologues from "storytellers" were most popular during the Han era. The Tang court was fond of performances in which a pair of actors, accompanied by an orchestra, improvised comic dialogues based on famous topics. The process of urbanization that began in the Song era led to the ascent of "variety plays," a genre not unlike *opera buffa,* whose texts took aim most of all at the public administration and which was highly appreciated by businessmen, landowners, and city dwellers. The earliest stage settings to survive date to the period of the Mongolian occupation, and many components of the musical theater from that creative period have become typical of Chinese theatrical opera in general: the characters are stylized, recognizable by their elaborate costumes, masks, and gestures; stage scenery is reduced to the minimum; the recitations and songs are accompanied by an orchestra. Such operas were originally composed of four acts, while the "drama" that became popular in southern China around the end of the Yuan era had a more open structure and could include many acts. The 16th century saw the arrival of a more refined theatrical genre called "Kun melodies," a form of opera written and appreciated most of all by officials and literati.

◄ Figure of an actor, Yuan dynasty, Xifengfeng in the Jiaozuo district, Henan, brick decorated in high relief, 35.8 cm high, Henan Provincial Museum, Zhengzhou.

Terms
Storytelling (*shuochang*)
Theater (*xi* or *ju*)
Variety play (*zaju*)
Act (*zhe*)
Stage setting (*juben*)
Chinese drama (*chuanqi*)
Chinese opera (*kunqu,* lit., "Kun melodies")

Related entries
Novels, Acrobatics and the circus

The world of the dead

◄ Terracotta statues of soldiers
in battle formation, Qin dynasty,
Pit 1 of the tomb complex of
Emperor Qin Shi Huangdi,
Museum of Qin Terracotta
Warriors and Horses, Lintong.

"Wan Zi offers me long-life drugs, Xian prepares strange potions for me. With these foods I escape the rites of death, lengthen the thread of my days, and become immortal" (Cao Zhi)

The quest for immortality

Terms
Primordial unity
(*yuanyi*)
Exterior alchemy
(*waidan*)
Interior alchemy
(*neidan*)
Immortal (*xian*)

Related entries
Yin and yang and the
five phases, Daoism,
Sacred mountains,
Healers and drugs,
Physical exercise

The desire to overcome death and transcend the limits of space and time is common to all humanity. In the thinking of ancient China, every human being represented a microcosm that was an accurate mirror of the macrocosm, so the quest for immortality was related to the study of the principles of the formation and function of the universe, which thus became a field of Daoist research. Reproducing the cyclical transformations of nature with an accelerated rhythm, initiates hoped to reach the "primordial unity," the origin of life. There were two basic methods. "Exterior alchemy" proposed the attainment of immortality through the consumption of drinks and drugs composed of certain natural ingredients prepared in accordance with a set of rigid ritual procedures. A central role was given to cinnabar, mercuric sulfide, because of its ability to transform itself into mercury when heated and then to easily return to the solid state. Cinnabar, of essence yin, was often combined with lead, of essence yang, with results that often proved lethal for the believer. As for "interior alchemy," the dominant trend beginning in the Song period, the proposed elixir was instead transcendental wisdom, and the body was prepared for rebirth by way of introspective practices and breathing exercises, along with certain foods and sexual practices.

▶ Cicada, Han dynasty,
206 BC–AD 220, jade,
length 6.4 cm, British
Museum, London.

Only in the Han period were members of the imperial family and certain high officials permitted to wear a funeral robe of jade plates covering the entire body.

Jade was attributed with the power to protect the body from decomposition: since Neolithic times the dead had been buried with objects made of jade, and the tradition of filling the mouth and body orifices with jade dates to the 2nd millennium BC.

A bi disk was inserted in the head-covering in the area of the fontanel, called the "plug of the celestial soul" (tianlinggai), creating a circular hole 3.2 cm in diameter.

Bi disks had apotropaic functions, warding off evil; the nine jade plugs served to prevent the escape of the corporeal soul through the body's orifices.

The body of the wife of Han emperor Wudi's older brother is covered with about two thousand jade plates joined by gold wire and bordered with ribbons in yellow fabric.

The ancient Chinese did not sleep on soft, stuffed pillows but rested their heads on a solid material like ceramic or bronze.

▲ Funeral robe, Western Han dynasty, 2nd century BC, from the tomb of Princess Dou Luan, district of Mancheng, Hebei, stone, bovenite, gold thread, gilt bronze, Hebei Provincial Museum, Shijiazhuang.

*Painted in the
classical blue-and-
green style, which
originated in the
Tang period, a
monumental
landscape opens
before the eyes of
the viewer.*

*Visions of the
world of the
immortals appear
in several Han-
period tombs, but
they multiplied
around the end of
the Ming dynasty, a
period of political
instability and
personal insecurity.*

*Given the presence
of the water, which
dominates the lower
part, and the
majestic mountains
above, the work
may well depict both
the mythical island
of the immortals,
located in the
Eastern Sea, and the
Cosmic Mountain
to the west.*

▲ Zhu Dan, *Mountains and Palaces
of the Immortals*, Qing dynasty,
1683, hanging scroll, ink and color
on silk, 394.9 x 135.5 cm, Freer
Gallery of Art, Smithsonian
Institution, Washington, DC.

"Even if a man is in possession of abundant vital energy . . . it is extinguished as soon as the purified soul returns to the heavens and the corporeal soul returns to the earth, and both die" (Zhu Xi)

The two souls of the dead

In the 2nd century BC, seeking to rationalize contemporary beliefs, the literati of the Han period elaborated a theory of life after death based on the idea that the dead have a double soul, in that way integrating the afterlife with the dual system of yin and yang. After death, the "purified soul," of yang essence, returned to the celestial world, passing through the "Heavenly Gate." The "corporeal soul," of yin nature, went instead to the underground world, located near the Yellow Springs or, according to other beliefs, in the region of Mount Tai. The position of the corporeal soul within the bureaucratic structure of the afterlife depended on the state of preservation of the body and on the funerary objects that accompanied it. In its journey to the heavens, the purified soul visited the home of the immortals, located in the 2nd century BC on islands in the Eastern Sea but relocated over the course of the 1st century BC to the Cosmic Mountain to the west, ruled by the "Queen Mother of the West." Even so, various inscriptions on stone steles from the 2nd century AD contrast the "body" of the dead person, composed of its two souls, with its "spirit," free in the sky. Although not uniform, the various theories do have in common the concept that the most spiritual portion of a human can exit the tomb to be present in the offering chamber or in the family temple during the celebration of sacrifices.

Terms
Purified soul (*hun*)
Corporeal soul (*po*)
Heavenly Gate
(*tianmen*)
Queen Mother
of the West
(*Xiwangmu*)
Body (*hunpo*)

Related entries
Ancestor worship,
The quest for
immortality, Tomb

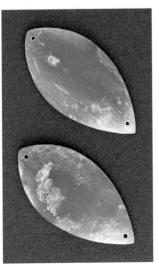

◀ Jade eye plaques, for plugging the orifices of the eyes, length 4.8 cm, Han dynasty, British Museum, London.

The urn's rich iconographic repertoire presents visions of the goods and pleasures that surround the soul of the dead in the afterlife, such as the palace at the top and the four vases surrounded by birds, indicating they are full of grain.

Some examples similar to this bear an inscription on this small stele, which helps to date the use of urns of the soul in the tombs of southern China in the brief period between the early 3rd century AD and the first decades of the 4th century AD.

During this period a type of hard stoneware was developed in the north of today's Zhejiang. Its glaze contained iron oxides that when fired in reducing atmospheres created an olive-green glaze known as celadon.

These urns, unopenable, were placed in tombs after the funeral and served the function of hosting the purified soul of the deceased, thus also protecting descendents from any possible malignant influences.

▲ Funerary urn (hunping), Western Jin dynasty, AD 280–316, glazed porcelaneous stoneware, 44 cm high, Fondazione Giovanni Agnelli, Turin.

Auspicious images from Chinese tradition, such as the turtle, symbolic of long life, alternate with figures inspired by Buddhism, which was spreading among the people of China during this period of disunion.

The incised date can refer to more than one year, for in the sexagesimal calendar of ancient China, the denominations of years were repeated cyclically. Even so, the work probably dates to the period when this foreign custom was in widespread use.

In all probability, this small urn, with its somewhat rough modeling and decoration, contains the ashes of a humble person.

Cremation, introduced and favored by Buddhism, was condemned by Confucian morality, which abhorred the destruction of the body, seen as a supreme act of filial irreverence.

Incised on the sides are the names of the figures symbolic of the cardinal points: the green dragon of the east, the red bird of the south, the white tiger of the west, and the dark warrior of the north.

▲ Urn for ashes, Song or Yuan dynasty, dated to 1206, 1266, or 1326, glazed stoneware, 28 cm high, Victoria and Albert Museum, London.

> "Moved, in a shared lamentation of grief, the many mouths together intone a chant. The fresh graves blend into the green of the grass. New tombs every day are put in order" (Bai Juyi)

Funeral rites

Terms
Rites (*li*)

Related entries
Ancestor worship,
Tomb, Virtual
companions

▼ The emperor's
funeral cart, Ming
dynasty, woodcut print
from the volume
Sanlitu, Chapter 19.

The rites accompanying death and burial were based on a host of customs and rules. Alongside Confucian precepts, which called for a period of mourning and a funeral ceremony in keeping with the rank of the deceased, was a great quantity of magical-religious customs intended to protect the deceased and family members from the potentially evil influences resulting from contact with death. The family members stayed awake during the passage from life to death, making offerings of food to and ritual invocations of the purified soul repeated three times after the death. The relatives then dressed in clothing of rough fabric and communicated the sad news to non-family members, in that way beginning the period of mourning. After the ceremonial cleansing there was the ritual dressing, which was accompanied by sacrifices and went on for several days. In the end the deceased was put in a coffin, closed with ceremonial knots. At times it was necessary to wait months before the right day for the funeral could be found, identified by specialists on the basis of information about the deceased and the relatives. The cortege departed the ancestral temple as musicians and exorcists drove off malignant spirits. Offerings and objects allotted to the deceased were carried directly in front of the coffin, followed by the family members, arranged in order of kinship. When they arrived at the sepulcher, the sacrificial rites were repeated several times before the coffin was positioned in its destined place.

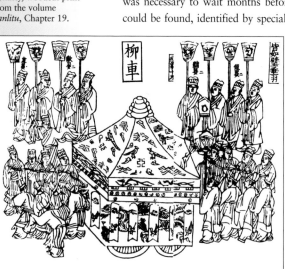

This diagram of one of the more enduring customs of ancient Chinese society is the earliest document on this theme that can be dated with certainty.

Collected under a large red canopy, nineteen squares are discernible, which originally must have been twenty-three, and which are based on numerological principles and tied to cosmological meanings.

There are written explanations of the diagram.

◀ Diagram of funeral rites, Western Han dynasty, circa 168 BC, from Tomb 3 at Mawangdui, Changsha, Hunan, ink and color on silk, 26.2 x 48.4 cm, Hunan Provincial Museum, Changsha.

The diagram presents in a schematic way the funeral rites and the practices of mourning, differentiated according to the rank of relationship with the deceased.

A funeral ceremony is being performed on the wings of a bird with white feathers, the color associated with death but also with immortality.

The ding *tripod is a ritual vessel from the Shang period (16th–11th centuries BC) made to hold food.*

Under a red umbrella held by a servant, two people face each other with arms crossed, identifiable thanks to their headdresses as princes or religious officials.

The anthropomorphic legs of the tripods emphasize the importance of the funeral ceremony, performed to assure the deceased a high rank in the social hierarchy of the afterlife.

▲ Model of a bird bearing two (*ding*) tripods, Western Han dynasty, from Wuyingshan, Shandong, terracotta, pigments, 53 cm high, Municipal Museum, Jinan.

"The state in which the dead find themselves remains hidden to us, they follow different routes from those of the living and . . . all is uncertain and indistinct to us, difficult to understand" (Wang Chong)

Afterlife

The continuity of kinship relationships after death had a profound influence on Chinese thinking about the afterlife, where the deceased was inserted in a hierarchy that did not differ at all from the hierarchy in force among the living. The distinction between a subterranean world, obscure and ruled by water, and a celestial world, a sort of paradise, led to differing concepts about the nature of the afterlife. The cult of immortality, which arose among aristocrats but then spread to all of the population, presented the possibility of continuing in some way to live on the earth or in the abode of the immortals. Echoes of this multitude of beliefs show up in the arrangement of tombs, in which the corporeal soul was provided with all the supplies of food and drink, objects of daily use, and models of figures and earthly goods that would help maintain social rank while also abiding comfortably in the subterranean world. Beginning in the 4th century BC, an inventory of these goods was provided to bring them to the attention of the bureaucracy of the afterlife. Decorations of cosmological significance, such as the ceilings of funeral chambers painted with heavenly bodies and constellations and mirrors with representations of the cardinal points or cyclical signs, put the deceased in harmony with the universe. Depictions of auspicious animals—dragons, deer, tigers, phoenixes—and certain divinities, such as the Queen Mother of the West, helped the deceased in the ascent to the celestial world.

Terms
Purified soul (*hun*)
Corporeal soul (*po*)
Queen Mother of the West (*Xiwangmu*)

Related entries
The quest for immortality, The two souls of the dead, Tomb

▼ Sarcophagus decorated with divinities and fantastic animals, Western Han dynasty, circa 168 BC, from Tomb 1 at Mawangdui, Hunan, painted wood lacquered in red inside and black outside, 114 x 256 x 118 cm, Hunan Provincial Museum, Changsha.

This standard, which was originally rolled around a bamboo staff, served in rites of evocations of the soul of the deceased and was perhaps carried in a procession during the funeral before being laid on the coffin.

The deceased, an elderly woman, is presented on this platform, protected by a canopy and framed by a winged animal and by the heads of the two dragons. Behind her are three women; kneeling in front of her are two men.

An atlantid supports the base, above which are evocations of the celebration of the sacrificial rites in honor of the deceased and reproductions of numerous tomb offerings.

Two guardians oversee access to the celestial world, which is dominated by the red sun with the black crow and by the sliver of moon with the frog and hare and is populated by dragons, birds, and hybrid divinities.

Two dragons weave through a green jade bi disc and rise from the underworld toward the celestial realm. The dragon, vehicle of divinities and immortals, also transported hun souls in their journey toward immortality.

▶ Painted standard, Western Han dynasty, circa 168 BC, from Tomb 1 at Mawangdui, Hunan, painted silk, 205 cm long, Hunan Provincial Museum, Changsha.

Two interwoven fish symbolize the underground world, cold and obscure.

Several coin trees have been found in tombs from western China dating to the period between the 1st and 3rd centuries AD.

In Chinese mythology the cosmic tree, symbol of fertility and eternal life, created the connection between the heavens and the earth; at the top lives the red bird of the south.

Fixed to the trunk are rings decorated with engraved waves and pierced plates decorated with mythological scenes; inserted in these are four levels of side branches, arranged at right angles.

The hope to achieve immortality is reflected in the decoration of the branches, from which hang typical Chinese coins, circular with square holes, that would perhaps provide the deceased with an easy life in the afterlife.

Dragon heads, elephants entering the gates of a city, and the King Father of the East (Dongwanggong) flanked by deer express the aspiration for immortality.

▲ Money tree, Eastern Han dynasty, 2nd–3rd century AD, partially gilt bronze and terracotta with traces of pigment, 139 cm high, Fondazione Giovanni Agnelli, Turin.

"Like a green ridge is the ancient tomb, deep is the palace like a purple terrace. . . . The soughing pines can be clearly heard, sounding like the wail of the people" (Wang Wei)

Tomb

Beginning in the period of the Warring States, a green tumulus indicated the presence of a tomb. The mausoleum of the first emperor, unusual in terms of size but traditional in its structure, was built in wood and hermetically sealed, but over the course of the Han period tombs appeared furnished with entry doors that stood at the end of Sacred Ways flanked by pairs of stone animals. Tombs with openings resulted from changes in funeral customs that later became generalized: spouses were buried in the same tomb, and funeral rites were celebrated inside the tomb. Tombs were divided into various sections, and over time preference was given to tombs laid out on the basis of an axial plan, in imitation of the homes of the living. Homes and palaces were built in timber; the need to construct solid structures led to a different choice in the building materials of tombs, with preference given to baked bricks or stone. The tombs of the imperial family of the Tang dynasty transmit a brilliant image of the period because their structures, arranged horizontally along a north-south axis, are embellished with wall paintings that depict the

▼ Sepulchral tumulus of the Qin Shi Huangdi, Qin dynasty at Liantong, Shaanxi.

surrounding landscape, including the parks at the heart of the imperial palace. The tombs of the Song rulers are less sumptuous, while the Ming emperors dissipated a large part of their public funds to erect their mausoleums, most of which were built above ground.

The pit of this funnel-shaped tomb, 16 meters deep and covered by a tumulus with a radius of 25–30 meters, is located on the north-south axis and is almost 20 meters long on the surface but only 7.60 meters long at the bottom.

From the end of the Neolithic period, a wooden structure called the outer coffin (guo) was built at the bottom of the vertical pits that constituted tombs.

The outer coffin became a symbol of rank during the Shang and Zhou periods, and it was divided into a central space reserved for the actual coffin, while side compartments contained burial goods.

The central space contained four coffins inserted one inside the next, with the last holding the corpse, laid on its back and dressed in about twenty articles of clothing held together by silk ribbons.

The outer coffin was protected by a layer of coal and white clay more than 1 meter thick, which for two thousand years safeguarded the contents from the penetration of oxygen and damp.

▲ Plan of Tomb 1 at Mawangdui at Changsha, Hunan, Western Han dynasty, circa 168 BC.

The tomb is part of a homogeneous group composed of three tombs that hold three descendents of Wu Zetian. The three royal children had fallen victim to the empress, but after her death they were rehabilitated and relocated to these tombs.

Eight niches line the access ramp (four on each side); these held terracotta figurines, while the funeral offerings and objects for the personal use of the prince were located in the coffin. The ramp was also fitted with several conduits for the aeration of the tomb.

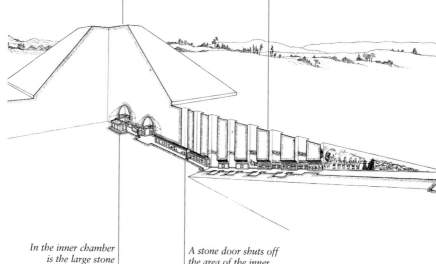

In the inner chamber is the large stone sarcophagus that held the remains of Prince Li Zhongrun, killed at only 19. The decorations engraved there and the wall scenes evoke life in the palace.

A stone door shuts off the area of the inner palace, which has a central corridor and which consists of the antechamber and the burial chamber.

▲ Tomb of Prince Li Zhongrun (also known as Prince Yi De), located in the area of Qianling, Xi'an, Shaanxi, Tang dynasty, AD 706.

The tombs of the three royal children who fell victim to Empress Wu Zetian are oriented along the north-south axis. At the top of the access ramp to Princess Li Yongtai's tomb, near the entrance, are painted the green dragon of the east and the white tiger of the west, preceded by several courtiers.

This view gives an idea of the size of this subterranean palace, which is almost 88 meters long.

Depicted on the walls of the access ramp are scenes of the entertainments and daily life of the noblewomen of the period, dressed in "Western-style" garments.

▲ View of the access ramp of the tomb of Princess Li Yongtai, located in the area of Qianling, Xi'an, Shaanxi, Tang dynasty, AD 706.

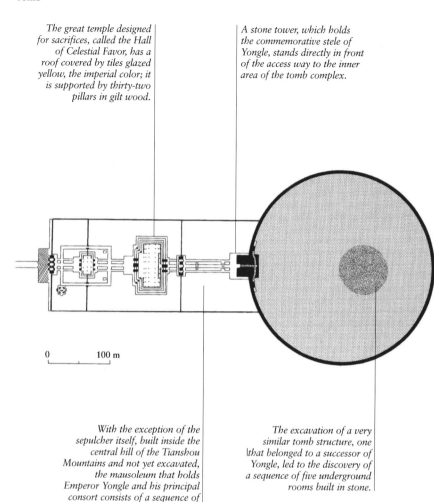

The great temple designed for sacrifices, called the Hall of Celestial Favor, has a roof covered by tiles glazed yellow, the imperial color; it is supported by thirty-two pillars in gilt wood.

A stone tower, which holds the commemorative stele of Yongle, stands directly in front of the access way to the inner area of the tomb complex.

0   100 m

With the exception of the sepulcher itself, built inside the central hill of the Tianshou Mountains and not yet excavated, the mausoleum that holds Emperor Yongle and his principal consort consists of a sequence of above-ground buildings.

The excavation of a very similar tomb structure, one that belonged to a successor of Yongle, led to the discovery of a sequence of five underground rooms built in stone.

▲ Plan of the tomb of Emperor Yongle, located at Changling near Beijing, Ming dynasty, 1409–1427.

About 50 kilometers northwest of Beijing is a group of mausoleums that held thirteen Ming-dynasty emperors.

Each of the tombs, connected by a wide Sacred Way flanked by larger-than-life marble statues, is located at the foot of a hill, which constitutes the natural tumulus in which the coffin is located.

This five-arched portal, nearly 30 meters high, leads to the main entrance to the sepulchral area.

▲ Marble portal located at the entrance to the complex of mausoleums of Ming emperors at Changling, near Beijing, 1540.

"The human statuettes and the representations of chargers are carved and decorated to seem alive, for the sole purpose of dazzling passersby" (Old Book of Tang)

Virtual companions

Terms
Objects of substitution
(*mingqi*)

Related entries
Qin Shi Huangdi,
Tomb, Afterlife,
Tomb guardians

▼ Three statuettes of literati, Ming dynasty, 1500–1600, stoneware with lead glaze, 21.6 cm maximum height, Victoria and Albert Museum, London.

The presence of both sacrificial victims and scale models in the first emperor's sepulchral complex may indicate that this was a transitional period during which "objects of substitution," which appeared in the 5th century BC, could perform certain generic functions of defense and service, but certain subjects who had close personal relationships with the ruler had to accompany him in the tomb. The majority of the figures—aside from seven thousand soldiers, the figures thus far extracted include officials, acrobats, and animals—demonstrate that the production of terracotta objects was organized on an industrial scale. During the Han period the use in tombs of objects of substitution expanded to the entire population, and in addition to the ranks of soldiers there were figures of servants, women, dancers, and eventually even more humble subjects, such as peasants, sties, and farmyard animals. During the Tang period a government office was created to supervise the production of funerary objects, but the severe limits it imposed on the number and size of the objects were often violated, and the tombs swarm with statuettes that reproduce every aspect of the daily life at the time. With the rebirth of Confucianism in the Song era, tombs were given simpler furnishings, with preference going to ceramics with classical or literary themes. All these figures became rare in the Ming epoch, when it became customary to burn paper models during the funeral service.

Naturalistic coloration initially accentuated the realism of the bird's shape, and some of the mineral pigments remained in the dirt that held the bird for more than two thousand years.

Dozens of water birds have been brought to light in recent years, all of them placed along a wooden embankment at the sides of a subterranean pit in the sepulchral area of the first emperor.

The heron has just caught something in its beak.

The deep impressions left by workers in the ground of the canal suggest that the setting was a water course or swamp populated by birds.

This hypothesis is given support by the historian Sima Qian, who tells of a subterranean reproduction of the great rivers of China, made in the vicinity of the mausoleum.

▲ Model of a heron, Qin dynasty, area of the tomb of the first emperor at Lintong, bronze with traces of pigment, circa 90 cm high, Museum of Qin Terracotta Warriors and Horses, Lintong.

Furnishing tombs with personal objects and figures created a welcoming and comfortable setting in which the corporeal soul of the deceased could continue to live in happiness.

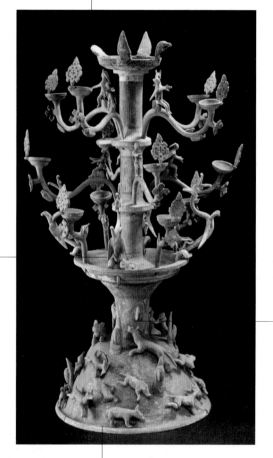

Made to illuminate a banquet, reproduced in ceramics in the antechamber of a tomb, this candle stand was placed beside a table set for a feast along with a group of musicians, comics, and acrobats.

The structure, which consists of a mountain-shaped base on which stands a majestic branched tree, and the decorative motifs, which evoke fantastic animals and immortals, put the scene of the banquet in a transcendent realm.

The objects of substitution, located in niches and antechambers, both of which would have been visited during the celebrations of certain rites, also served to demonstrate to society the filial piety of the descendents.

▲ Hundred-flower candle stand (*baihuadeng*), Eastern Han dynasty, 2nd century, from Jianxi Xilihe, Henan, terracotta, pigment, 92 cm high, Board in Charge of Cultural Relics, Luoyang.

"The exorcists wear bearskins, four gold eyes, clothes in dark colors and purple; they . . . exorcise by rushing through the homes eliminating the contamination" (Rites of Zhou)

Tomb guardians

Special attention was given protection of the deceased in his tomb, finding expression in multiple variants. The early sealed burials were protected by ranks of terracotta soldiers. Beginning in the Han period, the Sacred Way, flanked by stone animals and guardians, led the visitor to the entrance to the funeral park, symbolically closed by a pair of pillars that evoked the guard towers of the city, and thus to the feet of the central tumulus. Often depicted to the sides of the access ramp are the green dragon of the east and the white tiger of the west, which insert the tomb in the universal order. The entrance to the tomb is blocked by a stone door decorated in bas-relief with apotropaic motifs, among them the ancient "masks" with a ring in the mouth. The Han-period statues and wall paintings of exorcists were probably inspired by real exorcists, engaged to purify the location during the funeral rites using magical formulae and incense. Around the end of the 5th century, pairs of crouching beasts began appearing in the tombs of the Northern Wei, one with a human face, the other with leonine features. These beasts became a fundamental element in the tombs of the Tang period. Beginning at the end of the 7th century AD, they were joined by another pair of guardians with anthropomorphic appearances, related to Buddhist iconography.

Terms
Sacred Way (*shendao*)
Stone pillars of the city (*que*)
Masks (*pushou*)
Exorcists (*fangshi, fangxiangshi*)
Animal-face guardians (*zhenmushou*)
Human-face guardians (*zhenmuyong*)

Related entries
Exorcists and magicians, The animate world, Tomb, Virtual companions

◄Pair of tomb guardian creatures, Tang dynasty, first half 8th century AD, terracotta, pigments, 57 and 60 cm high, Museo di Arte Orientale, Turin.

The contorted features and threatening grimace denote the western origin of the figures, with their round eyes, long noses with dilated nostrils, and thick lips.

As late as the 6th century AD, figures of armed guards protected the entryways to the heart of tombs, but they were later replaced by the Heavenly Kings

The iconography of the Heavenly Kings was inspired by the "guardians of the four directions" (lokapala) from the Buddhist pantheon, which were located at the four sides of a sacred space to protect the faithful.

Each of the guardians treads upon an evil demon (raksas), also from the Buddhist world.

▲ Pair of statues of the Heavenly Kings (*Tianwang*), Tang dynasty, first half 8th century, terracotta with "three-color" (*sancai*) glaze, slip decoration, pigment, Museo di Arte Orientale, Turin.

The Sacred Way (shendao), which leads to the "Dragon-Phoenix Gate," the main entrance to the complex of the imperial mausoleums of the Ming, is flanked by twelve pairs of animals and six pairs of anthropomorphic statues.

Anthropomorphic guardian statues are called wengzhong in Chinese after the name of a valiant soldier in the Qin army whom the first emperor had immortalized in stone after his death.

The statue was carved from a single block of marble.

Two pairs of statues with human features depict civilian officials, another two impersonate military functionaries, and the third group is carved in honor of courtiers with meritorious records.

▲ Statue of guardian, Ming dynasty, 1435, white marble, circa 200 cm high, complex of the mausoleums of the Ming emperors, Beijing.

Capitals

Xianyang
Chang'an (Western Han)
Luoyang
Chang'an (Tang)
Kaifeng
Hangzhou
Nanjing (Nanking)
Beijing (Peking)

◄Formerly attributed to Zhao Boju, *Entry of Emperor Gaozu of Han into Guanzhong* (detail), Southern Song dynasty, 12th century, ink and color on silk, 29.7 x 312.8 cm, Museum of Fine Arts, Boston, William Amory Gardner Fund and Annie Anderson Hough Fund.

"Every time Qin conquered one of the feudal states, copies were made of the palaces and the pavilions and these were reconstructed to the north of Xianyang, facing south toward the Wei River" (Sima Qian)

Xianyang

▼ Hollow brick, Qin dynasty, mold-decorated terracotta, Municipal Museum, Xianyang.

Capital of the Qin kingdom beginning in 350 BC, Xianyang was revolutionized by the first emperor in keeping with his new policy of unity and centralization: according to the *Records of the Grand Historian*, a series of palaces was built to the north of the Wei River in the styles of the residences of the conquered kingdoms. Archaeological finds—the unearthed fragments of tiles in various styles—would seem to confirm this. The same literary source says that 120,000 patrician families from all over the empire had been obliged to settle in the part of the city south of the river. This information, together with the description of secret passageways that connected the palaces, making it possible for the first emperor to conceal his movements, will in all probability remain without archaeological confirmation. In fact, all that remains of the building complexes are various platforms in beaten earth bearing the impression of wooden structures, along with a few accessory items. On the basis of this information the outlines of two palaces have been reconstructed. Divided into various units, they were built on terraces of beaten earth and connected with a complex system of galleries, porticoes, and halls, paved with river stones or hollow bricks. The walls were plastered and whitewashed or painted with murals, the wooden beams decorated with bronze ornaments, the roofs covered with tiles with relief-decorated antefixes.

N

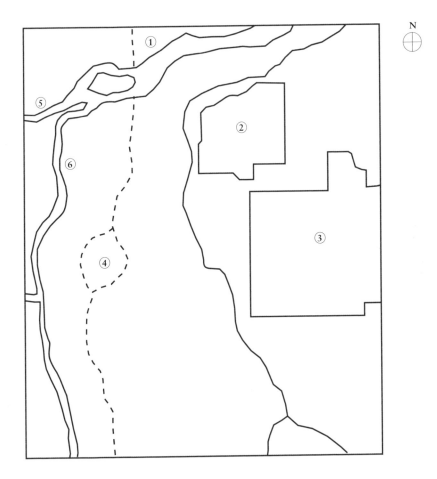

▲ Plan of the three cities located near today's Xi'an, in Shaanxi.

Legend

1. Xianyang, capital of the Qin dynasty (221–206 BC)
2. Chang'an, capital of the Western Han (206 BC–AD 8)
3. Chang'an, capital of the Tang (AD 618–907)
4. Lake Kumming (partially restored)
5. Wei River
6. Feng River

All that remains of the immense palace of Xianyang is this large platform 60 meters long and 45 wide, that served as the podium for the wooden structure of the palace.

Visible at the sides of the podium are the well-compacted layers of earth that were raised more than two thousand years ago and that are being reduced by natural erosion as well as agricultural activity.

The elevation shows an oblong palace composed of two symmetrical wings over a canal.

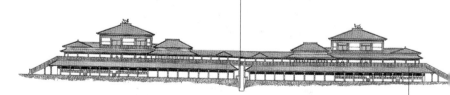

The construction method, with large raised bases and palaces built with frameworks of wooden columns and beams, was to become characteristic of the architecture of ancient China.

▲ Remains of the platform of the palace of Xianyang and elevation of its reconstruction.

"I extended my power through the entire universe, and I return to my natal land. And now, how to find the heroes that will stand watch on all my frontiers?" (Gaozu)

Chang'an (Western Han)

Gaozu, the first emperor of the Western Han dynasty, established his capital to the southeast of Xianyang and began populating it in 198 BC by way of decrees that obliged every inhabitant within a range of 600 *li* to move there. A circle of walls in compact earth, destined to enclose an area of about 36 square kilometers, was raised between 194 and 190 BC. The five complexes of palaces, which at the time of Wudi occupied two-thirds of the area within the walls, were in part residential, in part reserved for public offices, and were constructed in the Qin architectural tradition. The residential areas and markets were located in the northwestern part of the city and were separated from one another by streets and walls with guarded gates that were closed at night. Broad three-lane avenues, with the center lane reserved for the emperor, ran through the twelve city gates, each of which had three openings 6 meters wide; the avenues divided the city into irregular rectangles. Outside the walls to the west was the immense Shanglin Park, a place of amusements and also the hunting reserve of Emperor Wudi. Literary sources tell of a pond with four artificial islands that were created in the park in imitation of the paradise of the Queen Mother of the West, and of a tower of great height that made it possible to enter into contact with the immortals.

Periods as capital
Western Zhou
(11th century BC–771 BC), named Hao

Western Han
(206 BC–AD 8)

Wang Mang
(AD 9–24)

Western Wei
(AD 535–556)

Northern Zhou
(AD 557–581)

Sui
(from AD 587 to 617), named Daxing

Tang
(AD 618–907)

Terms
Ancient measure of distance (about half a kilometer) (*li*)

Related entries
Wudi, The quest for immortality, Chang'an (Tang)

◀ Statuettes of two men, Western Han dynasty, 2nd century BC, from the tomb of Emperor Jingdi, Yangling, Shaanxi, terracotta, slip decoration, pigments, impressions of wood and fabric, 57 and 58 cm high, Archaeological Museum, Yangling.

319

China's traditional historiography glorifies the Han dynasty, which laid the ideological foundation for the supremacy of Confucianism, destined to endure more than two thousand years.

The first Han emperor, known by his family name, Liu Bang, or by his posthumous title, Gaozu, was of peasant origin.

▲ Formerly attributed to Zhao Boju, *Entry of Emperor Gaozu of Han into Guanzhong* (detail), Southern Song dynasty, 12th century, ink and color on silk, 29.7 x 312.8 cm, Museum of Fine Arts, Boston, William Amory Gardner Fund and Annie Anderson Hough Fund.

The location of the Weiyang Palace, founded by Gaozu and amplified by Wudi such that it numbered forty buildings connected by open galleries, was determined by its relationship to the position of the polestar.

This celebrative painting represents Chang'an as a large fortified city; in reality, it was Gaozu who besieged the capital, in the area of the ancient residence of the Qin.

Tradition gave symbolic meaning to various urban elements, thus attributing to the Han dynasty a fundamental role within the cosmic order.

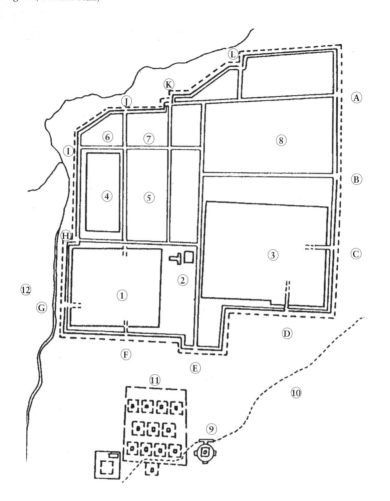

N

Legend

A–L: The twelve gates in the
city wall (194–190 BC)
1. Weiyang Palace (reign of
Gaozu, 206–195 BC)
2. Arsenal
3. Ch'angle Palace (reign of
Gaozu, 206–195 BC)
4. Gui Palace (reign of
Wudi, 141–87 BC)
5. Palace of the North
(reign of Wudi, 141–87 BC)
6. Western Market (reign of
Gaozu, 206–195 BC)

7. Eastern Market (reign of
Gaozu, 206–195 BC)
8. Mingguang Palace (reign
of Wudi, 141–87 BC)
9. Mingtang and Biyong
temples (AD 4)
10. Canal
11. Cultural complex (reign
of Wang Mang, AD 9–24)
12. Jianzhang Palace (reign of
Wudi, 141–87 BC)

▲ Plan of the city of
Chang'an in the Han epoch.

"I climb to the crest of Mount Bei Mang and look down on the city of Luoyang" (Cao Zhi)

Luoyang

From AD 9 to 24, Han rule was interrupted by Wang Mang, a Confucian politician who founded his own dynasty and sought in vain to introduce drastic reforms in favor of small property owners. In AD 25, a descendent of the imperial family succeeded in reestablishing the dynasty and moved the capital to Luoyang, a historical metropolis and prestigious capital of the Eastern Zhou. Although small in size in the 1st century AD, Luoyang already had twice the population of Chang'an, about 500,000. Located at the foot of Mount Mang, the capital was protected to the south by the Luo River and, like all the cities of ancient China, was surrounded by walls. Its plan formed an irregular rectangle, divided by large avenues arranged in a grid pattern. Two large palace complexes, one in the northern part and the other in the southern, dominated the city. Inside the walls were numerous gardens and parks, while several markets had been moved outside. In AD 68, the first Buddhist temple in China, the "monastery of the White Horse," was erected at Luoyang, destined to be rebuilt several times. Luoyang was destroyed before the end of the Eastern Han dynasty, only to rise to renewed glory beginning in 493 with the foreign dynasty of the Northern Wei, who moved their capital from Datong, on the northern border, to Luoyang in the heart of Chinese civilization, opening the door to Buddhism.

Periods as capital
Eastern Zhou
(770–221 BC),
named Luoyi

Eastern Han
(AD 25–220)

Wei
(AD 220–265)

Western Jin
(AD 265–316)

Northern Wei
(from AD 493 to 534)

Later Tang
(AD 923–936)

Terms
Monastery of the
White Horse
(Baima si)

Related entries
Foreign dynasties,
Chang'an
(Western Han),
Longmen

◀ Bas-relief with city gate, Eastern Han dynasty, district of Dayi, Sichuan, brick with molded decoration, 38 x 44 cm, Sichuan Provincial Museum, Chengdu.

323

Calamities of disastrous proportion—the gravest being the flooding of the Yellow River in AD 11, which brought five central-northern provinces to their knees—led to an insurrection against the usurper Wang Mang, who was killed in AD 24.

The strategic choice of Luoyang was based in part on the prestige of the ancient capital of the Eastern Zhou and in part on the need to find an alternative to the devastated Chang'an.

The change in course of the Yellow River following the flooding, along with incursions of nomadic peoples to the north, unleashed the first great wave of migration to the southern provinces, previously sparsely populated.

Proclaimed emperor in AD 25 by his relatives in the imperial clan, Liu Xiu, with the posthumous title Guangwu, spent eleven years bringing an end to the civil war and then established himself in the new capital at Luoyang.

▶ Qiu Ying, The Emperor Guangwu Fording a River, Ming dynasty, vertical scroll, 170.8 x 65.4 cm, ink and color on silk, National Gallery of Canada, Ottawa.

The policies of the Eastern Han were characterized by liberal rule in terms of the economy, with the growing autonomy of the large families, while the central power gradually ended up in the hands of the eunuchs.

Inside the walls lived peasants and their children, a private militia, servants, and slaves, all of whom tended the fields, took care of the animals, made tools and objects for their own use, and participated in commerce, all within a sphere of economic self-sufficiency.

The fertile lands of the large landowners were surrounded by guard towers and walls.

▲ Model of a tower, Eastern Han dynasty, 2nd century AD, from Mazuocun, Henan, terracotta, pigments, 148 cm high, Henan Provincial Museum, Zhengzhou.

Architectural models—guard towers, granaries, wells, sties, and so on—were part of the tomb furnishings of the landowners of the Eastern Han dynasty and provide precious information on the rural architecture of the period.

Chinese tradition looks upon the Han dynasty as the true beginning of the ancient empire and is thus the subject of constant reference. Even today, indigenous Chinese refer to themselves as "Han."

On a terrace overlooking the water, a member of the imperial family, protected by a small canopy, is enjoying the view of the distant landscape.

The banquets, ceremonies, and palaces of the Han became popular subjects for paintings in the Song dynasty.

▲ Li Rongjin, *Han Palace*, Yuan dynasty, mid-14th century, vertical scroll, ink on silk, 156.6 x 108.7 cm, National Palace Museum, Taipei.

Using only black ink, the painter has depicted a palace complex that rises along the rocky coastline in a series of courtyards, terraces, landscapes, and pavilions.

*"Long yearning to be in Chang'an. The grasshoppers weave
their autumn song by the golden railing of the well" (Li Bai)*

Chang'an (Tang)

A large-scale urban project was undertaken and completed under the brief Sui dynasty; it was then integrated with an efficient and tolerant administration under the next dynasty, the Tang. The new capital, located a short distance from the Chang'an of the Western Han, became the economic, cultural, and religious center of the entire ancient world, famous for its splendor and cosmopolitanism. The urban area of 84 square kilometers was symmetrically divided along a median axis that ran across the city from south to north, terminating in front of the tripartite complex of the imperial palace, the only building to lie along the axis. The imperial quarter, seat of ministries and administrative offices, was located to the south of the imperial palace. The image of Chang'an was dominated by the wall that surrounded the city, the imperial palace, the 108 residential neighborhoods, and the large tree-lined avenues that were flanked by open-air water canals crossed at each intersection by a small bridge. Each neighborhood was a small, self-sufficient community, with private homes, stores, wells of potable water, and at least one Buddhist or Daoist temple. Two large markets offered merchandise of every kind under the supervision of a state officer. Several canals provided water to embellish and irrigate the gardens and parks and to transport goods through the entire city.

Periods as capital
Western Zhou
(11th century BC–771 BC), named Hao

Western Han
(206 BC–AD 8)

Wang Mang
(AD 9–24)

Western Wei
(AD 535–556)

Northern Zhou
(AD 557–581)

Sui
(from AD 587 to 617),
named Daxing

Tang (AD 618–907)

Terms
Central imperial
palace (*taiji*)
Quarter (*fang*)

Related entries
Taizong, Xuanzang,
Wu Zetian, Li Bai,
Foreigners at the
imperial court,
Commerce,
Transportation,
Virtual companions,
Tomb guardians

◄ Pair of door handles in
the shape of masks
(*pushou*), Tang dynasty,
7th century AD, from the
ruins of the Daming Palace,
Xi'an, Shaanxi, gilt bronze,
26.4 cm diam., Collection
of Board in Charge of
Cultural Relics, Xi'an.

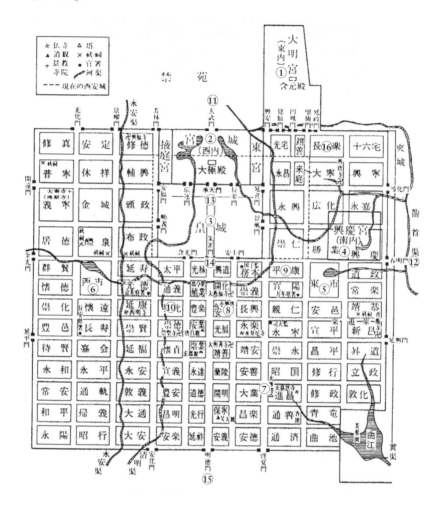

Legend

1. *Daminggong* ("palace of great light"): erected in AD 634, the complex was the residence of the emperor after considerable enlargement, begun in the 660s.

2. *Gongcheng* ("city of the palace"): imperial residence until the reign of Gaozong (649–683).

3. *Huangcheng* ("imperial city"): headquarters of administrative offices.

4. *Xingqinggong* ("palace of Xingqing"): another imperial palace instituted by Xuanzong (reigned 712–756).

5. *Dongshi* ("eastern market"): commerce in luxury goods.

6. *Xishi* ("western market"): similar to a bazaar, visited primarily by foreigners.

7. *Dayanta* ("Big Goose Pagoda").

8. *Xiaoyanta* ("Small Goose Pagoda").

9. *Pingkang fang:* amusement quarter.

10. *Xinghua fang* ("Xinghua quarter").

11–15. The city gates identified with certainty.

16. *Ch'angle fang* ("Ch'angle quarter").

This statue was found together with another very similar statue, but without weapons, that portrays the hunter, perhaps the dead general himself, a high official who in critical situations showed his faith to the emperor Xuanzang (reigned AD 712–756).

Funerary statues in marble are very rare, that material being used primarily for Buddhist sculptural art.

The servant bears two complete sets of hunting weapons: hanging from his belt on one side are his bow and a sword with a curved blade, similar to a Persian scimitar; on the other side is his quiver. On his back and in his arms, he holds the weapons of his master.

◄ Map of the city of Chang'an in the Tang epoch.

▲ Statuette of a servant, Tang dynasty, circa AD 740, from the tomb of General Yang Sixu at Dengjiapocun, Xi'an, Shaanxi, white marble, traces of pigments and gold leaf, 40.3 cm high, Museum of Chinese History, Beijing.

In 1970, in the basement of a home in Hejiacun, a small town in the suburbs of what is now Xi'an, a hoard of a thousand precious objects was discovered hidden in two large earthenware vases.

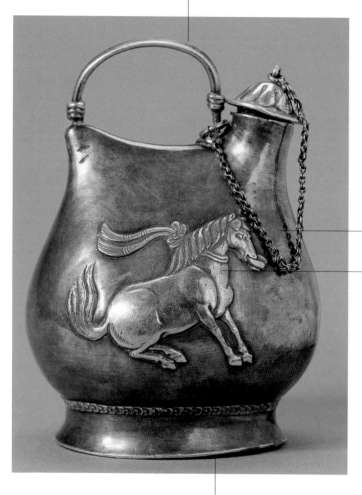

The shape of the flask repeats the shape of those made of sewn leather that were in widespread use among nomadic peoples and among pilgrims traveling to the "Western Regions."

The horse, embossed and gilt, seems to be suddenly stopping. Its striking pose and the cup in its mouth suggest that this is of one of the famous "dancing horses" trained to entertain at court.

▲ Wine flask in the shape of a canteen, Tang dynasty, 7th– first half 8th century AD, from Hejiacun, Xi'an, Shaanxi, partially gilt silver, 18.5 cm high, Shaanxi History Museum, Xi'an.

The hoard included coins of Sassanid, Persian, Japanese, and Chinese provenance that make it possible to date the hoard to the period of the An Lushan rebellion in the 750s.

"South and north of the bridge runs the main thoroughfare where old folks await His Majesty year after year" (Fan Chengda)

Kaifeng

Located along the Grand Canal near important coal and iron mines, Kaifeng, the "eastern capital" of the Northern Song dynasty, was a modern commercial center as well as headquarters of the central administration. The center of the city was dominated by the imperial quarter, with the home of the ruling family, government offices and ministries, and the painting academy. City walls around individual neighborhoods having been abolished, houses and stores faced one another along the streets, which were crowded day and night. Instead of the horizontal rows of homes broken up by courtyards and gardens of the past, the city now had multistoried buildings with fine decorative details and enclosed gardens with wide views. A corps of well-equipped firefighters and the wide central avenues reduced the danger of spreading fires always connected with timber structures. In China, bridges and pagodas had always been the only architectural structures to be made of stone or baked brick, and two pagodas from Song-era Kaifeng survive today: the hexagonal Po Ta, three of the original nine stories of which have been preserved, and the so-called Iron Pagoda, which reaches the height of 55 meters, divided into thirteen floors. The temple of the Jewish community, documented as early as the Song, was composed of several single-story wooden buildings, in keeping with Chinese tradition. It was destroyed in the mid-19th century.

Periods as capital
Five Dynasties
(907–960):
capital of the Later
Liang, the Later Jin,
the Later Han, and the
Later Zhou, named
Bian or Bianliang

Northern Song
(960–1127), named
Bianliang

Terms
Eastern capital
(*dongjing*)
Iron Pagoda (*tieta*)

Related entries
Huizong, Su Shi, Zhu
Xi, Minor religions,
Architecture

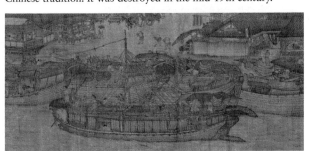

◀Zhang Zeduan,
*Going Up the River on
Qingming Day* (detail),
Northern Song dynasty,
early 12th century,
horizontal handscroll,
ink and color on silk,
25 x 528 cm, Palace
Museum, Beijing.

Zhang Zeduan, member of the Hanlin Academy during the rule of Huizong, created this splendid panorama of life in the Northern Song capital shortly before it fell to the Jin in 1127.

Handscrolls, which could extend several meters in length, were read from right to left: the user unrolled the painting with one hand while rolling it up with the other, enjoying the succession of scenes like frames of a film.

The sudden conclusion of the scroll, which ends just inside the city walls, has made scholars think it may be incomplete. Ming-period copies continue the scenes to arrive at the imperial palace, reinforcing this hypothesis.

This detail, which is part of the final scenes of the handscroll, depicts one of the city gates: a caravan of laden camels is setting off toward the distant desert zones of the northwest.

▲ Zhang Zeduan, *Going Up the River on Qingming Day* (detail): city gate.

Emperor Huizong, a great promoter of the arts, favored certain styles and subjects, preferring and thus commissioning scenes based on real life, rather than on the images of ancient paintings.

The streets leading to the city are lined with teahouses and shops. Such commercial enterprises are open to the view of the spectator, but the painter never penetrates into the private sphere of homes.

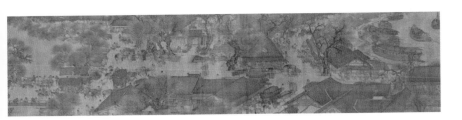

▲ Zhang Zeduan, *Going Up the River on Qingming Day* (detail): stores and teahouses.

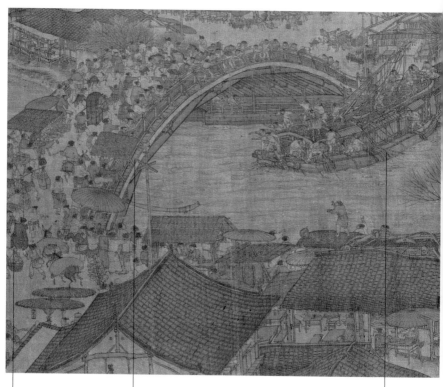

The city is crowded, but only men are visible, although they belong to every social level; women, living in seclusion inside their homes, were not part of public life.

On the occasion of the festival, a day of remembrance of the dead, numerous stands have been set up along the bridge offering food and trinkets.

The strong current of the Grand Canal is pulling a boat toward the shore as the boatmen, encouraged by yells from the crowd of idlers along the bridge, endeavor to fit the boat under the bridge so it can pass through.

▲ Zhang Zeduan, *Going Up the River on Qingming Day* (detail): bridge.

The boatmen usually lived on their boats with their families, a custom abandoned only in the last decades of the 20th century, under government pressure.

A boat was the fastest and most economical means of transportation for getting into the city. These wide, flat boats were designed for short-distance river transportation.

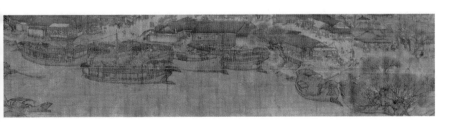

▲ Zhang Zeduan, *Going Up the River on Qingming Day* (detail): boat.

The first fields appear, along with the low huts of the capital's suburbs.

As the viewer slowly approaches the city, the countryside grows more populous; the first inns appear among the fields, along with peasants and their laden horses bearing goods to Kaifeng.

Here, at the beginning of the handscroll, the sun is rising, while toward the end the scenes are set in the late afternoon. Chinese painting does not take into account light and shadow, so the hours of the day are only deducible from the activities of the people: in the morning they are busy at their various occupations, while in the afternoon they have time to be idle.

The scroll begins with the depiction of the swampy and empty landscape that then existed around the ancient capital.

▲ Zhang Zeduan, *Going Up the River on Qingming Day* (detail): the countryside.

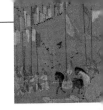

"If my position as governor lasts five years with you, I will spread my [fur coat] open to cover all the people of Hangzhou"
(Bai Juyi)

Hangzhou

In AD 1127, Kaifeng was taken by Jurchen nomads in the course of extending the territory of the Jin dynasty across all of northern China. A descendent of the imperial family took refuge first in Nanjing and then, in 1138, moved to what became the new capital of "temporary safety" of the Southern Song, Hangzhou. A city of limited size, it was by no means in keeping with the classical rules of urbanization. Set between the Zhe River and the "West Lake"—a famous body of water 5.6 square kilometers wide but not even two meters deep, created during the Tang dynasty by excavating and embanking the water from various streams—the city was crossed by a thick network of canals flanked by railings. The canals were cleaned once a year, while a daily service took care of the collection of excrement, used as fertilizer in the fields. The houses had two or three floors, the streets were narrow, and the city was packed with teahouses, restaurants, and bordellos arisen in response to the area's intense mercantile activity. Following repeated fires, watchtowers were erected in every neighborhood and an efficient and rapid fire brigade was organized. Given the paucity of free space inside the walls, several markets were located outside them. In 1148 the first emperor of the dynasty had the walls to the south enlarged and in that area built a complex of palaces and gardens that was ten times larger than the imperial palace of Kaifeng.

Periods as capital
Wuyue (907–978)

Southern Song
(from 1138 to 1279),
named Lin'an

Term
West Lake (*Xihu*)

Related entries
Huizong, Kublai Khan,
Foreign dynasties,
Technology and
industries, Commerce

▼ Plate in the shape of
a mallow flower (see
page 338), bottom
with inscription,
Southern Song dynasty,
glazed porcelaneous
stoneware, border
17.3 cm diam.,
Palace Museum,
Beijing.

The plate is an example of guan *ware* ("official ware") produced at one of the two kilns set up at Hangzhou following the relocation of the imperial court to the south.

Such "official" ceramics were made for the exclusive use of the court and government officials.

Although similar to the ru ceramics produced under the patronage of the Northern Song emperor Huizong, guan *ware has a thicker glaze because it was applied in several layers before firing.*

Beginning in the first half of the 15th century, the practice spread of applying a mark to the bottom of ceramics that indicated in four or six characters the name of the dynasty and the current reign (see page 337).

From the foundation of the empire it was customary to mark certain ceramics with the name of the workshop or the artisan as a means to facilitate administrative control.

▲ Plate in the shape of a mallow flower, Southern Song dynasty, glazed porcellaneous stoneware, border 17.3 cm diam., Palace Museum, Beijing.

N

0 1 2
km

◼︎ Gates

══ Principal canals

▲ Temples and monasteries

▲ Map of Hangzhou during
the Southern Song dynasty.

Legend

1. Imperial palace
2. Central avenue
3. Baidi Causeway
4. Commercial quarter
5. Inner city wall
6. Outer city wall
7. West Lake
8. Zhe River

Yue Fei (1103–1142), of humble origins, was commander of the Song troops after the flight of the court to Hangzhou and the revival of the dynasty under the ninth son of Emperor Huizong.

A brilliant strategist and valiant solider, Yue Fei succeeded in freeing large areas of central China from the control of the foreign Jurchen invaders, who had founded the Jin dynasty. When the emperor made a secret peace agreement with the Jurchen, the general was called back.

In 1163 two tombs were built, later integrated with a large temple complex that was restructured and enlarged several times after Yue Fei became emblematic of patriotic resistance to the foreign invaders.

Falsely accused of having plotted against the emperor, Yue Fei was secretly killed together with his young son, but only twenty years after his death he was rehabilitated.

▲ Temple dedicated to General
Yue Fei at Hangzhou, founded
during the Southern Song dynasty.

West Lake is crossed by two causeways, the Bai Causeway, named for the poet Bai Juyi (AD 772–846), who promoted construction of a tree-lined barrier in the year he was governor of Hangzhou (around AD 821), and the longer Su Causeway, named for the poet Su Shi (1037–1101).

West Lake not has been paved over, as has occurred with numerous other artificial lakes built inside the large parks of imperial palaces. On the contrary, it has become emblematic of the city.

From the lake emerge four small islands created during the Song and Ming dynasties and site of splendid aquatic parks, pavilions, and recreational spots.

▲ West Lake (Xihu) at Hangzhou, Ming dynasty, end 14th–early 15th century, album page, Cleveland Museum of Art.

"Flowerless trees in the uncertain spring; from where does the breeze bring this perfume? Ah, next-door neighbor is brewing afternoon tea!" (Gao Qi)

Nanjing (Nanking)

Periods as capital
Capital of all the ephemeral southern dynasties that arose following the collapse of the Han dynasty (Wu, 222–280; Eastern Jin, 317–420; Song, 420–479; Southern Qi, 479–502; Liang, 502–557; Chen, 557–589), named Jianye or Jiankang

Southern Tang (937–975), named Jinling

Southern Song (from 1138 to 1279), named Jinling

Ming (from 1369 to 1402), named Yingtian, then Nanjing

Terms
Black Dragon Lake (*Xuanwu hu*)
Lion Hill (*Shi Shan*)

Related entries
Hongwu, Yongle, Foreign dynasties

▶ The Sacred Way (*shendao*) that leads to the tomb of Emperor Hongwu at Nanjing, Ming dynasty, 14th century.

During the period of disunity that followed the collapse of the Eastern Han in AD 220, Nanjing claimed to be the home of authentic Chinese culture in contrast to the foreign cultures that dominated the north. For this very reason the city was razed to the ground in AD 589 by the new unifying force of the Sui, who restored cultural and political authority to central-northern China. Nanjing flourished again under the Tang, rising again as a capital city under the local dynasty of the Southern Tang. The architectural structures built by this brief dynasty have proven enduring: the imperial palace became the headquarters of administrative offices during the later Song and Yuan dynasties, and more than 400 years later the southern part of the city walls served as a base for the walls built by the first Ming emperor, Hongwu. Even before coming into total control of the imperial throne, Hongwu began construction work on a new imperial city, located to the east of the earlier city, with its layout based on that of the Forbidden City in Beijing. For strategic reasons the walls were enlarged to enclose the Lion Hill to the northwest, while Black Dragon Lake, an area where the imperial family had a retreat, was excluded. The northern banks of the lake hosted various government offices, and the fiscal censuses were filed on one of the islands.

The gate consisted of three massive stone constructions that could hold up to three thousand soldiers.

After the transfer of the capital to Beijing in 1407, Nanjing remained important as a site of commercial exchanges and industrial production, and also as a cultural center, since it was still the home of a branch of the imperial academy.

Nanjing was razed to the ground in 1864 during the repression of the Taiping Rebellion, whose leaders had chosen the city as the capital of their revolutionary government and named it Tianjing ("Heavenly Capital").

▲ The old city walls, southern gate (*Zhonghua Men*), Ming dynasty, 14th century.

"This city is built in the form of a square, with all its sides of equal length, and a total circumference of twenty-four miles. It is enclosed by earthen ramparts, twenty paces high and ten paces thick" (Marco Polo)

Beijing (Peking)

Located on the periphery of ancient Chinese civilization, Beijing served as the stronghold for the various foreign powers that occupied northern China in the 10th–12th centuries: the Liao dynasty made the city its southern capital, the most influential among the kingdom's five capitals. The later foreign Jin dynasty set in motion a vast building effort, reconstructing the city in the image of the capital of Kaifeng, the capital of the Northern Song. In 1215 the Mongols razed the city, but fifty-two years later Kublai Khan decided to rebuild it as his new capital. To the northeast of the old center, a rectangular space was laid out with a circumference of 28.6 kilometers that marked off the boundaries of the outer city. The imperial city was enclosed in the central-southern sector of the checkerboard layout; it in turn enclosed the complex of imperial palaces ("The Great Within"). The first Ming emperor, Hongwu, put the seat of his government at Nanjing, but his son Yongle had his splendid capital made at Beijing. The walls on the northern side were moved to the south so that the Forbidden City would be located at the exact center of the city's expanse. The layout of the new Beijing represented the culmination of traditional Chinese city design, based in part on the arrangement given the city by the Mongols, in part on the structure of the imperial palace at Kaifeng and then at Nanjing, and in part on notions derived from the classical science of geomancy.

▶ Signal tower in front of the "Gate of Moral Victory," Ming dynasty, 1439.

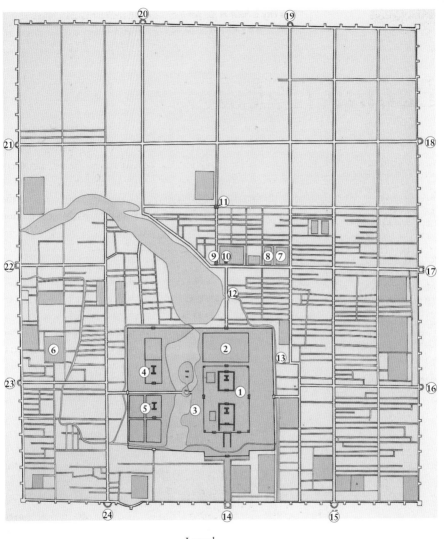

Legend

1. Palace complex
   (*Daming dian*)
2. Imperial garden
3. Imperial City
4. Palace of the Rising
   Monarch
5. Palace of Prosperity
6. Altar of the Land and
   Grain

7. Confucian Temple
8. Imperial College
9. Drum Tower
10. Central Tower
11. Bell Tower
12. Bridge of Peace
13. Tonghui River
14–24. Gates in the city walls

▲ Plan of Dadu (Beijing) during
the Yuan dynasty.

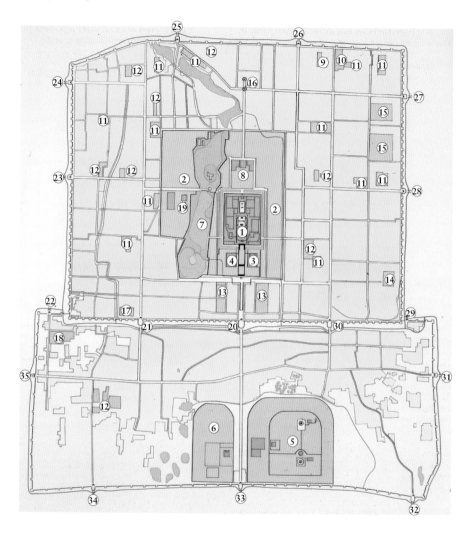

Legend

1. Forbidden City
2. Imperial City
3. Ancestral temple
4. Altar of Land and Grain
5. Temple of Heaven
6. Altar of the God of Agriculture
7. Central Lake (created under the Jin, 1127–1234) and Southern Lake (first Ming period)
8. Prospect Hill
9. Imperial College
10. Lama Temple, called Palace of Peace and Harmony (*Yonghegong*), erected in 1735
11. Residences of the princes of the imperial family
12. Temples
13. Government offices
14. Metropolitan examination hall
15. Warehouses
16. Bell and Drum towers
17. Elephant House
18. Barracks
19. Church
20–35. City gates

The Forbidden City was divided in two parts, the Outer Court (Waichao), site of the emperor's contacts with the external world, and the Inner Court (Neiting), where the imperial family lived together with the women of the court and the eunuchs.

Thick layers of cloud make it possible to discern the physical structures of the Forbidden City without, however, revealing anything of the areas belonging to the private life of the imperial family.

In the area called "The Hall for Paying Tribute to Heaven" (Feng Tian), built in 1420, the emperor, seated on his dragon throne, held audiences and received the highest state officials.

The clouds also indicate the celestial sphere that surrounds the emperor.

◀ Map of the city of Beijing during the Ming and Qing dynasties.

▲ Zhu Bang, *Portrait of an Official in Front of the Forbidden City*, Ming dynasty, 16th century, hanging scroll, ink and color on silk, 169 x 109 cm, British Museum, London.

The axis of the city extended outside the area of the Forbidden City to terminate in the north at the Bell Tower, the ringing of which awakened the inhabitants in the morning, and with the Drum Tower, the sound of which signaled the hours of the closing of the gates.

▲ Panoramic view of the Forbidden City.

Today's Beijing has little in common with the ancient capital, and the Forbidden City is the only large complex that has escaped the destruction of the various revolutions as well as modern progress.

The structure of the Forbidden City reflects the cosmic order: the constructions are arranged on a central axis that goes from the entry gate (Wumen) across the entire complex.

At the center of the world stands the Forbidden City, surrounded by a moat of water and by its red walls, the color of the polestar.

Buddhist cave temples

◄Ceiling of Cave 390 (detail),
Mogao, Dunhuang, Gansu,
Sui dynasty.

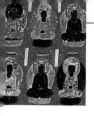

"The emperor [Ming of the Eastern Han] sent envoys to the Western Regions in search of the god [Buddha] and . . . acquired Buddhist scriptures and images" (Yang Xuanzhi)

Images of the Buddha

Terms
Western Regions
(*Xiyu*)

Related entries
Xuanzang, Foreign
dynasties, Buddhism,
Commerce

Dreams of a giant man with an aureole of flames around his head drove the emperor Ming (reigned AD 58–75) of the Eastern Han dynasty to introduce Buddhist writings and images from the "Western Regions" and from India. These were preserved at Luoyang in the first Buddhist temple on Chinese soil. Without doubt, Chinese authorities had news of the new religion during the reign of this ruler, who succeeded in briefly extending Chinese control up to the important oasis cities around the basin of the Tarim River. The spread of Buddhism was facilitated by the decline of central power in China, which favored the expansion of the Kushan empire from today's Afghanistan up to China's distant former colonies, beginning in the second half of the 2nd century AD. The first anthropomorphic depictions of the Buddha had been created at Kushan, influenced by the Hellenistic figurative tradition. Missionary activity, which took place just as the Buddhist canon was being translated, led to the practice of transmitting the new doctrine with the help of images. Many cave temples, decorated with wall paintings and sculptures that represented the entire Buddhist pantheon, were created along the Silk Route and even in the heart of China itself, in the provinces of Henan, Shanxi, and most of all Sichuan.

▼The Silk Route and
some of the principal
cave sites.

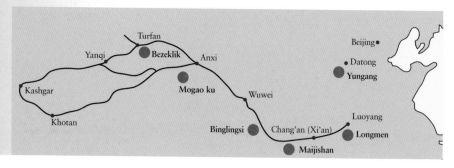

"During the Eastern Jin, a gilt bronze Buddha pedestal was floating in the ocean. It emitted light" (Inscription 4, southern wall of Cave 323 at Mogao)

Mogao

When it became a prefecture at the extreme northwestern tip of the Han empire, the Dunhuang oasis, located in western Gansu, represented the point of encounter between China and the lands of Central Asia. Beginning in AD 366 the most important Buddhist cave temples in China, known as the Mogao Caves, came into being there, about 25 kilometers from the oasis, near the Jade Gate Pass of the Han epoch. More than a thousand caves may be been dug into the rock of Mount Mingsha, 492 of which have been preserved, dating from the end of the 4th century AD to the end of the 14th century. The combination of interior architecture, sculpture, and wall paintings presents a magnificent spectacle: the principal figures in the scenes are often presented as fully round painted sculptures, while narrative episodes of the life of the Buddha, mythical figures, floral and ornamental elements, depictions of the patrons of the work, and landscapes are painted in mineral pigments on the walls, rendered uniform with a mixture of mud, dung, and plaster covered with whitewash. The oldest caves present Central Asian and even Indian schemes; especially in the Tang epoch these are combined with figures that recall Chinese aesthetics. The exceptional value of the caves was further increased in 1899 with the accidental discovery of about 40,000 objects, including manuscripts, paintings, and fabrics dating to the period between 406 and 1004. Most of these finds, all of them well preserved, are today in the museums of London and Paris.

Terms
Jade Gate Pass
(*Yumen Guan*)
Mogao Caves
(*Mogao ku*)

Related entries
Wudi, Images of
the Buddha

▼ The Mogao Caves, located near the Dunhuang oasis in Gansu province.

The thematic relationship between polychrome sculpture and wall paintings is a constant aspect of the Mogao Caves.

Three small caves are all that remains of the first phase of construction because the collapse of the central rock wall destroyed others that dated to the closing decades of the 4th century.

The square central insert, called the "dome of heaven" (tianjing), is based on a certain kind of wooden roof structure widespread in all of Asia.

The sculpture is modeled with loamy stucco on a wooden armature and probably represents Maitreya, the Buddha of the future, flanked by about twenty divine beings (devas).

▲ Section of the ceiling and western wall of Cave 272, Northern Liang dynasty, AD 421–439.

The four sides of the ceiling, shaped like a truncated pyramid, are decorated with motifs of the Elysian Fields of Chinese mythology.

The southern section presents the Queen Mother of the West (Xiwangmu), ruler of the Daoist paradise.

Figures belonging to Daoist mythology are inserted in a setting of Buddhist inspiration, emphasizing the all-inclusive character of the universalistic religion.

The queen's cart is drawn by two phoenixes and is surrounded by other fantastic beasts, among them the green dragon of the east and the white tiger of the west.

▲ Southern side of the ceiling of Cave 249, Western Wei dynasty, AD 535–556.

During the Tang period, the teachings and scriptures of Buddhism were spread among the common people by way of simple, unambiguously illustrated renditions.

A dancer wrapped in stoles and fluttering clothes moves at the center of a group of musicians. During this period agitated dances of Central Asian origin were popular not only on the outskirts of the empire but even at the central court.

▲ Southern wall of Cave 112 (detail), Tang dynasty, end 7th–early 8th century AD.

Illustrations of the most important sutras appear in the caves of this period, including these images of the paradise of Amitabha, the Buddha of "infinite light."

In 1899, thousands of manuscripts were found in the so-called Library Cave, along with hundreds of paintings on paper and silk and the first printed works that can be dated with certainty, all hidden early in the 11th century and forgotten by time.

Most of the material found was sold early in the 20th century to two Western researchers, Aurel Stein and Paul Pelliot, and the rarest works from the Dunhuang treasure are today held by the British Museum in London.

▲ Statue of the monk Hongbian, in front of the wall painting on the northern wall of Cave 17, Tang dynasty, 9th–10th century AD.

The cave was originally designed as a commemorative chapel to Hongbian, leader of the monks when a local magnate managed to turn over the entire area to the Chinese empire, ending a Tibetan occupation that had lasted more than half a century.

The statue of the monk had been hidden in the rock wall above the cave and was found and put back in its original location only in the 1960s.

Yungang

The Yungang caves were constructed over a period of a few decades, primarily while the nearby city of Datong, located just inside the Great Wall, was capital of the kingdom of the Northern Wei. Between AD 460 and 523, about 250 niches and caves were carved in the rock wall of Mount Wuzhou along the Shi Li River. These have suffered large-scale damage from erosion as well as from looting by art thieves in the early decades of 20th century. The five oldest caves are called the Tanyao Caves after the monk who convinced the emperor Wen Cheng to create a place of worship here as penance for the crimes committed by his predecessor, who had persecuted Buddhists. These caves have an upside-down U layout and enclose an enormous statue at their center, symbol not only of the glory of Buddha but of political authority. The figures are carved with simplicity, the massive bodies adorned with tight-fitting mantles with flattened folds and with jewels that recall Central Asian models as well as those Indian and Hellenistic. During the period of imperial patronage from AD 471 to 494, various twin caves were made with square layouts, often provided with a terrace made of stone but modeled on the wooden structures of the period. The iconographic repertory and sculptural works reflect Chinese influence, and they grow increasingly complex; the sensual bodies are concealed by the profusion of folds.

▼ The great seated Buddha of Cave 20, circa 12 m high, Northern Wei dynasty, AD 460–470.

The statues in the oldest caves, dating to AD 460–470, were cut directly into the rock walls, and timber roofs were constructed in front of them as protection; later, terraces were built instead that served as antechambers.

Niches with votive images are carved in the rock wall between the larger caves.

The columns, today eroded by time and weather, were originally octagonal, built on the model of the wooden columns decorated with numerous carved small Buddhas in meditative positions, generically called "thousand Buddhas" (qian fo).

▲ The rock wall and the terraces of Cave 10, Northern Wei dynasty, circa AD 480.

The austerity of the first period gave way to iconographic exuberance. The columns, walls, and ceiling of the terraces are entirely carved and glow with brilliant colors.

The decorative motifs are derived from the vast Buddhist pantheon, which absorbed an enormous variety of styles during its long journey from Persia and India to China, where they were combined and blended with the indigenous tradition.

Even the small Buddhas often present the physical characteristics prescribed by classical iconography of Indian origin: the cranial protuberance (ushnisha), the central "third eye" (urna), the elongated earlobes, etc.

The cave, carved during the period of great activity under imperial patronage, forms a pair with Cave 10, located beside it.

In addition to the various configurations of the Buddha, other divinities and celestial beings are depicted, including winged apsaras, warriors, musicians, and animals.

▲ Decoration on the interior of the terrace of Cave 12, Northern Wei dynasty, circa AD 480.

The entire lower strip of the cave is enlivened by scenes from the Jataka tales depicted in essential lines.

Episodes from the life of the Buddha—shown here is the departure of Sakyamuni from the palace in which he was born—illustrate Buddhist teachings in a simple and unambiguous way.

The willingness of the powerful to financially support the construction of caves, shrines, and pagodas spread with the Mahayana school, which saw the patronage of sacred images as a meritorious act, contributing to salvation.

▲ Detail of the wall decoration in Cave 6, circa AD 490.

*"When one tries to see from close up, the view is obscure. . . .
Moving back slowly one begins to make out [the figure] and
outlines and signs become clear" (Yang Xuanzhi)*

Longmen

Terms
"Dragon Door"
(*Longmen*)

Related entries
Wu Zetian, Foreign
dynasties, Buddhism,
Yungang

▼ Guardians and
demons in the cave
of Fengxian, Tang
dynasty, AD 672–675.

The transfer of the capital of the Northern Wei in AD 493 from the
border to the heart of China reflects the desire of the ruling house,
of foreign origin, to enter and become part of Chinese civilization.
Since Buddhism was an integral part of the state ideology, work
immediately began on construction of new rock temples, located
12 kilometers to the south of the historical city of Luoyang. The
hard gray limestone of the Yi River permitted more detailed working than the sandstone of Datong, and it has also proved more
enduring, although it has been damaged by pollution and the looting that took place early in the 20th century. Since new caves are
still being discovered, it is not possible to establish an exact number, but the statues alone number more than 100,000. Chinese
influence is visible even in the earliest phase of the work, which
corresponds to the period of the domination of the Northern Wei
at Luoyang, from 493 to 534; the walls around the principal figures are crowded with small niches with figures surrounded by
flowers, clouds, and divine messengers, all carved with a linear
dynamism. The figures have refined features and long-limbed bodies and wear broad,
angular robes. The cul-
mination of Longmen
art was reached under
the Tang emperor Gao-
zong and his consort,
the empress Wu Zetian,
who patronized the
execution of giant natu-
ralist statues with mer-
ciful expressions.

For many years Chinese and foreign scholars have been working to identify the great number of objects, like this head, that were removed from the Longmen caves and distributed to museums in Europe and the Americas.

The crown, dominated by a small Amitabha Buddha at the center, suggests that this is the Bodhisattva of compassion, Guanyin.

Stylistic and technical features—including the characteristic limestone—indicate the provenance of this head, one of the many elements removed from walls and taken to the West during the 19th and 20th centuries.

The desire of the Wei to assimilate Chinese culture is made clear in the sculptural style of the period following the relocation of the capital: the bodies become less bulky and grow slender; the features become linear and serene.

▶ Head of a Bodhisattva, Northern Wei dynasty, circa AD 495–575, limestone, 47.6 cm high, Freer Gallery of Art, Smithsonian Institution, Washington, DC.

The cave is named for the all-important flower of Buddhism, the symbol of purity and one of the religion's "eight treasures": the lotus. The fruit, flower, and stalk of lotus represent the past, present, and future.

The limestone of Longmen made it possible to work subjects in even the smallest detail, and every surface of the cave has been carved with the exception of the floor.

The many niches opened in the side walls are populated by configurations of the Buddha and Bodhisattvas and are decorated with festoons, clouds, lotus flowers, and geometric figures.

Standing in the rear of the cave is a statue of Buddha Sakyamuni, the historical Buddha, more than five meters tall.

▲ The Cave of the Lotus Flower (*Lianhua ku*), Northern Wei dynasty, circa AD 527.

A second high point of Buddhist sculptural art was reached at Luoyang under the rule of Emperor Gaozong (ruled AD 649–683) and Empress Wu Zetian (ruled AD 690–705), who moved the court there.

A seated Buddha Vairochana, more than 17 meters high, is symmetrically flanked by pairs of Bodhisattvas, celestial guardians, warriors, and demons.

The statues, which were originally protected by a wooden roof, are now exposed to sunlight, at the center of the southern wall of rock, on the southern bank of the Yi River.

One of the few Chinese sculptors whose name has survived is Li Zhi, who is thought to have created the nine colossal sculptures depicted in the cave of Fengxian.

▲ Fengxian cave, Tang dynasty, AD 672–675.

"As if one were to mount a carriage and pierce the mountain . . . an infinity of stars overhead and the land spinning around far below" (Inscription in Cave 4 at Maijishan)

Maijishan

Terms
Maijishan ("Wheat-pile Hill")

Related entries
Xuanzang, Buddhism, Binglingsi

A stupendous naturalistic panorama is the background to the majestic cliff in which the Maijishan caves were carved. Part of the Qinling mountain chain, Mount Maiji is located in Gansu province, about 45 kilometers to the southeast of Tianshui, which was the first city in which the monk Xuanzang stopped on his pilgrimage to India. The site's geographical isolation has contributed to safeguarding the wall paintings and sculptures, most of which are made in friable clay around wooden armatures that were inserted in the perforated rock. The stone needed to make the other figures and the bas-reliefs had to be brought from a distance, since the rock at the site would not have made possible such precise execution. Today there are 194 caves distributed in two sections, on the western and southern faces of the cliff, while the central area was destroyed by an earthquake in 734. Each of the two fronts is dominated by a three-figure group dating to the Sui dynasty, about 16 meters tall and clearly visible from

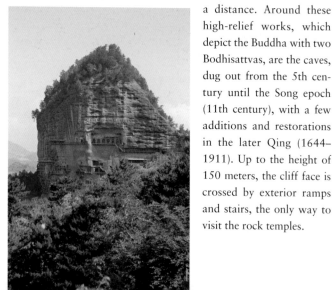

▶ The great cliff of Maijishan.

a distance. Around these high-relief works, which depict the Buddha with two Bodhisattvas, are the caves, dug out from the 5th century until the Song epoch (11th century), with a few additions and restorations in the later Qing (1644–1911). Up to the height of 150 meters, the cliff face is crossed by exterior ramps and stairs, the only way to visit the rock temples.

The clay, of compact quality, has resisted the weather somewhat well, but the original polychrome decoration has vanished.

Even from a distance the holes can be seen that were made to hold the wooden structure that supports the dried clay.

The largest sculptural groups in the rock caves were made during the Sui and Tang periods, and the figures reflect their aesthetics: although massive, they are sensual, elegant, and well proportioned.

▲ The great Buddha flanked by two Bodhisattvas, in the southern wall of the cliff, Sui dynasty, AD 581–618.

"With the passage of the years and the dynasties, the sacred images had been ruined, collapsed and fragmentary. I restored them . . . repainting and clothing them" (Zhizhou)

Binglingsi

The natural setting of the Bingling temples has been praised by many travelers who were thrilled by the bizarre rock formations of the Xiaojishi mountain chain that flank the Yellow River. A 27-meter-tall statue from the Tang period, depicting a seated Maitreya, the Buddha of the future, signals the presence of the caves to navigators on the river, the only means of access to the caves, which are about 70 kilometers from Lanzhou. The upper part of the figure was carved out of the sandstone wall; the lower part is composed instead of a wooden structure covered in clay. In 1967, the level of the river was raised by a new dam, which submerged about 170 caves, including one with a great sleeping Buddha. Today there are 216 caves and niches at Binglingsi, made between the early 5th and the 18th centuries. The 183 on the western side, protected by an embankment, are the best preserved and hold hundreds of clay and stone sculptures as well as

▼ Niche 28, Tang dynasty.

numerous fragments of wall paintings. Binglingsi has the oldest inscription in China's Buddhist caves, datable to AD 420. More than thirty caves date to the Northern Wei period, while two-thirds of the rock temples are from the Tang. During the Mongolian domination, Bingling, then called Lingyan, was an important monastery: this is indicated by several murals with esoteric and tantric themes.

Erosion has carved bizarre shapes in the soft sandstone.

Prior to the creation of a dam downriver in the late 1960s, the water level was notably lower.

Pilgrims from "Western Regions" planted rare and exotic plants around the caves, and many of these plants still survive, as for example a hundred-year-old Indian sandalwood tree.

▲ The Yellow River near the Binglingsi caves.

Two women are depicted among the followers of the Buddha.

An inscription inside the natural cave, 19 meters long and 27 wide, fixes the date of creation of the painting at AD 420. This would make the work the oldest wall painting in China dedicated to the Buddha.

The calligraphic touches that create the outlines and the interior details, as well as the features of the faces, seem to reflect Chinese influence.

Precious pigments made of copper, azurite, and malachite have been used in abundance, and the face of the Buddha still shows traces of the original covering in gold leaf.

▲ Seated Buddha, wall painting on the northern wall of Cave 169, Western Qin dynasty, circa AD 420.

Maitreya, one of the most widespread configurations of the Buddha, is the Buddha of the future, successor to the historical Buddha Sakyamuni and destined to unite the entire world under his guidance.

Modeled in the Tang epoch, the monumental sculpture has been restored many times.

The great Buddha was commissioned by a governor of the Liangzhou region during the Tang period.

▲ Monumental Maitreya Buddha,
Tang dynasty, AD 645.

Bezeklik

Terms
Flaming Mountains
(*Huoyan Shan*)
Western Prefecture
(*Xizhou*)

Related entries
Foreign dynasties,
Minor religions

The wall paintings in the rock temples of Bezeklik document the numerous, multicolored facets of the multiethnic culture of the cities of the Silk Route. Dug into the rock walls along the western slope of the Murtuk River, the caves are located in the Tian Shan's Flaming Mountains, almost 50 kilometers from the Turfan oasis. Early in the 20th century the archaeologist Albert von Le Coq had some of the best-preserved paintings removed, and they are today in the Museum für Indische Kunst in Berlin. Of the 83 existing caves, only a few more than 40 still contain paintings, many of them in a precarious state of preservation. Most of the paintings date to the period of greatest splendor in the Uyghur kingdom at Gaochang (late 9th–11th century AD), when Bezeklik was the most important center of worship in the country, and many of the oldest caves were renovated. The subjects of the 10th-century works testify to the conversion of the Uyghur royal house from Manichaeism to Buddhism. A passageway has preserved the image of a wooden coffered ceiling datable to the period of the rule of Qu Gaochang, installed by the descendents of the Huns in the 5th century AD. During the Tang period the city of Gaochang, founded by the Western Han as a military outpost, rose to be capital of the Western Prefecture. The wall paintings of that period evoke the style and motifs of the Mogao Caves at Dunhuang.

▼ The Bezeklik caves, located in the Flaming Mountains in Xinjiang.

Nothing has remained of the first period of activity in the Bezeklik caves except the design of a coffered ceiling, painted in the hallway around Cave 18, which dates to the period of the local kingdom of Qu (AD 540–600).

Some caves testify to the later period, in the mid-7th century, when the area, called the Western Prefecture (Xizhou), was under the control of the Tang empire.

Cave 16, with a rectangular outline and vaulted ceiling, dates to this period and bears images of the sutras and the paradise of Amitabha, along with portraits of the painter's patrons.

The individual features, the long colored cloaks with tight sleeves and circular collars, and finally the inscriptions in Uyghur make clear the Turkic origin of these men.

▲ Portraits of patrons, Cave 16, Tang dynasty, AD 7th century.

When, around AD 840, the Uyghurs were forced to move their khanate, founded in 744, from the steppe of today's Mongolia toward the southwest, they settled at Gaochang, in the Turfan oasis.

The first paintings the Uyghurs commissioned after their arrival indicate their adherence to Manichaeism: a large "tree of light" painted in Cave 38 is the clearest proof of this.

The inscription beside the first figure calls him "Tutuq Burgra [of the house of] Sali." The Uyghur writing, written vertically, consists of five vowel signs and twenty consonants.

This painting, removed early in the 20th century, is thought to date to the period immediately after the conversion of the Uyghur royal house to Buddhism.

In some prayers of Uyghur origin, reference is made to the dead by way of the periphrasis "those who bear the flowers [in their hands]." The flowers in the painting seem to have been added later, perhaps as a way to complete the portrait after the death of the artist's patron.

▲ Portraits of Uyghur princes, Tang dynasty, 9th century, wall painting from Bezeklik, Cave 9 (today Cave 20), 62.4 x 59.5 cm, Museum für Indische Kunst, Berlin.

During the long period of weakness
of the Chinese empire, the Uyghurs
succeeded in maintaining their
domination until 1124, when the
Jurchen Jin dynasty brought
northern China under its control.

The painting
depicts heretics
exulting at news
of the death of
the Buddha.

This period painting does not reveal
any Chinese influence, even if there
are parallels with certain paintings
in the Mogao Caves at Dunhuang.

▲ *Musicians*, Uyghur kingdom
of Gaochang, Song dynasty,
10th–11th century.

References

◄ Figure of Budai ("Laughing Buddha"), Ming dynasty, dated to 1486, stoneware with "three-color" (*sancai*) glaze, 119.2 cm high, British Museum, London.

Map of China

0 250 500 mi
0 250 500 km

N
W — E
S

Ulaanbaatar

TIAN SHAN MOUNTAINS

XINJIANG-UYGHUR AUTONOMOUS REGION

PAMIR MOUNTAINS

TAKLIMAKAN DESERT

ALTUN SHAN

• Dunhuang

KUNLUN SHAN

QILIAN SHAN

QINGHAI

NINGXI. AUTON◯ MOUS REGIOI

River

GANSU

Yellow

Mount Maiji ▲

TIBETAN PLATEAU

QINLIN

HIMALAYA SHAN

TIBET AUTONOMOUS REGION

• Lhasa

Yangtze

Chengdu •

Kathmandu ★

SICHUAN

★ Thimphu

River

GUIZHOU

★ Dhaka

YUNNAN

BAY OF BENGAL

378

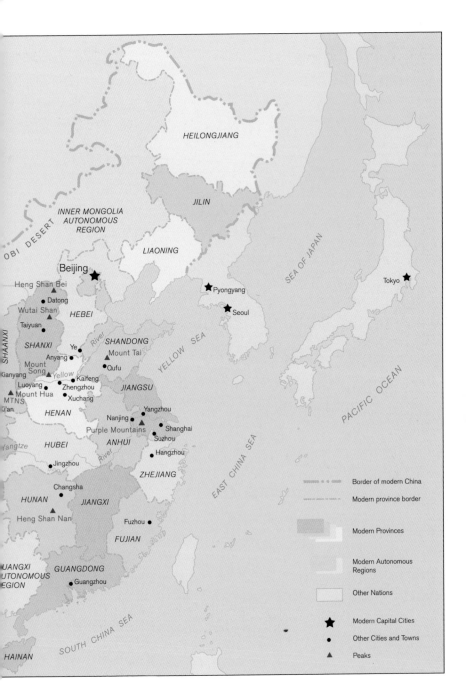

HEILONGJIANG

JILIN

INNER MONGOLIA
AUTONOMOUS
REGION

GOBI DESERT

LIAONING

SEA OF JAPAN

Beijing ★

Tokyo ★

Heng Shan Bei ▲
• Datong
Wutai Shan ▲
HEBEI
Pyongyang ★
Taiyuan •
Seoul ★

SHAANXI

SHANXI   Ye •   SHANDONG
Anyang •   ▲ Mount Tai
Mount
Song ▲ Yellow • Qufu
Xianyang Kaifeng •
Luoyang • Zhengzhou •
▲ Mount Hua   • Xuchang   JIANGSU
MTNS
Xi'an   HENAN

YELLOW SEA

PACIFIC OCEAN

River

Yangzhou •
Nanjing • ▲
Purple Mountains • Shanghai
HUBEI   ANHUI   Suzhou •
• Jingzhou   • Hangzhou

Yangtze   River

ZHEJIANG

EAST CHINA SEA

Changsha •
HUNAN   JIANGXI

Heng Shan Nan ▲

Fuzhou •

FUJIAN

GUANGXI
AUTONOMOUS
REGION

GUANGDONG
• Guangzhou

SOUTH CHINA SEA

HAINAN

Border of modern China

Modern province border

Modern Provinces

Modern Autonomous
Regions

Other Nations

★ Modern Capital Cities

• Other Cities and Towns

▲ Peaks

Chronology

DYNASTY	DATES	CAPITAL
Shang	ca. 1500–1050 BC	Anyang from ca. 1300 BC
Zhou		
Western Zhou	11th century BC–771 BC	Hao (Xi'an)
Eastern Zhou	770–256 BC	Luoyi (Luoyang)
Spring and Autumn period	770–476 BC	
Warring States	475–221 BC	
Qin	221–206 BC	Xianyang
Han		
Western Han	206 BC–AD 8	Chang'an (Xi'an)
Wang Mang	9–24	Chang'an (Xi'an)
Eastern Han	25–220	Luoyang
Three Kingdoms		
Wei	220–265	Luoyang
Shu	221–263	Chengdu
Wu	222–280	Jianye (Nanjing)
Western Jin	265–316	Luoyang
Eastern Jin	317–420	Jiankang (Nanjing)
Northern and southern states		
Southern dynasties		
Song	420–479	Jiankang (Nanjing)
Southern Qi	479–502	Jiankang (Nanjing)
Liang	502–557	Jiankang (Nanjing)
Chen	557–589	Jiankang (Nanjing)
Northern dynasties		
Northern Wei	386–534	Pingcheng (Datong), Luoyang from 493
Eastern Wei	534–550	Ye
Western Wei	535–556	Chang'an (Xi'an)
Northern Qi	550–577	Ye
Northern Zhou	557–581	Chang'an (Xi'an)
Sui	581-618	Daxing (Xi'an) from 587
Tang	618-907	Chang'an (Xi'an)
Five Dynasties		
Later Liang	907–923	Bian (Kaifeng)
Later Tang	923–936	Luoyang
Later Jin	936–946	Bian (Kaifeng)
Later Han	947–950	Bian (Kaifeng)
Later Zhou	951–960	Bian (Kaifeng)
Ten Kingdoms		
Wu	902–937	Yangzhou
Wuyue	907–978	Hangzhou
Southern Han	907–971	Guangzhou
Chu	907–951	Changsha
Former Shu	908–925	Chengdu
Min	909–944	Changde (Fuzhou)
Nanping–Jingnan	913–963	Jingzhou
Later Shu	934–965	Chengdu
Southern Tang	937–975	Jinling (Nanjing)
Northern Han	951–979	Taiyuan
Song		
Northern Song	960–1127	Bianliang (Kaifeng)
Southern Song	1127–1279	Jinling (Nanjing), Lin'an (Hangzhou) from 1138
Liao	916–1125	Yanjing (Beijing, southern capital)
Jin	1115–1234	Zhongdu (Beijing)
Yuan	1279–1368	Dadu or Khanbalik (Beijing)
Ming	1368–1406	Yingtian, later Nanjing
	1406–1644	Beijing
Qing	1644–1911	Beijing

Museums

Many Chinese museums, as a result of the steady stream of important archaeological discoveries, have been reorganized, and many new ones have been founded. As examples, there are the Provincial Museum of Hunan at Changsha, which holds the splendid lacquers and silks from the Mawangdui tombs; the Provincial Museum of Shaanxi at Xi'an, which holds precious finds from the area of the ancient capital; and the Provincial Museum of Hubei at Wuhan, which has the unique collection of musical instruments dating to the Bronze Age of Marquis Yi of Zeng, who died in 433 BC. Various new museums have arisen near or directly on sites of important discoveries, such as the Museum of the Nan Yue King at Guangzhou in Guangdong, the Museum of Sanxingdui near Chengdu in Sichuan, and the Museum of the Terracotta Army near Xi'an. The burial area around the ancient Chang'an capital has been transformed into large open-air museums, as is true of the tombs of the Ming emperors in the area around Beijing.

Beijing: Palace Museum
www.dpm.org.cn
The ancient Forbidden City constitutes a single very large (720,000 square meters) museum, enclosing art objects and artisan work of every kind, most of it belonging to the imperial court of the Qing dynasty.

Berlin: Museum für Indische Kunst
www.smb.spk-berlin.de/smb/samm lungen/details.php?objectId=11
The heart of this museum is composed of the so-called Turfan Collection, which presents wooden and stone sculpture, paintings on silk and paper, and fragments of wall paintings dating to the period from the 3rd to the 13th centuries. The finds, from cave temples around the oasis of Turfan, were collected in the early years of the 20th century by A. Grünwedel and A. von Le Coq.

Boston: Museum of Fine Arts
www.mfa.org
Some of the most important works of ancient Chinese civilization are today in American museums. The vast Chinese selection in the Boston museum includes many paintings, most of all portraits and works of the "birds and flowers" genre. Also present is a panorama of ceramic art from the Song to the Qing periods.

Kansas City: The Nelson-Atkins Museum of Art
www.nelson-atkins.org
Ritual vases and weapons present an overview of Chinese culture during the Bronze Age, while various rare paintings dating from the 10th to 13th centuries offer indications of the birth of landscape painting in China. There is also a notable collection of ancient furniture.

Lintong: Museum of Qin Terracotta Warriors and Horses
www.bmy.com.cn
This museum is built on the site where the terracotta army of Qin Shi Huangdi was excavated. The excavations have been ongoing since the 1970s and bring to light new surprises; in 2003, for example, an artificial underground pond was discovered with bronze aquatic birds.

London: British Museum
www.thebritishmuseum.ac.uk/ world/asia/china/china/html
The large collection covers five thousand years of Chinese history and contains many masterpieces, such as the paintings by Gu Kaishi and Song Huizong. Also of fundamental importance are the Buddhist paintings and texts on silk, including the first printed book, acquired by Aurel Stein at Dunhuang.

Paris: Musée Cernuschi
www.cernuschi.paris.fr
Recently restructured, this museum is located in the welcoming palace of its founder, Henri Cernuschi, and presents a broad panorama of Chinese funerary art, from the Neolithic to the 14th century, with an impressive selection of archaic bronzes and a series of funerary statuettes (mingqi) that date from the Han to the Tang periods.

Paris: Musée National des Arts Asiatiques Guimet
www.museeguimet.fr
The Chinese section of the museum is famous for its wall paintings and works on paper and silk collected by Paul Pelliot during his trips to Central Asia and Dunhuang. These include a vast collection of mingqi objects (substitution burial objects) from two private collections dating primarily to the Han and Tang periods.

Taipei: National Palace Museum
www.npm.gov.tw/index.htm
Founded in 1949, after the withdrawal of Jian Jieshi (Chiang Kaishek) to Taiwan, the museum holds numerous historical works from the imperial collections, and in fields of painting and calligraphy the quality of its collections is unique. The works are shown by turns in large, well-documented exhibitions.

Washington, DC: Freer Gallery of Art, Arthur M. Sackler Gallery, Smithsonian Institution
www.asia.si.edu
These two large collections, based on the donations of Charles Freer and Arthur M. Sackler, present a notable collection of ritual bronzes and archaic jades as well as many paintings dating primarily to the Ming and Qing dynasties.

Zurich: Museum Rietberg
The Chinese collection here is famous for Buddhist stone sculptures dating from the 6th to 9th centuries. They are integrated with a representative selection from India, Indochina, and Central Asia. The paintings of the Ming and Qing periods, held in another pavilion within the museum's large park, offer a panorama of the culture of the literati of the period.

Bibliography

The following list is meant to indicate ways for the interested reader to further study the history and culture of China.

Chang, Kwang-chih. *The Archaeology of Ancient China*. New Haven: Yale University Press, 1986.

Chase, W. Thomas. *Ancient Chinese Bronze Art: Casting the Precious Sacral Vessel*. New York: China House Gallery, 1991.

Childs-Johnson, Elizabeth, curator. *Ritual and Power: Jades of Ancient China*. Exhibition Catalog. New York: China House Gallery, 1988.

Debaine-Francfort, Corinne. *The Search for Ancient China*. New York: Harry N. Abrams, 1999.

Fong, Wen C., and James C.Y. Watt. *Possessing the Past: Treasures from the National Palace Museum, Taipei*. Exhibition catalog. New York: Metropolitan Museum of Art; Taipei: National Palace Museum; New York: distributed by Harry N. Abrams, 1996.

Hansford, S. Howard. *Chinese Carved Jades*. Greenwich, Conn.: New York Graphic Society, 1968.

Herberts, Kurt. *Oriental Lacquer: Art and Technique*. New York: Harry N. Abrams, 1963.

Idema, W.L., and Lloyd Haft. *A Guide to Chinese Literature*. Ann Arbor: Center for Chinese Studies, University of Michigan, 1997.

Lee, Sherman, ed. *China, 5,000 Years: Innovation and Transformation in the Arts*. Exhibition catalog. New York: Solomon R. Guggenheim Museum, 1998.

Lippiello, Tiziana. *Auspicious Omens and Miracles in Ancient China*. Sankt Augustin: Monumenta Serica Institute; Nettetal: Steyler Verlag, 2001.

Li Zehou. *The Path of Beauty: A Study of Chinese Aesthetics*. Beijing: Morning Glory, 1988.

Loehr, Max. *The Great Painters of China*. New York: Harper & Row, 1980.

Loewe, Michael. *The Pride That Was China*. New York: St. Martin's Press, 1990.

Loewe, Michael, and Edward L.

Shaughnessy. *The Cambridge History of Ancient China*. Cambridge, UK, and New York: Cambridge University Press, 1999.

Miller, James. *Daoism: A Short Introduction*. Oxford: Oneworld, 2003.

Morris, Edwin T. *The Gardens of China: History, Art, and Meanings*. New York: Scribner, 1983.

Paludan, Ann. *The Chinese Spirit Road: The Classical Tradition of Stone Tomb Statuary*. New Haven: Yale University Press, 1991.

Pirazzoli-t'Serstevens, Michèle. *The Han Civilization of China*. Oxford: Phaidon, 1982.

Rawson, Jessica, ed. *The British Museum Book of Chinese Art*. London: British Museum Press, 1992.

Roberts, J.A.G. *A Concise History of China*. Cambridge, Mass.: Harvard University Press, 1999.

Scarpari, Maurizio. *Splendours of Ancient China*. London: Thames & Hudson, 2000.

Sullivan, Michael. *The Arts of China*. Berkeley: University of California Press, 1999.

Temple, Robert K.G. *The Genius of China: 3,000 Years of Science, Discovery, and Invention*. London: Prion Books, 1998.

Tregear, Mary, and Shelagh Vainker. *Art Treasures in China*. New York: Harry N. Abrams, 1994.

Vainker, S.J. *Chinese Pottery and Porcelain from Prehistory to the Present*. London: British Museum, 2005.

Watson, William. *The Arts of China to 900 AD*. New Haven: Pelican History of Art, 1995.

Welch, Holmes, and Anna Seidel. *Facets of Taoism*. New Haven: Yale University Press, 1979.

Yang, Xiaoneng, ed. *The Golden Age of Chinese Archaeology: Celebrated Discoveries from the Peoples Republic of China*. Exhibition catalog. Washington, DC: National Gallery of Art, 1999.

Zwalf, W. *Buddhism—Art and Faith*. London: British Museum Publications, 1985.

General index